Mobile Pastoralists

Mobile Pastoralists

Development Planning and Social Change in Oman

Dawn Chatty

Columbia University Press
New York

Columbia University Press
New York Chichester, West Sussex

Library of Congress Cataloging-in-Publication Data
Chatty, Dawn.
Mobile pastoralists : development planning and social change in Oman / Dawn Chatty.
p. cm.
Includes bibliographical references and index.

ISBN 978-0-231-10549-1 (pbk.)

1. Nomads—Oman. 2. Pastoral systems—Oman. 3. Rural development projects—Oman. 4. Indigenous peoples—Oman—Politics and government. 5. Social change—Oman. 6. Oman—Ethnic relations. 7. Oman—Politics and government. I. Title.
GN635.043C48 1996
305.8'0095353—dc20

95-45923
CIP

Casebound editions of Columbia University Press books are printed on permanent and durable acid-free paper.

Printed in the United States of America

To
MLR

Contents

Maps

**Map 1 prepared by Peter Hayward; all the rest by Jane S. Davis*

Note on Names and Transliteration of Arabic Words

I have used pseudonyms where I have felt the privacy of an individual or family might be at risk. I have not changed the names of people now deceased or in the public domain.

For the most part, I have not fully transliterated Arabic words. Instead I have attempted to reproduce the pronunciation of the area into a common English form. Except where otherwise noted, only the singular form of an Arabic word is indicated, with *s* added for plurals. In the case of words that end in the "ta marbuta" (for example, jiddah and haylah), I have rendered them with a final *t* as they would appear and be pronounced before an attached noun (for example, Jiddat-il-Harasiis and Haylat-il-Harashiif).

Acknowledgments

This project has occupied more than ten years of my life, and I find it very hard to isolate just a few individuals for special thanks. I owe so much to so many. I am particularly grateful for the encouragement and support extended to me by Brigadier Malcolm Dennison, His Excellency Khalfan bin Nasser Al-Wahaibi, His Excellency Yahya bin Mahfudh Al-Manthri, Mr. Basri Danisman, and Mrs. Barka Bakry when I embarked upon this project.

In the course of the earlier fieldwork, I was particularly indebted to Ann Watts, Elisabeth Mitchell, and David Fenner. They struggled with me to see the project on the road and traveled a very bumpy journey with me always in good spirits and infinite optimism. I am particularly grateful to David and Elisabeth for quickly adapting to my pace and working so well with me as a team. Many of the earlier special reports to government were first drafted by them. I am sure they join me in thanking the Harasiis people, especially those families that accepted, so graciously, our constant questioning, often about matters they did not wish to discuss. To our guide, Hamad, his wife, and children as well as Jamal, our driver, a particular thanks for working so hard to understand what it was we needed to know.

During the middle years of this project, I was particularly grateful to Michael Hyland for his unfailing encouragement to write this book. I sincerely appreciated his efforts to make me stand back from the morass of cable traffic to look at it objectively. Any success I had was due to his hard work.

I am grateful to Dale Eickelman, John Peterson, and Nancy Lindisfarne for their steady support and academic interest in my work. I also thank Stephanie Ramamurthy for her research assistance. To Mark

Stanley Price, Karen Stanley Price, Roddy Jones, Gigi Crocker Jones, and Ralph Daly my thanks as well. Their work on the oryx reintroduction project and my own overlapped. Although we often "agreed to disagree," I am grateful for their flexibility, humor, and warm hospitality.

To Shirley Ardener and the staff of the Centre for Cross-Cultural Research on Women, University of Oxford, a particular thanks for making the period of time I spent with them revising the manuscript so stimulating.

Finally there are two individuals I owe more to than a few words can ever convey: my husband, Nicholas Mylne, my deepest appreciation. His total support and on-the-ground backup saved the project from disaster many a time. To my professor, mentor, and dear friend, Hilda Kuper, a sadly belated thank you. She, more than any other of my teachers, shaped the way I think. I only regret she did not live to see this project to completion.

Abbreviations

DLF	Dhofar Liberation Front
DTCD	Department of Technical Cooperation and Development
ECWA	Economic Commission on Western Asia
FAO	Food and Agriculture Organization
NGO	Nongovernmental Organization
PDO	Petroleum Development Oman
PDRY	People's Democratic Republic of Yemen
RO	Omani Rials
SOAF	Sultan of Oman's Air Force
UNDP	United Nations Development Program
UNESCO	United Nations Education Science and Culture Organization
VFUNDW	Voluntary Fund for the United Nations Decade of Women

Mobile Pastoralists

1

Introduction:

The Stirrings of a Development Plan

Development plans aimed at nomadic pastoral populations in the Arabian Peninsula and Fertile Crescent have meant, as a rule, projects to settle them.[1] For most of the twentieth century these peoples have been subjected to schemes that either deprived them of their livestock, their traditional grazing lands, or their freedom. Only in the past two decades has a more flexible and open-minded attitude found a niche in development planning for these mobile and often marginalized people.

Two theoretical themes are fundamental to an understanding of this phenomenon. One is the question of the nature of pastoralism, which some regard as a throwback to an earlier stage of human development and others as a unique and sophisticated adaptation to a harsh environment. The second revolves around the question of development: what is the nature of planned change, what is the relationship between the donor and the client, and how do people actually integrate change into their lives? These two theoretical concerns are brought together in this study. They underpin the description and analysis of a development plan aimed at permitting a nomadic pastoral community in the Sultanate of Oman to benefit from modern social services without being forced to give up their traditional way of life. These issues are also foundations to an understanding of how this community has changed and adapted to the profound forces on the margins of their universe.

For centuries the highly mobile, adaptable, and close-knit nomadic pastoral peoples in the Arabian Peninsula have been regarded with suspicion as well as admiration by their settled and more urbane cousins. Consequently, the relationships between pastoral communities and agrarian and urban ones have not always been smooth or easy. At times they were characterized by competition and strife, at other times by symbiosis and cooperation. The ecological and environmental requirements of each of these population groups were such that a crisis among one sector would trigger a reaction in the other. Often the result was that the whole area was thrown into turmoil.

With the consolidation of state power and authority in the "nation-state" after the Second World War, most of the nations of the Middle East turned to their pastoral populations with a view to settling them in one place. Such measures, it was assumed, would assure control over them. Jordan, Iraq, Syria, Saudi Arabia, and Egypt all attempted the "sedentarization" of these communities with limited success. Indeed the resulting disintegration of the pastoral community frequently created new problems for the nation-state.

In one corner of Arabia, however, the pastoral population was left to its own devices. The Sultanate of Oman has a small nomadic pastoral population representing perhaps 6–7 percent of the total. Because of the peculiarities of Oman's own modern history, this population was largely ignored until the second half of the twentieth century, when oil exploration teams began to move into the desert areas of the interior of the Sultanate. Only by the late 1970s, with government services reaching most of the agricultural and urban centers in the country, did the desert inhabitants come under scrutiny. With the example of so many sedentarization and settlement schemes before it, the government chose to follow a different course.

The first half of this work is the description of that process: of the decision to find a way to extend basic social services to a highly mobile pastoral population without destroying their traditional way of life; of the involvement of three "cultures"—the pastoral tribe targeted for development, the government agencies, and an international development agency (the United Nations Development Program, or, UNDP)—in a process that had no predictable outcome; and of the role of the anthropologist/project leader as mediator, spokesperson, interpreter, and finally, activist for the program and the pastoral community.

The second half of this work focuses on the pastoral people themselves: on the way in which they reacted to the presence of outsiders, government and other officials; on the adaptation they have made to the changes in their environment—both planned and unplanned; and on the ways in which they are accommodating themselves to the changes in their own society.

The Nature of Nomadic Pastoral Societies

Nomadic pastoral societies in the Middle East have a number of features in common, and it is possible to formulate some generalizations about them. The definition of pastoralism I use in this study is *animal husbandry by natural graze and browse with some access to crop cultivation.* As no pastoral group is ever entirely self-sufficient, it must maintain reciprocal and interdependent relations with sedentary communities on the margins of its grazing areas. The pastoral adaptation to the ecological environment has always presupposed the presence of sedentary communities and access to their products. Today, with even more sophisticated technology in the form of trucks, water bowsers, metal utensils and frames, bottled gas, and other trappings of late twentieth-century life, the dependence on people outside their own group is particularly apparent.

The nomadic pastoral way of life is shaped by migration. A combination of seasonal and regional variability in the location of pasture and water makes movement from deficit to surplus areas both logical and necessary. Pastoralists have a double reliance on land in the form of pasture for graze and browse and in the form of water sources for themselves and their herds. Each discrete unit or tribe seeks to control sufficient land and water for the livestock holdings of the group, particularly during the hot summer months. The borders between tribes have always been fairly fluid and subject to reinterpretation as the relative strength of one group vis-à-vis another fluctuated or as pasture conditions became desiccated. Up until the mid-twentieth century, tribes were in constant competition with each other for the use of these precious resources, and the weaker units, or less ably represented ones, were often forced to give up their rights to use certain areas. In some cases this meant only minor readjustments in the allocation of resources within the tribe. In other cases it meant wholesale tribal displacement.

The basic features of the pastoralist's territory include winter pasture, permanent watering places for summer, and access to an urban market. The relatively stable dominance of such territory over a period of time by a group of genealogically related agnatic segments identifies a nomadic pastoral tribe. The pivotal position in that organization is the Sheikh. He is the central leader and traditionally enjoys a vast and ill-defined field of privileges and commands. He regularly exercises authority over pasture allocation, settling of disputes, and representation of the tribe to sedentary peoples or central authorities. The first function, pasture allocation,

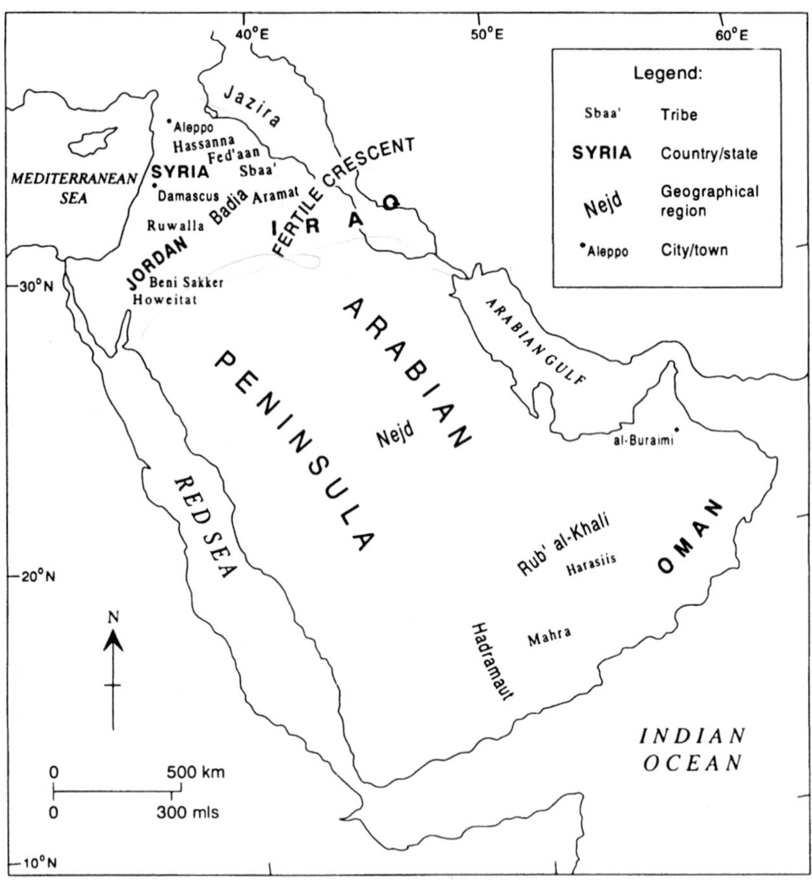

MAP 1 Arabian Peninsula and Fertile Crescent

is basically one calling for coordination of migration. The more rugged the terrain or complex the migration, the more formal the administrative apparatus at the Sheikh's disposal and vice versa (see Barth 1961). The second function, settling disputes, is generally achieved informally, being governed by custom and compromise and regulated by diffuse sanctions. When a Sheikh is asked to arbitrate, he has no power to enforce his decision and must rely on his moral authority as well as the concurrence of the community with his point of view. The recent works by Lancaster (1981:85), Dresch (1989:100), and Caton (1990:13) elaborate on this aspect of a Sheikh's role in tribal society. The third function, and perhaps the most important in recent decades, is the settling of conflicts with sedentary communities. Again, the decision of the Sheikh and his informal council of elders cannot be carried out by force. Its implementation rests upon the personal influence and moral standing of the man himself. Although ultimate authority rests with the Sheikh, it is based upon meticulous evaluation of tribal sentiment. Too frequent disregard of tribal consensus could, and does, result in a gradual shift in authority and influence to another tribesman of a sheikhly family.

The nomadic pastoral tribes of the Arabian Peninsula are often referred to as *Bedouin*, a term derived from the Arabic word, *bedu*, meaning an inhabitant of the *badia*—the large stretch of semiarid land or desert that comprises nearly 80 percent of the Arabian landmass (see map 1). They have, for centuries, pushed their frontier regions into border areas of agricultural settlement and have, as often, been repulsed when central governments have had the strength to do so. This tug-of-war between agricultural and pastoral-based modes of existence often encompassed populations that moved between both types of economic orders. When central authority was weak, the pastoral tribes conquered the land and associated agricultural villages and oases by *ghazu* (raiding) or by collecting the tribute of *khuwa* (brotherhood).[2] When central authority was strong, however, the tribes were forced to make payment to the government or retreat into the badia.

Along the northern frontiers of settlement that arc around present-day Jordan, Syria, and Iraq, elements of the nomadic pastoral tribes invariably settled in the border villages and combined agriculture with raising of small livestock and paying their taxes to the representatives of the central authority. When that authority was too weak to impose order and taxation on the border areas, these families frequently abandoned their farms and joined their kin in full-time pastoral activities.

Historical Expansion and Retreat of Nomadic Pastoralists

For centuries expansions and retreats have characterized the history of the pastoral tribes of Arabia in their special relations with central authorities. Examples of tribal invasions during times of weak central governments go back to the third century *a.d.* and earlier. For that time (a period of anarchy in the outlying regions of the Roman Empire) there is documented evidence of Bedouin invasions into areas of agriculture. The seventh-century Islamic conquests into the area known as Greater Syria or Bilad-ash-Sham were initially made possible by the weakened condition of the rival Byzantine and Persian Empires. Anarchy after the passage of the Mongols in the fourteenth century made possible another Bedouin expansion into the same region. The most recent occurrence of Bedouin expansion was during the second hundred years of Ottoman rule. At this time the Ottoman military presence in the area was withdrawn in order to support the Empire's war against Austria (Hourani 1991:225). Large numbers of pastoral tribes from the Aneza and Shammar confederacies of the Nejd moved into the area, attracted by the richer pastures of the region. Villagers fled to larger towns and cities or turned to nomadic pastoralism, swelling the ranks of the sheep herding units that attached themselves as clients to the invading camel-raising tribes (Volney 1959 [1787]:377–379).

This expansion of pastoral tribes was to continue for nearly 150 years, pushing the frontiers of pastoralism west through the borders of dry farming near the Mediterranean coastline. The initial impetus behind the expansion is not fully understood. The later phase of expansion, however, was a direct reaction to the growing strength of an important religious reform movement in the Nejd. Some pastoral tribes refused to submit to the exigencies of the government that had been formed by Ibn Saud under the banner of the Wahhabi reformers. The first of these was the camel-raising Shammar confederacy (Oppenheim 1939:1:132). By the beginning of the eighteenth century, the camel-raising Aneza confederacy arrived and attempted to penetrate the region. These tribes were the Hassanna, the Fed'aan, and, later, the Sbaa', the Wuld Ali, the Amarat, and, in the early nineteenth century, the Ruwalla.

Throughout the nineteenth and into the twentieth century, these tribes continued to jostle and fight for control over large stretches of pastureland and associated agricultural villages on the borders. Sometimes they formed alliances among themselves to contest pasture rights of former supporters. As each tribe attempted to establish its hegemony over a region, the nature of the ghazu became almost desperate among the tribes as well as settlements in the region. The khuwa, which was being extorted in greater quantities from weaker tribes and farmers, no longer represented a guarantee of security as it once had.

This period of tribal unrest and disruption of both trade and communication came to an end soon after the close of the Crimean War (1867); an event that had distracted Ottoman attention from its southern provinces. A period of reform of central government was initiated in the Arabian Peninsula—especially under Abdul Hamid II. Ottoman military authority was restored to the border areas of agriculture, initiating a period of greater safety and economic benefit for cultivators. The nomadic pastoral tribes were encouraged to fight among themselves and an army of thirty thousand agents was actively engaged in instigating feuds between tribes. On some occasions troops were lent to one side or another with an ensuing massacre by rifle-bearing troops against sword- and lance-carrying tribesmen (Nutting 1964:374).

Agricultural expansion was actively sponsored by the Ottoman authority at this time as a way of reasserting control over the frontier zones. Government soldiers armed with modern weaponry—Snider Breech-Loaders and Winchester Repeaters—manned new border garrisons, giving farmers the security they needed to increase in numbers and strength.[3] The most aggressive of the new settlers were the Circassians fleeing from the Russian occupation of the Caucasus. The Druze communities pushed out of South-Central Lebanon established border settlements and maintained themselves in the face of opposition from the nomadic pastoral tribes, such as the Ruwalla, that were also claiming the area. Along the entire border units of sheep-raising tribes returned to agricultural settlements and took up a mixed economy of farming and livestock raising. Land reforms, tax remissions, and other special privileges further pushed the balance in favor of agriculture, leaving the nomadic pastoral populations to find a new ecological niche for themselves.

At the close of the First World War, Northern Arabia, nominally an Ottoman province, was partitioned by the League of Nations. The semi-arid lands of the badia were divided up and distributed, under "mandate status," to France and Great Britain. The southern wedge alone remained in the hands of Abdul Aziz Al-Saud. This step, along with the subsequent establishment of British and French administrations in their respective regions, the development of road and telegraph infrastructure, and the introduction of mechanized transport, had a tremendous impact on the nomadic pastoral tribes of the region as well as on the population as a whole. Many were to prophesy that these developments spelled the death of the nomadic pastoral way of life. Most of these changes, however, were quickly absorbed by the Bedouin and altered to meet the needs of their own highly adaptive system.

Nomadic Pastoralism in the Sultanate of Oman

The Sultanate of Oman in the southeastern corner of Arabia, covering an area of about three hundred thousand square kilometers, presents a unique and puzzling case for nomadic pastoral studies.[4] Here a situation of total neglect, benign or otherwise, was the case until just two decades ago. The entire country had been deliberately kept apart from the rest of the world. Some called Oman the "Tibet" of the Middle East (Eickelman 1989:368), so little was known about it. The ruling Sultan kept very tight control over all aspects of the country's administration.

Development was limited to a Dutch Reform Church hospital and school in the capital of Muscat (established in 1894) and, in the late 1960s, a hospital at Tanam. All imports had to be cleared through the Sultan personally. Vehicles, a rarity even in the late 1960s, had to be personally approved by him for import into the country. These were limited to employees of the palace, the national oil company, the armed forces, and a few very privileged wealthy merchant families. Many families smuggled their young sons abroad to educate them. And, as the Sultan's behavior became more repressive, whole families began to go into exile in search of a better life. The pastoral populations of the interior desert regions of the Sultanate of Oman had little contact with or access to the central government of the Sultan on the coast and marginally more with the Ibadi Imam in the northern Oman mountains. For much of the first half of the twentieth century, the country was known as the Sultanate of Muscat and Oman. The Sultan held power in Muscat and along the coast, while the Imam (elected leader) of the dominant Ibadi sect of Islam held sway in the mountains and foothills of the north of the country. The Sultan and Imam maintained a power-sharing compromise up to the early 1950s, when a newly elected Imam began a play for power and a rebellion ensued. Only then did some of the nomadic pastoral tribes perfunctorily take sides in the struggle for control over the interior of the country between the Imam and the Sultan.

With the accession of Sultan Qaboos bin Saiid in 1970, a concerted program of development occupied the young government. Education, health, and other social services, together with plans for developing the country's physical infrastructure—roads, telephone, radio, and television—were implemented in rapidly expanding waves out from the capital area along the coast and from Salalah in Dhofar. By the late 1970s the government had reached a point where it felt that its health, education, and other social services covered most of the urban and rural population of the country. The time had come, some officials felt, to extend the same services to the highly mobile, difficult-to-reach nomadic population in the interior desert areas of the country.

Earlier in the 1970s the government had been almost totally preoccupied in winning the "hearts and minds" of the Dhofari population in the south of the country, after a protracted insurrection had been narrowly won. It was felt that some elements of that transhumant pastoral population were harboring rebels or remained indecisive about the new government. Thus an elaborate program of civil aid for the Dhofar region was established. A mobile medical service was set up to reach the more inaccessible settlements weekly, using four-wheel drive vehicles and, when necessary, helicopters and small aircraft. Comprehensive community centers were built throughout the mountain ranges. These consisted of schools, health clinics, mosques, and an assortment of government offices where requests were accepted for water well drilling, for welfare subsidies, and for assistance in house construction. A high frequency (HF) radio provided the link between the center and Salalah in cases of emergency. The rationale behind these administrative centers was not only to "win over the population," but also to attempt to settle them permanently around the centers or around the new water holes. Keeping a close watch over a fairly settled population was far easier than trying to keep up with the seasonal movements demanded in their traditional way of life.

After a decade of guerrilla activity in the Dhofar Mountains, government efforts to pacify the population through the extension of generous social services proved successful. The traditional pastoral way of life has, however, been severely disturbed, as has the unique monsoon-based rangeland ecosystem of the mountains. This situation requires a separate study and cannot be dealt with in any depth here. It has, however, contributed to the formation of a unique policy toward Oman's other nomads—the pastoral population raising camel and goat in the interior of the country. That policy is the extension of services that have reached the rest of the population—health facilities, schools, mosques, administrative offices—to the desert dwellers, but without forcing them to give up their traditional way of life.

Summary of current situation

Oman, like so many of the states of the Middle East, has been inhabited by and continuously subjected to successive waves of peoples. Settlement has come mainly from the desert fringes; one along the southern coast of Arabia and the other through the northern gateway of Al-Buraimi. The legendary ancestry of all Arab tribes is traced back to two brothers—the northern Qais (or Adnan) and the southern Yemen (or Qahtan). The first groups to enter Oman spread out along the southern coastal region and began to settle in the Ja'laan and along the western side of the Jebel Akhdar mountain. These were a Qahtani group, the Malik ibn Fahm, as well as some Mahra, South Arabian language-speaking tribal groups (Wilkinson 1972). The migrations of these groups from the southern route continued for probably four to five centuries until early Islamic times. Most other Arab groups apparently arrived in Oman from the north, the last major one being the Azd Shanu'a. Their arrival seems to have coincided with a period of weak Persian rule along the Batinah coast, and they were able to penetrate into the very heartland of Persian Oman. The Persians recognized their leading families and lineages as "kings of the Arabs." These Arabs, with Persian support, were able to exercise a loose control over the majority of the Arab groups in Greater Oman. With the rise of Islam, the Persian ruling groups were removed and power transferred to the Arabs. For the next hundred years, until the first Ibadi Imamate was formed shortly after 720 A.D., the country was left entirely in the hands of the Arab ruling families and subjected to a form of tribal rule (Wilkinson 1987).

The tribal structure of Oman has undergone deep changes over the centuries. Many nomadic tribes have arrived and sedentarized far from their original tribal territory. Other Bedouin tribes, adapting to the changing rhythm of history, have established settled branches in widely dispersed regions of the country, specializing in either farming, fishing, or pastoralism. Families within one tribe have been known to change their economic focus, given the general ecological conditions at any one time.[5]

Of the numerous pastoral tribes in Oman, four stand out either because of their size, the peculiar nature of their ecological niche, or their responses to the political and legal events of the last one hundred years. They are the Wahiba, the Duru, the Jeneba, and the Harasiis (see maps 2 and 3).

The Wahiba tribe occupies an area between Sufra-ad-Dawh and the southern coast of Oman. They are bounded on the west by Wadi Halfayn

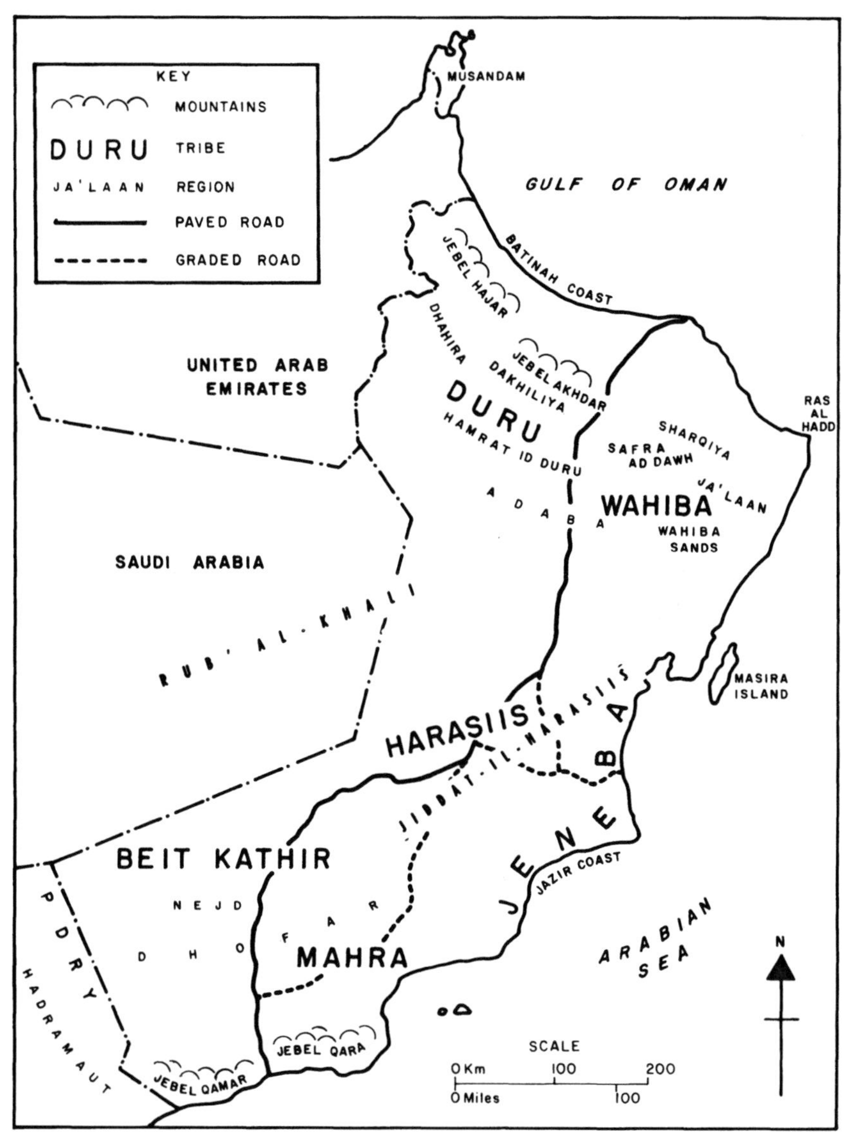

Map 2 Tribes and Geographical Regions in the Sultanate

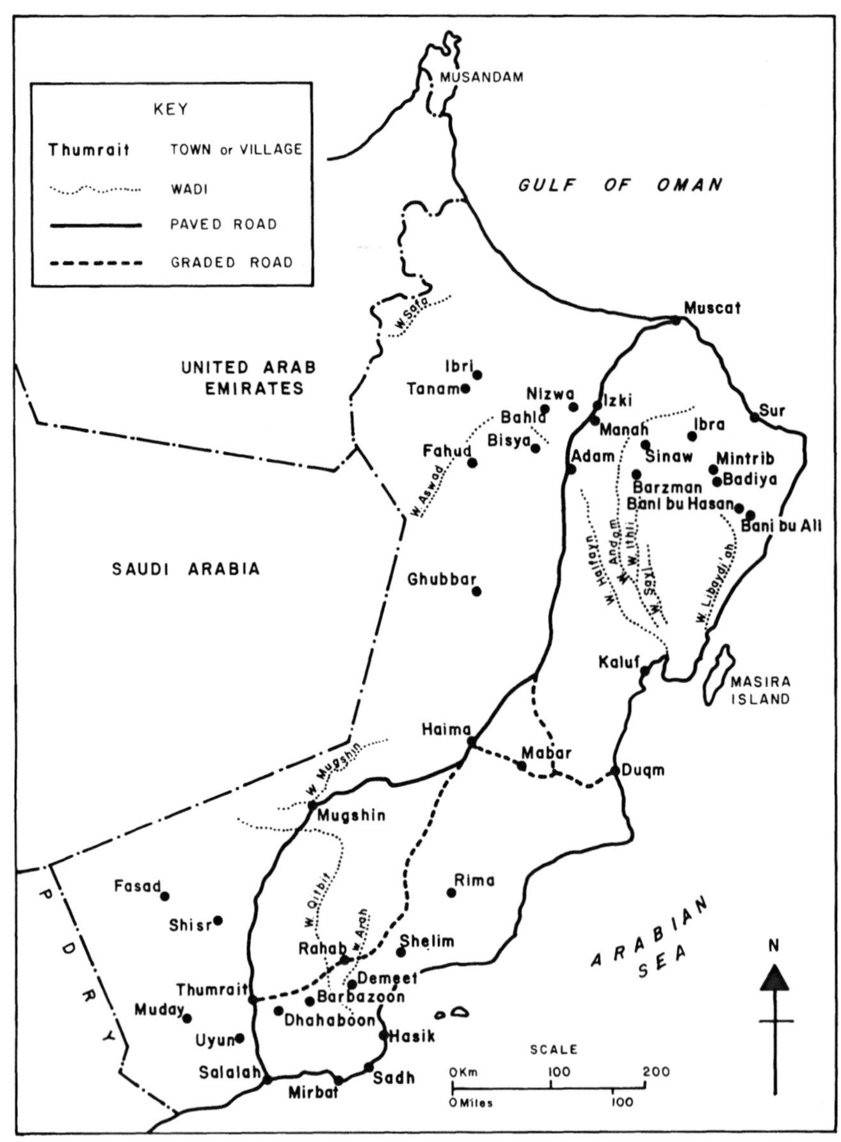

Map 3 Towns and Wadis in the Sultanate

and on the east by the settled areas of the Sharqiyya. They are primarily a pastoral people numbering around seven thousand. In winter they migrate within their desert territory in search of grazing for their livestock. In summer they move to the edge of the Sharqiyya, where the tribe owns numerous date gardens. Fishing is an important activity among the Wahiba coastal population. In summer, when the monsoon winds make this pursuit less attractive, families from the coast tend to migrate to the Wahiba settlements on the fringe of the Sharqiyya for the date harvest.

The Duru tribe is spread over a large area, from Wadi Safa and the sands in the west and northwest right across the semiarid plain almost to the Wadi Halfayn. It is a widely spread tribe divided into a number of sections, each living in a fairly well-defined area. They engage in camel, goat, and sheep husbandry. In autumn, winter, and spring they are nomadic, but as the heat increases and the dates ripen they come in from the desert and settle outside various towns. They own most of the date groves in Tanam and about one-third of the gardens in Ibri. The Duru—as most of the other nomadic pastoral tribes in Oman—never actually live in the towns, but put up palm frond huts nearby during the summer.

The Jeneba is a large and widely dispersed group comprising several sections. South of Adam they practice nomadic pastoralism. They also form a substantial part of the population of Sur and of the Ja'laan and have historically had seafaring interests up the Gulf to India and to East Africa. Along the southern coast of Oman they are fishermen. They predominate on Masira and between Duqm and Dhofar. Their total numbers easily reach twelve thousand.

The Harasiis tribe appears to have been originally a Dhofari tribe and they continue to speak a South Arabian Mahri-related language. They are small in number, totalling not more than three thousand people and occupying the once waterless gravel and limestone desert plateau known as the Jiddat-il-Harasiis. This region, which separates south Oman—Dhofar—the northern mountains, and coast of Oman, was once a particularly inhospitable and difficult tract to cross, let alone survive in. And until very recently it was, in effect, the "backwater" of both Dhofar and northern Oman (Janzen 1986). The Harasiis tribe was probably pushed progressively into this vast uninhabited desert by stronger pastoral groups moving northward from the Hadramaut valley of Yemen. Although the tribe's claim to the area has, on occasion, been contested by rival groups, no other tribe has actually attempted to move into the Jiddat. It was, until recently, the most desolate of landscapes, with little if any seasonal grasses and totally unfit for habitation during the scorching summer months. Events over the last twenty years have transformed the Jiddat and profoundly affected its population. In the 1980s it became the location of a joint government/United Nations Development Program project that is the focus of this study.

Oil activity in this corner of the Arabian Peninsula started only after the Second World War, with the explorative work near Al-Buraimi in 1948. It was seriously hindered by the reluctance of the Ibadi Imam in the Jebel Akhdar to permit Christians into the territory he controlled. However, the potential for oil wealth in the region encouraged the Sultan and the national oil company administration in Muscat to search for a way into the most promising desert areas. In 1955 an exploratory search party landed at Duqm on Oman's eastern coast, made its way across the Jiddat-il-Harasiis, and finally arrived at Fahud in the territory of the Duru tribe. The local tribal leaders gave the party permission to explore for oil. The Ibadi Imam, however, was enraged and ordered that the date gardens of the Duru at Tanam be burned. After a series of skirmishes, and with serious assistance from the British military, the Sultan was able to impose his authority over the region and oil exploration, and, later, production, took place without opposition. In 1958 an oil exploratory party came to a point called Haima in the middle of the Jiddat-il-Harasiis and sank a water well as a support for their oil activity. Another well was sunk at a point seventy kilometers toward the coast, at a point called Al-Ajaiz. These two wells were the first water sources on the Jiddat-il-Harasiis and the Harasiis tribal leader, Sheikh Shergi bin Akis, lost no time in requesting that the wells be left open after the oil party moved on elsewhere (see chapter 4 for further details of the oil activities). For the following decade there was very little oil exploration activity on the Jiddat itself. Al-Ajaiz became something of a magnet attracting pastoral families to its well and its seasonal browse. Haima was also used, but not to the same extent as Al-Ajaiz, as the area surrounding it was a salt flat with very little graze or browse available for the herds of camels and goats.

In the late 1970s a government decision under the sponsorship of the Ministry of Social Affairs and Labor was taken to try to extend social services to the nomadic pastoralists of the desert areas by building a number of experimental tribal centers. Approval to build the first of these centers was made at about the same time as the Royal Oman Police Force's search for an appropriate spot to build a border station to patrol its long and fairly ambiguous border with Saudi Arabia on the margins of the Rub' al-Khali (Empty Quarter). As water was the crucial factor, both Haima and Al-Ajaiz were under consideration. The Minister of Social Affairs and Labor as well as the Inspector General of the police considered that a combined border patrol station and a tribal center would be the most effective use of government funds. A British firm of architects was given the tender to build the center, which was to consist of the government representative's office, a medical clinic, a four-roomed school, a mosque, a reverse osmosis water plant, a police station, and an assortment of villas to house the government employees. By 1980, with no special consideration for the peculiar features of the country nor the particular difficulties of the desert, a "tribal" complex of buildings was under construction. The choice of location proved to be fortuitous indeed, but the physical structures were in danger of becoming "white elephants" in a landscape renowned for its heat mirages. During this construction I was approached and asked whether I could help find a way to encourage the nomadic pastoral community in the area to use the soon-to-be opened center.

Changing Attitudes Toward Nomadic Pastoralists

In spite of a lingering sentimentality toward the Bedouin that has deep historic roots, the popular consensus over the past few decades has been that these tribes are a major obstacle to social and economic development. The recently established governments of Northern Arabia generally regard their nonsedentary populations as tribes forming a state within a state and constituting a "national problem." The local concern is that nationhood in the Arab world cannot be achieved on a stable and permanent basis unless the tribal segment becomes fully integrated with the rest of the nation. At the same time, pastoralism is associated with antiprogressive forces. Administrative policies in agriculture, health, education, and land reform often appear to be obstructed by the pastoral tribes. These people are seen by local administrators as a source of trouble, a backward entity standing in the way of national progress. Hence, the only overall solution envisaged by national administrators is the settling of the tribe.

The United Nations and its agencies came into being at about the same time as the nation-states of Northern Arabia achieved independence. Its position on the nomadic pastoralists was closely attuned to and legitimated that of the Arab nation-states. A series of meetings and, later, studies were organized by various United Nation agencies to examine the problems of the member states. The course these sessions took is clearly revealed by Bocco (1990:97–121). Starting in 1952 a policy of settling nomadic pastoralists and turning them into farmers was proposed in order to raise their standard of living. Between 1956 and 1957 the World Health Organization recommended the settling of nomads in order to improve their health and to stop them from transmitting diseases. In 1959 there was a lone voice of dissent as Food and Agriculture Organization experts signaled the importance of improving the animal husbandry practices and rangeland of the nomadic pastoralists. Returning to the majority opinion, the International Labor Organization set out a number of recommendations, which reflected the unanimity of expert and national opinion that settling the nomadic pastoralists was synonymous with development and progress (Bocco 1990:101; also see Awad 1962; Barth 1962; International Labor Organization 1962). This sedentarization meant the transforming of the pastoralist, who lived upon the products of the herd and flock, into a settled cultivator of the soil (see, for example, Awad 1959).

The key factor in this attitude is the "anxiety" of many Arab administrators that pastoralism as a mode of life is a holdover from an irrational past and therefore lacking modern rational use of the world's resources (Cunnison 1977). In the 1980s much of the focus of the literature shifted to African pastoralists, but the arguments remained very similar. Political motivation to settle or control pastoralists was couched mainly in ecological terms—their abuse of the environment (Sanford 1983; Aronson 1980; Galaty 1980; Gilles and Gefe 1990; Saleh 1990). The label of environmental degradators was also applied to pastoralists in the Arabian Peninsula (Janzen 1983; Chatty 1980; Hobbs 1989). These studies highlight the cultural and value gap between many local administrators and pastoral people within the nation-state.

Much of the recent literature concerned with the nomad problem is a reflection of the attitude highlighted above. A selection of United Nations publications during the past few decades reveals some common themes: 1. Pastoralism is both self impoverishing and inimical to national development. 2. Nomadic grazing practices have led to loss of ground cover, and, as an effect of the politically drawn borders, pastoralists take less interest in range management and conservation. 3. The habits of pastoralists isolate them from whatever social, educational, and medical services may be available to the rest of the society (UNESCO 1961, 1962, 1963; UNESOB 1970; FAO 1972, 1985, 1988, 1989). Much of this literature on the nomad problem reveals an emphasis, particularly puzzling to me, on the "resistance to change" of nomadic populations when compared with other societies (Schneider 1959; Sahlins 1967; Weulersse 1946; Yacoub 1970, 1972; Coon 1951; Warriner 1959). The focus is adjusted in more recent analysis to explain the regular failure of pastoralists to respond to development aid (Dyson-Hudson 1991; Behnke and Scoones 1993; Hurskainen 1990).

Historical Imagery of Nomadic Pastoralists in Arabia

Nomadic pastoralists, and particularly the Bedouin tribes of the Middle East, have fired the imagination of historians, poets, travelers, and academics for centuries. Many colorful and highly imaginative passages have been penned about these peoples by Western as well as Arab writers. At the root of the work of both groups is the philosophical image of the "noble savage." Ibn Khaldun, the fourteenth-century North African historian, court adviser, and judge, developed the concept of the pure and noble Bedouin in his introduction to the History of Civilization (*The Muqaddimah*). In it he expands his theory of the way in which Islamic civilization has risen and fallen over the centuries, always being renewed by fresh blood from the desert. An image of the human being as a social animal, unspoilt by the trappings of civilization and still holding tightly to the concept of the blood tie and the kin relationship, is given special prominence. This, he wrote, was the basis of the "group solidarity" (*asabiyah*) that held the Bedouin together as a society and brought them both closer to nature and to God. Civilization, he propounded, destroyed group solidarity. Given these "facts," he developed his philosophy on the cyclical course of history. Bedouin moved out of the desert and, because of their superior group solidarity and strength, easily conquered existing urban civilizations. Once in place, these formerly desert dwellers were corrupted by the trappings of urban life and fell prey to the next wave of attack from the desert dwellers who still had a sense of group solidarity. Ibn Khaldun's work started out as a general introduction to the subject of history—until that time generally a few lines or at most a few pages in many a work—and grew to the size of a substantial volume. Rather than going against accepted tradition, he went beyond it and proclaimed his lengthy elaboration of historical theory, *The*

Muqaddimah, as the origin of a new science. The work was almost universally accepted immediately and accommodated within the traditional framework of historiography.

However, for several centuries Ibn Khaldun's work suffered a decline, until it was revived in the late Ottoman period and many of his ideas were adopted by Western scholars. This was particularly true where it could be established that he was a precursor of a contemporarily fashionable theory. Thus the eighteenth- and nineteenth-century French philosophical traditions expounded by Voltaire, Jean Jacques Rousseau, and, later, Alexis de Tocqueville that extolled the virtues of the noble savage were very much in line with the ideas developed earlier by Ibn Khaldun.

For Arab historians there was a further dimension to the imagery of the nomadic pastoralist, which was the association of the Bedouin with the grandeur of the earlier Islamic civilization. The Bedouin were strongly affiliated with the first Islamic caliphate, the one hundred years of drama and brilliance centered around the Umayyid dynasty in Damascus. During the expansion of this caliphate, an ideology based on Bedouin society came to the fore (see Saleh Ahmad al-'Ali, quoted in Gavrielides 1993:147–158). It provided the rationale for the administration of the newly established garrison towns and conquered territories. Furthermore, to many an Arab historian Umayyid power represented the Bedouin reaction against the townsmen of Mecca and Medina. The lore of the desert, the solidarity, dignity and toughness of the blood tie, the scepticism in matters of dogma, together with imagination and good sense, were characteristics ascribed to the Bedouin and many of the caliphs of the Umayyid dynasty.

By the second half of the twentieth century the attitudes and imagery surrounding nomadic pastoralists and, in particular, the Bedouin of the Arabian Peninsula had become so highly colored and peculiarly ethnocentric that it was difficult to distinguish between fact and fiction, let alone the population that was meant to be encompassed by the term. At times urbanized Arab bureaucrats used it in a romanticized sense to indicate a people in a sort of primal state of goodness, whereas at other times it was used to indicate any population group that had not acquired the trappings of modern life such as cement housing, material possessions, and the general sophistication associated with a Western education. By the 1980s in Jordan, for example, the term *Bedouin* (Layne 1994:12) was often found used interchangeably with the terms *tribe, nomad, pastoralist,* and *desert Arab.*

In Oman the term is often qualified and government officials will discuss "pastoral" bedouin and "fishing" bedouin as being part of the same large, rural tribal-based society. As Eickelman (1989:74) points out and Wilkinson (1977:189) and Johnson (1969) before him, bedouin (*bedu*) is often used locally in contrast with settled (*hadhar*) ways of life (also see Lewis 1987:3). In this instance what is actually important is not so much the mobility or economic organization of the society but its social organization as a tribal society. The Egyptian villager working in Oman, Wilkinson illustrates, would probably tend to label all Omanis as "bedu" even though they may be village dwellers, because their social organization is tribal. To Omanis themselves the definitions are different and a marked distinction between bedu and hadhar holds (also see Altorki and Cole 1989:18). In the northern parts of the Arabian Peninsula, the term is used with more precision to indicate pastoral segments of the population, though there as well it is used, on occasion, in a pejorative sense to indicate a rural, unsophisticated, and simple person.

Settlement Policies in the Middle East

First Saudi Arabia, then the countries contiguous to it—Jordan, Syria, and Iraq—have attempted to settle their nomadic pastoral population. Perhaps the first example of this type of forced settlement is the Hijra scheme in Saudi Arabia, established by King Abdul Aziz for political as well as religious reasons early this century. His goal was, first, to "purify" the religion of the Bedouin, which was considered by him and his fundamentalist Wahhabi followers to be far removed from Orthodox Islam. And, second, it was to control the movements of these Bedouin and make them available for the Al-Saud expansionist military activities whenever necessary. This large effort to settle the Bedouin began in 1910. Those who were successfully recruited into these Hijra schemes were called Ikhwan. In 1912 the Al-Artawiya settlement was established  and by the late 1920s had a population of over thirty-five thousand. It was destroyed, however, after the 1929 revolt of the Ikhwan. Over the decades it has been repopulated by other Bedouin and today the population numbers nearly sixteen thousand. Little agriculture is practiced there. The population depends mainly upon trade, transport, government employment, and National Guard salaries. Another Hijra established in 1912, Al-Ghutghut, reached a peak population of ten thousand Ikhwan before it too was destroyed by loyal supporters of Ibn Saud in 1929 (Fara

1973). By 1950, however, most of these settlements were minor administrative centers, the Bedouin having abandoned them to return to their pasturelands with their herds of camels, sheep, and goats.

The situation in the mandated states of Syria, Jordan, and Iraq was somewhat different. The British and French mandate authorities had permitted and encouraged the pastoralists under their administration to maintain a separate political identity, and, in some cases, such as under the Contrôle Bedouin in Syria, separate courts were established to deal with Bedouin affairs. The nation-states were understandably opposed to this situation of a state within a state and viewed such a phenomenon as inimical to the ideal of national unity (Glubb 1942; Ministère des Affairs Etrangères 1923–1937). These difficulties between the tribal political system and the modern "Western-based" one were veiled in an economic idiom by government officials. Consequently the settlement and transformation of pastoralists into cultivators was urged for the economic integration and advancement of a "marginal" and "primitive" people—not for political integration. Needless to say, most of these imposed settlement projects failed to achieve an economic, let alone political, integration.

The case of Jordan is particularly interesting in this context. At the time of its creation as a state under British mandate to the League of Nations in 1921, its population was estimated at three hundred thousand, with over half (one hundred and seventy thousand) classified as "nomads" or "semi-nomads" (Bocco 1990:109). Throughout the mandate period the British attempted to integrate the population into the nation for the same political reasons discussed earlier. The strategies were settlement schemes, army recruitment, and agricultural development efforts. With independence, and for the next thirty years, the policies remained the same, as did the strategies. Between 1960 and 1980 a total of eleven settlement schemes were undertaken, and Bocco (1990:110) shows that the expert opinions throughout this period were divided and contradictory, some claiming the "nomads" were unable to break with their traditions and others that they were interested in and capable of adapting to sedentary life.[6] The irony of such statements was that the basic premise of breaking down Bedouin tribal strength was overlooked. Recent studies (Bocco 1989; Layne 1989, 1994) show that, contrary to the detribalization of the Bedouin, something far more complicated has emerged. The model of tribal organization common to the Bedouin has not only remained intact, but has come to be associated with the identity of the state's ruling monarch—King Hussein—and the nation itself.

Recent Changes in Nomadic Pastoral Life

Over the last three decades—the 1960s, 1970s, and 1980s—tremendous changes have taken place throughout the Middle East. In cities enormous economic growth and development have occurred along with a rural-urban migration of individuals seeking to join the labor market. In villages economic growth has in places stagnated as people are drawn away in search of wage labor, while in other rural communities economic growth can be observed as a result of the introduction of modern agricultural methods and equipment. In the pastoral tribal sector emigration and sedentarization are also occurring. This phenomenon is erroneously regarded by national administrators as a "recent" change and a sign of the deterioration of the pastoral way of life. Outmigration through extremes of wealth or poverty has always existed among pastoral populations (Barth 1961:109–111). Although data on population dynamics among these peoples are sketchy, the balance between births and deaths tends not to give as high a rate of natural growth as among sedentary communities (see Meir 1987). What population increase there is tends to be drained off through the mechanisms of emigration and sedentarization. The core of the pastoral group thus remains demographically in balance with the land and the herd. The historically documented migration and sedentarization of some of the Shammar Bedouin tribes in Jordan in the eighteenth century (Caskel 1954), the emigration of some Syrian Aneza tribes back to the Nejd of Saudi Arabia between 1934 and 1938 (Lewis 1987), and the sedentarization of the Al-Shabana in Iraq (Fernea 1970) are but a few examples.

Perhaps the most far-reaching development to affect the nomadic pastoral tribes was the establishment of a regional infrastructure during the Interwar Mandate. Originally intended as an aid to military control of the area, a system of roads begun by the French and British was to dramatically affect the pastoralists' organization. Camels, the major economic wealth of many Bedouin, were increasingly rendered obsolete as new systems of transport became operative. Slowly at first, and then with increasing urgency, sheep, the traditional herding animal of the "common" client tribes, replaced camels as the herding animals of the "noble" tribes.[7]

This general pattern is widespread throughout the region. Cole

(1971) and Bonnenfant (1977) both remark on the shift to sheep raising among the noble tribes in Saudi Arabia. In Iraq and Syria the noble Shammar and Aneza tribes raise mainly sheep (Ministère des Affairs Etrangères 1931; Lancaster 1981:223–246). In Jordan the noble Beni Sakker and Howeitat tribes have also shifted to modern sheep raising. These Bedouins' recent emphasis on sheep as the principal grazing animal and their accompanying shift from camel, as beast of burden, to truck represents a modernizing form of pastoralism wherein new relations with sedentary communities are expressed in heavier trade and closer symbiosis in cultivation. Throughout this region the truck is used to transport sheep for sale from the desert to distant market centers, to transport households and animal holdings from one camp to another and water to the herds in the desert. The truck also provides for easy and continuous relations between the village and the tribal encampment, permitting many Bedouin families to undertake a secondary work activity in urban or village centers.

The very rapidity with which the truck is replacing camel transport in Syria, Jordan, and Saudi Arabia is becoming a threat to the long-term well-being of that way of life (Chatty 1986). In the past range usufruct depended upon two factors. First, up to two or three weeks were required to move from one pasture area to another. Today that can take a matter of hours or days by truck. This rapid mobility has, in the past two decades, led to increased overgrazing of the rangeland. Second, there was the almost universal seizure of tribal territory by the nation-state and its transformation into state-owned land. This has removed the tribal leaders from the protective and regulative role they once fulfilled in the pastoral community.

Over the years the ecologically fragile semiarid steppeland has slowly succumbed to the pressure of overgrazing, cutting of woody plants for firewood and ploughing of marginal areas for precarious grain production. Vast areas that once had been good grazing land have become barren and are now considered man-made deserts. With the advent of the truck, the pace of erosion has accelerated and vast areas of rangeland are lost annually to the desert. Furthermore, since the late 1940s most governments of the Middle East have maintained the belief that all the semiarid regions should be considered and kept as government-owned land. Previous grazing rights have progressively been canceled with no compensation, thus encouraging misuse and uncontrolled nomadic grazing throughout the steppe regions.

Over the last fifteen to twenty years some governments have begun to recognize the dimensions of the problem. Following the failure of most of the earlier attempts to sedentarize pastoralists and successfully transform them into farmers, the governments of Syria, Saudi Arabia, and, to an extent, Jordan, began in the 1970s and 1980s to reassess their priorities and search for better ways of reaching their goal of integrating these groups into their respective nation-states. Some have cautiously begun to develop programs that more effectively integrate their pastoral population into the regional economy. They have initiated plans designed to optimize the output of the desert steppe (nearly 90 percent of the total land area) in the only manner that it can be used—for grazing. Governments and international agencies involved in the Middle East have turned to a study of the deterioration of the rangeland.

Programs of rangeland development have become commonplace throughout the region. In a few cases the human factor in relation to land use, and land tenure, has held considerable weight (see Draz 1977). In the late 1960s and 1970s studies of the traditional system for graze management known as *hema* in Saudi Arabia showed it to be the oldest effective range conservation system known and still maintained—under different names—in many countries of the Middle East (e.g., *mahmia, marah, koze, mahjuz, masnuun*). Expert advice was that the former grazing rights of the pastoral tribes be restored—within the framework of a modern cooperative. Such action, it was argued, would result in a marked regeneration of the rangeland and a change in the prevailing destructive attitude toward the range as a no-man's land open for free grazing by the first flocks to arrive. In Syria land donated by the government in the 1960s and 1970s formed the foundation of a series of hema associations and cooperatives (see also Shoup 1990). The initial success of this program paved the way for the extension of the system to cover more than 1.5 million hectares of steppeland, with a total of twenty-two cooperatives by the end of 1976.[8]

In Saudi Arabia programs to settle Bedouin and turn them into farmers have only reluctantly given way to projects designed to improve the vast rangeland of the country. During the severe drought from 1957 to 1965, efforts were made to settle the nomadic pastoralists most seriously affected by the crisis. The Wadi al-Sarhan Project was first initiated in 1961 as a relief scheme near the sensitive Jordanian-Saudi border. Within a few years it was transformed into an agricultural project to raise the standard of living of the nomadic pastoralists. The project failed utterly after the first rains in 1965, when most pastoralists withdrew from the scheme and went off in search of fresh grazing land for their meager herds. It struggled along for a few more years until it was finally canceled in 1972. A second scheme to settle the pastoralists was initiated in 1964 in the area between the Rub' al-Khali and the Dahna Desert. Called the King Faysal Settlement Project at Haradh, it encompassed eight thousand acres of grazing land and was expected to provide for one thousand families.

The stated goal of this project was to integrate the Bedouin into the national fabric and to improve their socioeconomic conditions by providing them with new skills in agriculture. Although the project's administration attempted to learn from the earlier mistakes at Wadi al-Sarhan, it too suffered considerable setbacks. Within three years there was a reversal of goals, and the project was transformed into a massive scheme to grow fodder crops and raise sheep (Abdulrahman 1979).

The failure of these more modern and better-planned settlement schemes as well as the rising internal demand for meat and the rapid deterioration of the steppeland have gradually forced the government to reassess its rangeland resources. As in Syria, the traditional hema system was reactivated, on an experimental basis, in the late 1960s and early 1970s as a practical basis for a National Country Program for rangeland development. By the late 1970s the success of these few experimental stations encouraged the government to support the expansion of hema as a grazing management system throughout the country. This was accompanied by the revival of a traditional water spreading system, a modern feed reserve and storage facility, and livestock fattening stations on the margins of the steppeland in order to relieve the pressure of grazing on the rangeland.

The Bedouin population of Jordan, approximately 7 percent of the total (Abu Jaber et al. 1978), has not escaped the impact of modernization any more than nomadic pastoralists elsewhere in the Middle East. Indeed, many of the Jordanian Bedouin are actively striving for the benefits they see offered by modern society. Today a process of settlement in the small rural communities of Jordan's frontier zone between agriculture and pastoralism is taking place. This is partially because of sophisticated government planning but, more important, because "settled" life—but not necessarily farming—is becoming more attractive to the Bedouin themselves (Abu Jaber and Gharaibeh 1981). The continued existence of a pastoral community in Jordan is vital, given the fact that a large part of the fresh meat consumed in the country (around 25 percent by the 1990s) is still provided by Bedouin herders and landowners. Furthermore, the arid and semiarid land that defines most of Jordan can only be used effectively by the Bedouin. In this respect, the government has recognized that there is no easy substitute for the Bedouin and their role in the contemporary economy of the country. The present concern of the government and international agencies involved in the region's development is how to encourage the Bedouin to maintain, if not expand, the productive capacity of livestock raising in a terrain in which no one can replace them. To that end, a national study was undertaken by the University of Jordan in the late 1970s to ascertain the economic and social status and current attitudes of a representative sample of the population's Bedouin (Abu Jaber et al. 1978). Not surprisingly, the most critical characteristic to emerge from the study was the recognition of the degeneration of land usufruct as a result of overgrazing and poor management of the grasslands, which in turn resulted from earlier land registration and private ownership of small plots. The recommendation at the end of the study was for a planned program of man/land use that would make a modernizing form of livestock raising more attractive to the inhabitants of the Jordanian badia. A system of rangeland conservation in the form of livestock raising cooperatives—as sponsored by the Food and Agriculture Organization in other countries of the region—is particularly well suited for adoption in Jordan. This issue, still under discussion in 1991, has become more focused, and land rights, as well as controlled access to the range, have come to characterize the issues of the present decade.

The nomadic pastoralists of the Middle East are constantly changing their way of life to best suit their needs. The adoption of truck transport and the equally rapid obsolescence of the camel, the change in water and grass management and the experiments in fodder farming all point to the primacy of livestock raising to these populations. The reality of these changes should be of no surprise. Peoples everywhere are changing and, where there is freedom of choice, decisions are being made to optimize conditions. Few farmers today cultivate in exactly the same way they did fifty years ago. And few Bedouin today raise livestock in the same fashion as their grandfathers. Change is part of their life as it is part of life in all societies.

The Organization of the Study

In the following chapters I will describe and analyze how a development project aimed at nomadic pastoralists was conceived, drafted, implemented, and completed. Three distinct cultural perceptions affected this process: that of the nomadic pastoralists, the local bureaucracy, and the international aid agency. A fourth interpretation, if my own vision as an anthropologist is included, might also have played an important part in the way the pastoral population perceived some changes. The issues of importance, the conflicts, and the compromises all contributed to the course the project took and, finally, to the select way in which the nomadic pastoralists themselves controlled the course of change in their lives and their culture.

Chapter 2 discusses the relationship between anthropology and development. It deals with the way in which government ideas and structures came to be interpreted and set into a series of workable goals; how the demands of international development agencies were accommodated and how, through my mediating role as project leader, conflicts of goals, time frames, budgets, and ideologies were bridged. It also looks at the different perspectives from which development was viewed.

In Chapter 3 the plan of action negotiated between the international agency and myself as the project leader is described and its implementation through a series of practical activities is discussed. The setbacks and the unexpected difficulties during these initial few months are also examined. The place of primary health care delivery in creating social ties as well as obligations for the project personnel is analyzed. The way in which the repeated delivery of promises affected the relationship between the project personnel and the tribes is also discussed. This led to my inevitable transformation in the eyes of the tribal population from project leader to interpreter to catalyst and, finally, to activist. The early successes of programs for the boarding schooling, water delivery, and tent distribution all contributed to the pastoral population's determination to change my role and move me from the traditional category of participant observer to something more like tribal spokesperson.

Chapter 4 is a description and analysis of how the Harasiis tribe has come to terms with the radical changes in their environment. Long before the central authority of the Sultan was effectively imposed on the region, the national oil company and its exploration teams had become familiar sights in that desert. The relationship between the two was, on the surface, only one of employee and employer. But the Harasiis tribe were to learn much about the twentieth century from these sporadic contacts. In later decades the government-sponsored reintroduction project of the white oryx was to have an even greater impact on the tribe. First, there was the government selection of the comparatively lush wadi belonging to the tribe for the exclusive use of the base camp of the scheme. And, second, there was the almost total monopoly of employment for Harasiis men as oryx rangers and scouts. The relationship of the tribe with other government agencies, such as the police and the armed forces, is also discussed in relationship to a pattern of employment that begins to emerge: the Harasiis are quick to adopt and adapt elements of the modern twentieth century that suit them. They are just as adept at dismissing what does not work for them and maintaining their own tribal integrity.

Chapter 5 discusses the present Harasiis household, a blend of the traditional and the innovative. This section concentrates on the universality of daily existence. It discusses the traditional cultural patterns and the new adaptations and compares and contrasts the families of a full-time husbandman with one who is locally fully employed. An economic analysis is made of pastoralism and the newfound local employment opportunities in the Jiddat.

Chapter 6 focuses on the relationship between pastoralism and full-time employment opportunities. It analyzes the place of the entrepreneur in the society and the political broker. Two groups of brothers are discussed, one set being the tribal entrepreneurs and successful merchants, the other the political mediators and employment brokers. Both groups continue to strive for recognition as leading figures in the tribe. The role of the patriarch in the creation of strong sibling groups is also examined in an effort to understand the dynamics behind successful agnatic cohesion in the tribe.

Chapter 7 reexamines the popular position that women tend to be the conservative element in society. Focusing on the wives of the household heads discussed earlier, this chapter looks at the nature of gender relations among the Harasiis tribe. Women are seen to have a complementary role to play in society and the issue of inequality is largely missing from their lives. It is only in relation to the settled communities or the cultural expectations in the urban government facilities that their status seems to diminish. Contrary to the notion of their conservatism, Harasiis women have pushed for education for their daughters and for themselves, catching the national government off guard.

Chapter 8 looks at the future of the Harasiis tribe caught in a world of petroleum exploitation on a UNESCO World Heritage Site. It reviews the trends in herd management and subsistence patterns and the ways in which tribal identity can accommodate national identity. It critically examines the accomplishment of planned development and questions whether change that is not, in fact, actually initiated—even to a small degree—from within the tribe itself ever does take place. Finally, it looks to the changes the tribespeople have themselves supported and highlights the way in which formal education, among other developments, is being supported as the key to survival in the coming years.

2

Developing a Plan:

United Nations Project OMA/80/WO1

"I have the pleasure to send you [a] copy of the above report based on the excellent field work done by Dawn Chatty. . . . I have benefited greatly from her 'applied anthropology and rural sociology.' Indeed, would that my UN development system started more of its rural and community development work with such field studies first!"[1] This quote is drawn from a letter written by the Resident Representative of the United Nations Development Program in the Sultanate of Oman to accompany the distribution of the terminal report of findings and recommendations of project OMA/80/WO1. At first reading it gives the impression that anthropology, which commonly features in only selected aspects of the development process, has at last been recognized as having an important contribution to make during the crucial early stages. In fact the study referred to above was the closing report of a unique, if not peculiar, exercise wherein anthropological knowledge had been applied to a development aid process in the Sultanate of Oman from its national conception to the completion of formal international assistance.

Anthropology and the Development Process

Much of the literature on anthropology and development is ambiguous on the subject of the contribution of anthropological knowledge to the development process (e.g., Bennett 1988:1–29). Although some optimistic assessments have appeared recently (see Wulff and Fiske 1987; Pottier 1993; Green 1986; Brokensha and Little 1988), on the whole the work is negative and reinforces the impression that anthropological knowledge is largely irrelevant to a process concerned with economic parameters or production per se rather than with human life (see, for example, Price 1989; Clay and Holcomb 1986).[2]

The association of anthropology with development manifested itself in the period after the First World War, when the well-being and development of "peoples not yet able to stand by themselves" formed a "sacred trust" of Western civilization. Anthropologists at the time were mainly confined to giving information about local customs to those in authority. By the 1930s the civilizing mission of colonial rulers had changed emphasis to a qualified preservation of what was indigenous. Anthropologists, many of them trained by Malinowski,[3] began to apply themselves to solving problems concerning the small-scale simple societies of colonial Africa and Asia.

The creation of specialized national and international agencies to undertake development work (also referred to at first as reconstruction) came about at the close of the Second World War. Initially the role of anthropologists was simply to provide background information (e.g., Barnett 1956). Since then, and reminiscent of the situation in the 1930s, anthropologists have battled—with some success—to take a fuller part in all the stages of the development process (see Gow 1993:380–397; Escobar 1991; Grillo and Rew 1985; Cernea 1991a; Chambers 1989).

This fight for recognition has been widely discussed and debated for a number of years. It has produced a vast body of literature, which is largely beyond the scope of this study. Michael Horowitz (1988), in a concise and seminal piece, summarized the changes that have taken place over the last three decades. He underscored the very limited role anthropology had in development in the 1960s when the focus of assistance was on infrastructure, urbanization, and industrialization. In the 1970s it shifted to an emphasis on direct assistance to the poor, especially in rural areas. Since anthropologists were, in the main, the only professionals with much firsthand experience of the rural poor in the Third World, they could easily create a niche for themselves in the expanding development role in economic assistance to the Third World. That place, however, lay mainly in the final phase of the project cycle. Anthropologists were invited to carry out "social soundness" analysis for project designs that had already been completed, or to evaluate finished works and conduct postmortems. Very rarely did they join in the policy discussions that preceded the design of specific interventions.

While this limited role was better than no role at all, it was a little like gazing into a crystal ball in order to foretell the social impact of a proposed plan—such as the effect on an agricultural community of constructing a series of low dams. Even when the anthropologist's analysis indicated a very poor promise of socially beneficial results, such projects often went ahead anyway because the political and economic requirements of the agency were deemed more important. David Price's work, *Before the Bulldozer,* is an eloquent testimonial of just such a situation.

The need for most, if not all, development agencies to show accomplishments and to account for financial expenditure limited the role of anthropologists, for it was assumed that the necessary fieldwork would require too much time and money. The need to gain a population's trust and to understand the concepts and values that underpinned a society before planning and designing programs for them—let alone implementing development activities—was considered too expensive and time consuming to warrant serious consideration.

Anthropology and Local Participation in Development

By the 1980s anthropologists and their points of view began to influence the general course of development theory if not the practice. Michael Horowitz summed up the need to enlarge their role and to involve people at the grassroots level:

> In a variety of areas, anthropology affected the ways that some development planners viewed the problems, even if these planners only rarely applied those views in project implementation. Most planners, however, seem to remain well insulated from our findings, the most important of which is the necessity of involving local populations in the planning, design, implementation, and evaluation of development activities intended for their benefit. (1988:2)

By the close of the decade, evaluation offices of international development organizations were beginning to voice the same concerns as Horowitz. In-house evaluations frequently criticized the shortcomings of their own policy. For example, the World Bank unashamedly indicated that its sociological studies were inadequate and that it did not understand the socioeconomic and cultural features of the population expected to benefit from projects—particularly smallholders and women. The Bank recognized the need to encourage the participation of the rural poor in planning and implementation. The underlying assumption of all such studies was that local participation would contribute to the long-term sustainability of projects—the theoretically ultimate goal of most development organizations (World Bank 1988).

Project evaluation reviews within the United Nations Development Program during this same period yielded similar findings. Where the World Bank and other lending institutes tended to stress reform, the UNDP was more concerned with implementing government policy. Their concern for "long-term, self-reliant development," however, underscored the same problem—an inadequate understanding of existing socioeconomic conditions. This failing as well as overrigid blueprints in implementation of programs were commonly cited as factors that made local participation (or "beneficiary participation," to use UNDP jargon) in the development process difficult and inadequate. These reports generally highlighted the need for more tractability and diversity of ideas from the development specialists in the field.

It was during this decade that anthropology attempted, vaguely, to define its role. In an official publication of the American Anthropological Association (Partridge and Warren 1984:1), development anthropology is defined as "scientific research with scientific application within the development project cycle. Its objective is to enhance benefits and mitigate negative consequences for the human communities involved in and affected by development efforts." I take this to mean that anthropologists should ideally be actively engaged in all aspects of the process. This includes designing research, identifying and sampling populations, pulling together resources, recommending programs, and negotiating between cultural groups (Wulff and Fiske 1987:3).

Other disciplines more intimately involved with the development process—such as economics, policy sciences, and public management—have developed their own categories to describe the stages of the development process. In the following discussion of the development project aimed at nomadic pastoralists in the Jiddat-il-Harasiis, I will use Wulff and Fiske's descriptive categories:

1. Definition of the problem or the need by producing information;
2. Formulation of a policy by choosing an alternative;
3. Planning and implemention of interventions to achieve the chosen solution; and
4. Assessment of the results through evaluation (1987:3).

The Creation of the Project

This project sponsored by the United Nations Development Program came into existence at the junction in the history of development practice where "people's participation" was becoming important. It officially ran from May 1981 to July 1983 in the Sultanate of Oman and what follows is an analysis of the project, of the actors involved, of the struggle to establish lines of authority and power, of the babble of tongues and frequent misunderstandings within the local community and the international setting.

Historical Background

The modern development of Oman has been intimately shaped by the personal idiosyncrasies of Sultan Saiid bin Taimur, who came to power in 1932 when his father abdicated. Although poor health was given for the decision to abdicate, many felt that Taimur bin Faisal had been overwhelmed by the impossibility of governing a country hugely in debt to local Indian merchants and the government of British India (Townsend 1977). Sultan Saiid bin Taimur's first objective on his accession was to eliminate the debts he had inherited. Having accomplished this in a short period of time, he determined to avoid further debts by the most parsimonious financial management of the country.

A detailed history of Sultan Saiid's rule is beyond the scope of this study and is covered in a number of excellent works by Peterson (1978), Townsend (1977), and Skeet (1974), to name a few. It is, however, important to keep in mind that Sultan Saiid succeeded in reuniting Oman and Muscat in the 1950s. At the same time, he isolated himself politically from neighboring countries. And, worse, he became increasingly more withdrawn from his own people, until he finally secluded himself in Salalah—a place he regarded as his private property rather than part of the country. Except for the merchant community in the capital area of Muscat and its neighboring town, Mutrah, the population was entirely composed of highly dispersed subsistence agricultural, fishing, and pastoral communities. These enclaves were cut off from the capital area by their very inaccessibility and from the rest of the world as a direct result of the extreme isolationist policy of Sultan Saiid bin Taimur.

By the 1960s his control of the country was weakening. There was a rebellion in the mountains of Dhofar that he was unwilling to face in any manner other than violent repression. In the rest of the country disaffection for his policy of strictly controlling the rate of modernization was growing, and increasingly larger numbers of people were emigrating. But the more restive the mood, the harsher were the restrictions he placed on the population.

Oil had been discovered in commercial quantities in Oman in 1964 and the first exports started in 1967. Very slowly the Sultan began to move toward development. But always the philosophy was that "the rate of progress should not be too rapid."[5] By 1969 there were ten kilometers of paved road, three schools, and twelve hospital beds—all in the capital area—to serve a population of nearly five hundred thousand. Plans had been drawn up to construct hospitals, schools, roads, ports, and harbors, and to deliver water and electricity in the capital area. In the interior, special attention was to be given to the "oil-bearing area and the Duru tribe who live there." A hospital and housing units were under consideration for this pastoral tribe.

Sultan Saiid's government, however, was by this time regarded as the most reactionary and isolationist in the region, if not the world. Slavery was still common and many medieval restrictions were in force. Disillusionment and rebellion reached such alarming rates that a palace coup supported by the army was organized. On July 23, 1970, the thirty-eight-year reign of Sultan Saiid ended, when he signed a formal abdication document in favor of his son, Qaboos bin Saiid.

The situation in Dhofar—which many historians feel precipitated the palace coup against Sultan Saiid—was intricately tied up with the British policy in Aden. After years of poorly organized opposition to the rule of the Sultan over the tribal communities of Dhofar, a formal revolutionary movement—the Dhofar Liberation Front—was established in June 1965. The DLF's war took the form of simple guerrilla operations against the Sultan and his British supplied forces. The Front received moral support, arms, and supplies from the dissident forces fighting the British government in Aden.

By the summer of 1970 the Sultan's Armed Forces, in spite of British equipment and British officers, were completely on the defensive, and the Sultan controlled little more than the town of Salalah—which was protected by barbed wire fencing all around it—and its airfield—which was run and defended by SOAF and the British Royal Air Force. The tra-

Until the mid-1980s Harasiis shelters consisted simply of a tree with a blanket thrown over it for shade. Before fencing was introduced (in the mid-1980s), possessions were tied up on tree branches or wedged into a tree trunk to keep them away from the omnivorous goats.

ditional economy of Dhofar, which was based on the seasonal movement of people and livestock from the mountains to the coastal plains and back again—following the monsoon grazing—had been totally disrupted, possibly effectively destroyed.

Upon his succession Sultan Qaboos bin Saiid regarded himself as part of the opposition movement to his father and set out to counter the insurgency with the following strategy:

1. The offer of a general amnesty;
2. The incorporation of Dhofar as the southern region of Oman;
3. Effective military opposition to the rebels;
4. A rigorous program of development;
5. A diplomatic initiative to have Oman recognized as an Arab state and to isolate the People's Democratic Republic of Yemen.

The first and third elements of this strategy were of particular impor-

A Harasiis household in the late 1980s and 1990s. Canvas cloth is draped over a metal frame to create a temporary, easily moveable home.

tance to the way in which development for pastoral populations came to be conceived by those in authority in Oman.

Identifying the Problem

As part of the general amnesty of 1970, any rebel (meaning, primarily, members of the pastoral tribes of the mountains of Dhofar and Yemen) who surrendered and turned in his arms, would, after a screening, be rearmed, reequipped, and incorporated as a member of a tribal militia (*Firqat*) and returned to his old tribal area as part of a new internal security force. There a government center would be built. This center generally encompassed the drilling of one or more deep wells, the building of water troughs for the population's livestock, and the establishment of a school, a medical station, a mosque, a government shop, government accommodation as well as a Firqat unit. The new recruit would be encouraged to settle his family at the government center. By 1978 there were fifty-three such centers in Dhofar, the largest concentration being in the mountain ranges where resistance to the government had been strongest.

True to his word, in his first five years Sultan Qaboos bin Saiid concentrated on the rapid development of a social and economic infrastructure. Many of the development plans that his father had commissioned and planned to implement one step at a time the new Sultan undertook with a sense of immediacy and urgency. The country's development budget in 1971, during his first year, was $60 million; by 1975 it had grown to $1,000 million. In 1976 the government of Saudi Arabia was reported to have promised $180 million for development in the mountain region of Dhofar. This sum was to be used almost exclusively for building roads and digging water wells. By that same year the country had modern road, sea, and air communications with the rest of the world. Telegraph and telephones were becoming widespread, as were schools, health clinics, and hospitals. Social welfare services and the extension of water and electricity were also rapidly expanding in ever growing circles out from Muscat and Salalah.

By the end of the 1970s the Ministry of Social Affairs and Labor had established a network of community development centers under the direction of an Egyptian technical adviser attached to the UNDP. This program, which had only opened five years earlier—one of the first of many UNDP projects in Oman—started in a small cluster of villages just outside Nizwa, in the north of the country. Its activities included adult literacy programs, health and hygiene campaigns, some income-generating activities for women, and a welfare division.

By 1980 the joint UNDP/government community development centers were thinly stretched over the northern coastal and mountain areas of Oman. The UNDP field specialist in charge of the program was considering a plan to extend the project into the southern region and an office in Salalah was under discussion. The vast interior desert, which occupied over 80 percent of the country's landmass, was felt to be too difficult an environment to penetrate and thus not suitable for the UNDP sponsored project. Suitability, it appears, was being measured with an eye to quick results and field reports that tabulated progress by quantitative rather than qualitative growth. Thus the actual needs of each community were overshadowed by desk requirements when selecting an appropriate population.

Formulation of a Policy

The Minister of Social Affairs and Labor, however, was concerned with the small, but nonetheless significant, population of the country that had still not benefited from any of the basic government services established during the past decade. This population, the nomadic pastoralists of Oman, had been in contact with the national oil company over the last twenty years. Petroleum exploration and finally extraction had taken place in territories that they regarded as their own. Except for the Duru tribe, which had received special attention in Sultan Saiid's speech of 1968 (and in the hastily built hospital and housing settlement in their territory), most of Oman's nomadic pastoralists were hardly aware that the government of Sultan Qaboos was anything different from that of his father or grandfather.

The Minister of Social Affairs and Labor was himself a member of one of these tribes and had begun his early career with the oil company as a clerk. He was acutely aware of the isolation and marginality of most of the nomadic pastoralists of the country. He was also aware of the delicate nature of that way of life and the ease with which it could be irreversibly disrupted.

The example of Dhofar and the effect of the government-run "hearts and minds" program on the pastoralists of its mountain ranges was becoming all too well known. In less than ten years of civil aid—as the program was called—overstocking of livestock and overgrazing were seriously threatening to destroy a fragile ecosystem.

The government program of drilling water near the Firqat camps and, later, wherever the local population requested meant that the traditional grazing patterns—basically a type of transhumance that allowed certain pasture areas to rest while the herds moved off in search of water—were no longer practiced and overgrazing was common, especially near these water wells. Furthermore, the salaries and stipends generally made available to the local population through civil aid programs were regularly reinvested into livestock. Although the herders realized that pasture was finite, suddenly water appeared not to be. The camel-herding groups of the interior desert—once the elite of the pastoral community—began to invest in more camels to add to their herds. And the cattle-herding groups also invested in camels, more as a symbol of wealth and prestige than for any functional requirement.

The establishment of the comprehensive government centers and their modern services was also seriously undermining the traditional way of life. The idea behind these centers was to encourage the pastoralists to become less mobile and therefore more controllable. Housing assistance projects were also introduced at this time, and the population was encouraged to build permanent homesteads next to the community centers. Very rapidly a way of life and a delicate ecosystem was becoming seriously threatened as a result of a politically motivated and ill-conceived plan to extend services to a mobile population.[6]

Perhaps as a reaction to what was happening in Dhofar, the Minister of Social Affairs and Labor wanted to find a way of extending basic social services to the nomadic pastoralists of the desert areas without either settling them or changing their traditional way of life. With this goal in mind, he conceived of a plan to build six "tribal administrative centers" throughout the desert regions of Oman, where services would be offered to the local population. The search for a location for the first of these centers was conducted with finances as much in mind as appropriateness. The decision to build in the same place as the Royal Oman Police force was taken in order to cut costs. Choices were limited to where water existed—either at the well at Al-Ajaiz or those at Haima (see map 5). Haima was selected as the site because its water had fewer impurities and its location was closer to the international border with Saudi Arabia. Building started in 1979, and by August 1980 the physical structures were in place.

In the same year work was completed on the tarmacked road to connect the north of the country with the south. This road, extending for nearly seven hundred kilometers from Nizwa through to Thumrait, also ran adjacent to the combined border patrol station/government tribal administrative center at Haima. Its completion marked the first time that Haima could be reached either from the capital of Muscat or from Salalah in less than one day's driving time. For the pastoral communities in the central desert the road link was to be as meaningful to their development as the tribal administrative center itself.

At the close of 1979 I had the opportunity to meet the Minister of Social Affairs and Labor to discuss his ideas and goals for the nomadic pastoralists of Oman. His desire to see basic social services extended to this mobile population without adversely affecting their way of life was very strongly expressed. However, there was no plan to meet the altruistic aims he was outlining. The policy of the ministry was very clear and the construction of a site for implementing that policy was well underway. But it was obvious that the problem needed to be more clearly identified and alternative solutions addressed. After this a project needed to be conceptualized, and a plan of action designed. With the approval of all concerned, it could then be implemented in order to meet the goals expressed by the Minister.

Early in 1980 arrangements were made for me to visit the construction site at Haima in order to get a better idea of what facilities were to be part of the tribal center. On February 11, 1980, I flew to the site in a Police Air Wing aircraft. It was only just possible, because of a sandstorm, to make out the structures that were being built. With the help of the construction site foreman, I was able to find the following buildings: a mosque, a government representative's office—which would also house a four-room school—and a health center with an outpatient clinic and a maternity unit. There were also seven residences for the government employees who would be assigned jobs at Haima. These residences were earmarked for the Ministry of Health, the Ministry of Interior, and the Ministry of Education only. There was also a service center with generators for electricity and a reverse osmosis plant capable of transforming up to twenty-five thousand gallons of brackish water into drinking water per day. There was a small dormitory attached to the service center. A small garage capable of repairing tire punctures, a gas station under concession to a Harasiis tribesman, and a small cold store and café attached to the station filled up the complex. A short distance away (one hundred meters) was to be the police border station, which would be almost totally self-sufficient, sharing only the facilities of the service center.

From that short visit I drew a brief set of general observations and returned to meet with the Minister. My impression was that the center had been designed to serve a population of roughly four thousand people, although the water capabilities of the center were sufficient only for five hundred. The design and accidental placement of the center was such that it was very unlikely that much, if any, settlement of pastoralists would ever be found adjacent to the unit. Physically Haima was a *sabkha,* a salt flat where grasses would not be found. Nor was there any tree cover, which Oman's nomadic pastoralists depended upon for shelter. Furthermore, the school had no dormitory. This meant that its organization would have to be on a seasonal basis—when the nomads were the least mobile—or else a dormitory would have to be constructed in order to effectively use the structure already going up.

The biggest problem facing the government, however, seemed to be the sheer spread of the population. The area attributed to the Harasiis tribe covered more than 40,000 square kilometers. The center itself was meant to service a larger area, as it was not restricted only to Harasiis tribespeople but to any "Omani national" within the borders drawn up by the Ministry of Interior. The center was located literally in the middle of nowhere, halfway between Salalah and Muscat, 150 kilometers west from the Indian Ocean and about the same distance east from the Saudi Arabian border and its awesome Empty Quarter. Very little was known about the Harasiis tribe itself. Its population size was sheer guesswork. Estimates ranged from early explorers' figures of a few hundred armed men (Lorimer 1986 [1908]) to those of the oil company in the 1960s, which put their numbers up to four hundred able-bodied men. Their seasonal campsites as well as more permanent pasture and grazing areas were unknown. Except for a few heavily mineralized springs along the eastern coastline of Oman, they appeared to have no fixed or seasonal place that could serve as a focus for government activity.

Obviously Haima would have to become the focus for them, and the creation of that focus would have to be a fundamental goal of the project. But how much time that would take was anyone's guess. Furthermore, the perceived needs and problems of the population and how they might differ from those of a settled population had not been considered in designing the physical structures at Haima. Some fundamental information—it seemed to me—needed to be collected about the population in order to set up a program that would breathe life into the tribal administrative center that was near completion at Haima.

On my return to Muscat I met once again with the Minister and briefly outlined what I felt were the alternatives before him. I described what would be required to transform the buildings at Haima into a living center for the nomadic pastoralists. I outlined a program of action covering three, perhaps four years, during which time a one-to-two year sociological/anthropological survey would be conducted to gain an understanding of the tribe, its size, its needs, its problems, its present economic direction, and a course for the future that would not force the population to give up its present way of life. As part of this scheme I stressed the need to conduct some in-depth household studies in order to gain an understanding of the needs of the Harasiis families, particularly the women and children. Since women were commonly assumed to be the most conservative force in society and, in this case, the least likely segment of the population to utilize the facilities at Haima, it would be necessary to focus on their needs and, through them, on the needs of the family. Without such an emphasis it was very possible government planning that focused only on the men who made the effort to come to Haima itself might be formulated.

In very broad terms, my idea was that the first year would be spent in data collection and in the formulation and planning of practical programs. The second and third year would be devoted to implementing such schemes. A final fourth year would then be taken up in training Omani counterpart personnel to take over the activities designed to promote basic social services emanating from the Haima tribal center.

Governments in the Arab world do not often sponsor social science research. Most research of that nature tends to be part of international aid programs and the situation in Oman was no different. In my discussions with the Minister of Social Affairs and Labor and his Director-General of Social Affairs it soon became clear that they perceived my suggestions as falling within the parameters of the development program already established by the Ministry and the UN Department of Technical Cooperation for Development (DTCD). Since 1975 Oman had, with the assistance of its one United Nations adviser, undertaken a community development project as a means of providing its widely scattered communities with basic services that were *suitable* and *relevant* (emphasis the Minister's) to the conditions of the Sultanate. And, as mentioned earlier, the United Nations adviser had suggested that the community development project should extend its work not into the more remote desert areas but into the Salalah region, where "civil aid" had already been operating for almost a decade. Both the Minister and his Director-General felt that my suggestions should be incorporated into the already existing community development project, or as an appendage to it, and the UNDP Resident Representative was approached to discuss the feasibility of such an idea.

The idea was greeted with enthusiasm, and in March 1980 I was asked to prepare a rough draft of a proposal for a two-year project. I set about writing a request for two year's support—in the first instance—to study the needs and problems of the pastoral community within the jurisdiction of the Haima tribal center in the first year, and to plan, design, and implement practical programs for the local population in the second year. Within weeks the rough draft had been officially approved by the Minister and forwarded to the Ministry of Foreign Affairs for transmission to the UNDP Resident Representative.

A new stage in the development of the proposal, one that would bring additional actors into the process, had now been reached. Before proceeding further it is worthwhile to look briefly at the groups that would be involved and the parts that they would play. First, there are the bureaucrats (international civil servants), generally in the headquarters of the development agency. Then there are the development specialists in the field. Third, there are the national government employees. And, finally, there is the local community, or "target population." The totality of groups involved in a development project/program form a subculture of their own. In a sense, the development project has an ethnography of its own. Understanding the local society and culture becomes one of many tasks that have to be undertaken. The relations of the local population to the specialists may underpin the ethnography, but the relations of the specialists to the national government bureaucrats and the international aid officials also have to be understood. Each group has its own set of priorities as well as its own idea of what the future should hold for the local population and for themselves.

Within this subculture a number of different languages may be spoken. Even where literal, linguistic translations are made, the meanings and intents of each tongue are sometimes incomprehensible to the other groups. Hence when Egyptian expatriate social workers conducted a brief survey in 1980 among a group of pastoralists, inquiring whether they would like the government to provide them with homes (sing. *beit*, pl. *buyut*), the reply was positive. The pastoralists meant canvas—cloth shelters—but the social workers understood cement breeze block constructions. Frequently the rallying cry of local participation in the planning, design, implementation, and evaluation of development activities (Horowitz 1988) is lost among all the conflicting voices that are involved in the development process. Yet change does take place, and populations constantly strive, with varying degrees of success, to improve their situation and raise their standard of living. The role of the development agency, its bureaucrats and specialists, can only be regarded as of secondary importance. For without the will at the local grassroots level sustainable and directed change will not occur.

Setting the Stage for Implementation

The search to find a home for my proposal to study the needs of the Harasiis families had begun. The UN project adviser was approached to take it on as part of his comprehensive community development project, but he declined. The Economic Commission for Western Asia

(ECWA) was approached, but the response here was noncommittal. The project was in danger of becoming an orphan without an umbrella organization within the UN system to take responsibility for it. Only the personal interest of the Oman-based UNDP Resident Representative and the Minister of Social Affairs and Labor kept the idea alive. When the Omani government's request became official, the Resident Representative in Muscat nominally placed the project under the supervision of DTCD in New York.

Funding for the project became the next hurdle. Many, if not most, United Nations projects are paid for by the host country on a cost-sharing basis. The wealthier the nation, the greater the percentage of the costs it will carry. The situation in Oman was one in which most UNDP costs were carried by the country itself. In the case of this project, however, the local UNDP office decided to request funding for the project from within the United Nations system itself. The place of the family and, hence, women made this project seem ideally suited for funding by the Voluntary Fund for the UN Decade for Women (VFUNDW, later renamed UNIFEM). After numerous telegrams and lost correspondence to the ECWA Office in Beirut, an application for consideration by the VFUNDW was put forward by the Resident Representative and belatedly supported by ECWA on behalf of the Ministry of Social Affairs and Labor. The project was now given the title "Women's Component in Pastoral Community Assistance and Development: A Study of the Needs and Problems of the Harasiis Population" (OMA/80/WO1). The total society remained my focus, but for funding considerations the women's component was highlighted.

In September 1980 the VFUNDW approved funds for the project. The official project document—as it had been submitted to New York—was signed in November by the Minister of Social Affairs and Labor and a representative of the DTCD. Two weeks later, my name was put forward by the government to run the project as a DTCD technical assistance expert. At this point in the description of the events and actors that shaped the project, I need to digress and raise an issue that had a great impact. Thus far in the creation of this development project we have the national government, the local population, or target group, the in-country United Nations field office, the regional office (ECWA) in Beirut, the international division office at New York headquarters, and the funding source within the UN system. An official UN project document and budget had been prepared by the UN field office using the very rough budgetary minimums I had outlined in my proposal. Incredibly, my rough estimate of costs had not been revised to incorporate the sizeable UN administrational overheads and contingencies before being submitted to the VFUNDW for funding. No one in the field office in Muscat, in the ECWA regional office, or at UN headquarters in New York had noticed that the budget, as submitted, was totally unrealistic for a two-year project under UN sponsorship. Indeed, the resulting total sum requested for the project would hardly fund one year's activities.

The project proposal was carefully reviewed and approved for two years, the funding request granted and duly signed into being by the Oman government in the presence of a UN official and the UN Resident Representative. Only then was it was noticed that the UN system's overheads and other associated expenses could not be stretched far enough to run the project for two years. Without any consultation with the field office, the national government, or myself as the prospective project manager, UN headquarters (DTCD) decided to cut the project from two years to one year. It informed the field office of that change and requested that a revised program of work be immediately submitted to reflect this new time frame.

This was a powerful statement of the UN position in relation to the small project that had just been signed into being in Muscat. The project was not going to be generating any income, since it was almost totally funded from within the UN system itself. It would be focusing on a remote, marginal, and isolated community and involve only one "technical assistance expert"—in this case an anthropologist chosen by the government without any prior involvement from UN headquarters. The normal course of events had been turned around. In the UN mode of operation the host government usually has the final choice in the selection of candidates for development projects. The choice of individuals to forward as candidates, however, is at the discretion of the selection unit at UN headquarters. Effectively, the process of selection is controlled by the UN itself.

If left unchallenged, this decision to cut the project down to twelve months would have killed any sustainable development prospects for the pastoral community. At the most, an anthropological field study could have been conducted and become part of a socioeconomic background document for future projects. However, the international civil servants in DTCD were not prepared to see twelve months given to background studies only and demanded that the already tightly scheduled two-year work program be compressed into one year. Thus, they were demanding that fieldwork, identifying of problems, planning, designing, implementing practical programs, training of counterparts, and closing down were all to be accomplished within one year. As unrealistic as it would have been, the staff at headquarters also wanted to see potential reports enumerating accomplishments, results, and achievements. A year's work with no concrete result other than a "study" would, in their minds, not have been a justifiable use of time and money. The image their position conjured up was of a development project speeded up into Chaplinesque motion and marching off the condensed time frame to leave behind a sustainable development program for the local population to pursue with equal speed.

I have made this brief foray into the complexity of UN headquarters administration—its funding and financing, the competing divisions in its backup, and other technical units—to highlight the role that the individual personality sometimes does play in the development process. The role of the Resident Representative of the UNDP in the field is a particularly significant one. The effective practitioner can turn a small weak national program into an important and financially significant one (and vice versa). The local Resident Representative can effectively destroy the single local project—whatever its scale—or keep it afloat in spite of disinterest or mismanagement in headquarters. For the role of the Resident Representative dramatically reveals the two extremes found in the culture of development: the specialists whose fundamental concern is with the development process in the host country and the international bureaucrats whose primary focus of interest is the development organization itself and their place in it.

It was simply luck that the Resident Representative at the time, although a longtime international bureaucrat close to retirement, had a sincere interest in the national development process. Through his efforts and after repeated cables, telexes, and telephone conversations—as well as my own private visit to New York headquarters to argue the case for returning to a two-year program of work—the project was resubmitted for further funding. But it was only after a further ten months of squabbling and continual interference over the program of work (one-year or two-year) that funding was approved for a further nine months. Even that step, DTCD insisted, rested upon the Omani government's expression of continued interest in seeing the project into a second year. It was suggested that the government make a token gesture of interest by putting up $5,000 toward the budget requirements of the project extension—which they did.[7] These clashes of interest between the UN national field office, myself in the field as the project manager, and DTCD at UN headquarters were to seriously mar working relations in the actual effort of creating a sustainable development process among the local nomadic pastoralists.

Throughout the first ten months of financial crisis, I continued to hold to the original two-year program of work—the first year to study the needs and problems of the population and the second year to run practical programs to meet those needs. The only compromise I made was to commence a primary health care effort in the first year. This was partially as a vehicle for gaining the trust of the community and partially as a response to the extreme isolation and difficulty of the physical environment of the local population. Otherwise I repeatedly insisted to the UN headquarter's program coordinator that if the project were to run for only one year, then the first year's program of work from the original document would be the target. My position was ignored. Without any regard for the actual needs of the local community or the project team, the coordinator in New York submitted his own recommendations for a one-year program of work to the UN field office in Muscat for approval by the Omani government. He justified his report on the grounds that the project leader "has not been able to come up with any suggestions" that had been found acceptable.[8] Any hope for a positive working relation between the UN headquarters and the field was rapidly dying.

The tone had been set, and the correspondence between the program coordinator (in the technical backstopping unit of DTCD) in New York and myself continued in a similar petty and inconsequential manner. The Resident Representative and field office director in Muscat was totally preoccupied with the task of getting additional funding to complete the original two-year project proposal. Unusually, all other project correspondence was sent on to me. I had been given the responsibility of dealing directly with UN headquarters but had no authority to make any demands. These letters generally requested minor clarification, the detailing of the program of work, or summaries of preliminary data-gathering results. Some communications concerned technical suggestions, warnings, and guidelines for new avenues to take. Others were reprimands for not utilizing the right backup or support unit or for bypassing the accepted line of authority. In a few cases, a genuine effort to be of assistance was clearly the intent and might have been useful if the project had been a large one, with a development team of half a dozen or more. As it was, the project consisted of myself and a young Peace Corps couple

on loan from the Ministry of Health to assist in the delivery of primary health care.

National Level Project Involvement

Despite the friction between myself and the project coordinator in New York, relations with the national government were excellent from the early planning stage to the closing days of the project. Once it had been signed into being, the project should have left the Minister's office and become the responsibility of one of the directors in a Directorate-General in the ministry. At that time the ministry had three directorates, one for Social Affairs, one for Labor, and one for Housing. Furthermore, a ministry official should have been assigned as the national counterpart to be trained to take over the work once UN technical assistance had ended.

During the year that passed, and as the project grew from an idea into a fully funded development effort, the Director-General of Social Affairs had been the government official most likely to act as the link between the government and the project. Any requests for government action, funding, or permission to approach other ministries to involve them in the work at Haima would have had to be carefully put to him. As with so many government officials, this individual was extremely sensitive to any suggestion that his intellectual abilities were not on a par with those of the specialists. All ideas should emanate from him—a common enough position anywhere in the world. His particularly unique character trait, however, was his strong Muslim mysticism—Sufism—and the delight he took in sharing his philosophy with his guests and visitors. Time for him was always a relative value, and this was a major obstacle facing the project: how to accommodate the philosophical approach to time of the Director-General with a very tightly scheduled and budgeted UN project?

Just days before the official starting-up date of the project, a long-running power struggle between this Director-General and another official in the Ministry came to the fore. The other official came out ahead, and was appointed Under-Secretary to the Minister (equivalent to Deputy Minister), while the Director-General was removed from office and made adviser without portfolio to the Minister. A new Director-General was appointed, a very young man whose only prior managerial experience had been as director (secretary) of the Minister's office. At my official meeting with the Minister to formally initiate the project, I was surprised to learn that, although the new Director-General was nominally the project leader's counterpart, the project was to be assigned directly to the Minister's office and that a monthly meeting was to be scheduled with the Minister himself to monitor progress.

The Minister's justification for this direct link was that the success of the project required the input of several ministries in order to extend social services to the local population. The Ministries of Health, Education, and Water and Electricity, to name a few, would soon have to be involved in the project. The Minister felt that by keeping the project under his wing the other Ministers would feel obliged to do the same. This reasoning proved to be correct, and the lines of communication, responsibility, and authority for the project were out of the ordinary in terms of local field/national government relations. It was refreshing to work with such a clear, forward-looking man. And in some ways this linkage made up for the extraordinarily direct but far less pleasant contact between myself and UN headquarters.

Shortly thereafter another coincidence, the political reshuffling of some of the Sultan's cabinet, further set the stage for direct and smooth relations between the project and the Omani government. The Minister of Social Affairs and Labor was transferred to the Ministry of Water and Electricity, while the Minister of Education and Youth Affairs was appointed acting Minister of Social Affairs and Labor. The outgoing Minister carefully briefed his replacement on the project for the nomadic pastoral communities of Oman. The direct access to three of the ministries—through the persons of the former and present Minister of Social Affairs—quickly led to the introduction and similar access to the Minister of Health, the last vital link in the playing board of the project.

This uniquely direct access to those in authority meant that, like the situation vis-à-vis UN headquarters, the project was again orphaned. That is, it had no firm foothold in intermediate government circles. The remoteness of the fieldsite and urgency of the program of work meant that very little time would be available to spend in the corridors of the national government bureaucracy. Without that access there would be little opportunity to gain the confidence of middle-level government civil servants—precisely the individuals who would have an important role to play in any long-term sustainable development in the country. In the short term there was no need to attempt that integration. The decision to take a direct interest in the project had been made by those with the greatest power and authority.

The suspicion and lack of confidence that UN headquarters showed to me is perhaps best illustrated by their reaction to the direct access I was given to three Ministers (and by association the four Ministries most important to the project). In the first six-monthly progress reports that I prepared and sent for evaluation by DTCD in New York, I mentioned the monthly briefings the Ministers had set up as well as some of the outcomes of those discussions. These meetings had proved to be very successful and, in retrospect, it is doubtful whether the project would have been able to accomplish anything in its two years had it not been for that access and goodwill. The reaction from DTCD in UN headquarters, however, was negative. On learning of these meetings, an urgent cable was sent to the Muscat field office emphasizing the rule that

> progress reports and by extension all reports are to be submitted to DTCD and Resident Representative for review/comments prior to submission to governments. While we appreciate government's interest in "regular short reports" (quoted from my earlier justification for these meetings), we strongly suggest informal oral reports, as United Nations must exercise special care (to) avoid possible inadvertent commitments to governments in unreviewed documents. Appreciate yours and Chatty's continued cooperation as preventive action to avoid potential difficulties.

The initial reaction from the Muscat field office was to ignore this cable. But as the next few cables from headquarters repeatedly asked for copies of the reports and briefings that had already been conducted, I was asked to pouch copies of the briefing papers on to New York. Although project activities were neither delayed nor suspended pending the outcome of the review at headquarters, the field office and project personnel waited impatiently for the reaction from New York, fearful of another reprimand. Four weeks later the long-awaited reply arrived and consisted of an inventory of facts: "We have reviewed the two letters and have the following observations: The first letter dated 22 October, submits a plan of work, while the second letter, dated 14 November, provides information on the implementation of the immunization program and data collection." There was no further elaboration, no constructive comment, no criticism. However, the issue regarding these reports and briefings was never raised again.

The continuous conflict between UN headquarters and myself was not simply a personality clash, although personal temperament, age, education, and professional experience in development all contributed to making the situation more intense than it need have been. In many ways, the conflict was an institutional one: the development specialist in the field has different goals and perceptions of reality than those of the development bureaucrats. On a continuum of orientations from one extreme to the other, the development specialist is looking at the local population and seeking results and justification within that realm, while the development bureaucrat is primarily interested in results and justifications that are self-serving. Thus the administrator at headquarters is searching for a way to show his or her ability and skill. The easiest way to achieve this end is by undercutting the field officer and by being seen to take the interests of the headquarters seriously.

Those interests are totally oriented to measurable goals: how money has been spent, how much money has been saved by cost-cutting, and how many deadlines have been met. Thus the field officer who is totally project/people-oriented is undercut, second-guessed, and, on occasion, held up to ridicule by the headquarter's personnel.

In the ethnography of a development project, the field office generally serves as a buffer to this competitive but understandable conflict of interests. And during the initial year of the project's existence, the head of the field office, the Resident Representative, was enthusiastic and unusually supportive of the project and personally advised me to be more subdued and less impatient with the cables from headquarters. However, in the last nine months of the project, he was replaced, and the new Resident Representative had little interest in acting as a buffer. His concern was to reestablish a tight formal control over all aspects of the work of his office. His inflexibility and close adherence to the minutiae of all staff rules was only overshadowed by his lack of interest in the progress of the small projects operating in Oman at that time.

Development organizations and countries that are recipients of international aid must, by definition, hold the same long-term goals—sustainable development. However the means to those goals and the short-term interests of these agencies are inevitably ones where conflicts of interests will lie. For the UNDP the importance of short-term, continuous results, of budgets and closely monitored programs of work is an inevitable part of the running of a large multinational institution where the babble of voices can easily become a confusion of goals, ideologies, and attitudes to work. The individual bureaucrat in the massive civil service is naturally oriented toward proving his or her worth. The individual national programs and needs at field missions become of secondary importance.

For the local government, or the recipient of international aid, the ideology of development—the desire to improve the standards of living of the local population—is the same as the donor organization's in the long term. But the national government does not have the same concerns. The time frame of the individual project, the rush for results, the close monitoring of achievements is not a part of the local government's concerns. There a problem once studied tends to be regarded as solved, for identifying the difficulties means that they will eventually be overcome.

In this case the government's concern, quite rightly, was to identify the needs and problems of the community that the project addressed. The fact that there were only two years to expose the problems and begin setting up an establishment to deal with them was of no concern to the government. Somehow things would work out, just as the small details of running a remote desert station were always being worked out (e.g., the problems of the vehicles, of housing, of camping equipment, of emergency survival kit, of HF radios for communications, of food and water for the team). The government regarded the project as only the first step in the extension of basic services to the nomadic pastoral population of Oman. If it took another five, six, or seven years to take the next step, it would make no difference, as long as the stage had been adequately set. And in fact it was to take another six years after the close of the project for the next phase to be undertaken.

My roles in this development process were diverse. But whatever the role, the relative success of each stage was significantly affected by the personalities sharing the stage at the same time. First, I had the responsibility of acting as an interpreter of national policy vis-à-vis the pastoral community during the conceptualization of the project. This job was not very difficult, since most anthropologists assume they can speak for the communities they study and do not hesitate to represent their perceptions of the community as reflecting the same reality as that of the community members themselves. Next I had to attempt the role of international civil servant as leader of the UN project. This task was poorly accomplished, as striking a neutral position in discussion and in writing did not come naturally to me.

In the context of the project, the position of the UNDP Resident Representative was ideally suited for mediating and perhaps even passing on to me, by example, some of the tricks of the trade. But, as luck would have it, the unique combination of dedicated development specialist and seasoned international civil servant was not to appear in Oman until after the close of the project, in the person of the third UNDP Resident Representative to serve in Oman during the opening, running, and closing years of the project. Here the appointment of a charismatic individual in the field office was to play a positive and supporting part in helping me move from the role of disgruntled UN "technical assistance expert" to national government catalyst and, later, activist for the pastoral population targeted by the project.

Whatever personalities were represented on the side of the development agencies, the individuals holding senior Omani government positions during the project years were the lifeline to the project and directly responsible for any successes that were achieved. Without their firm conviction in the direction that development had to take in Oman (especially in relation to the pastoral population), without their accessibility and lack of formality in terms of the more commonly accepted channels of authority and decision making, and without their equally charismatic, enthusiastic, and responsible leadership, the project would never have achieved anything other than provide a salary to one more development specialist.

3

Implementing a Plan:

Transforming a Water Well Into a Tribal Center

The government policy underpinning the project to extend social services to the nomadic pastoral populations of Oman was that these communities should not be coerced into changing their way of life. How that policy came to be realized and how the water well at Haima was transformed into a tribal administrative center is the focus of this chapter. The planning and implementation of interventions were largely shaped by the ways in which competing demands between international, national, and local actors were balanced and in the way new directions were introduced and established.

In the recent literature on the subject of anthropology and the development process, many of the studies focus on the theoretical contribution anthropology or anthropologists can make in the early planning and project formulation stage (Justice 1986; Hoben 1982; Conlin 1985; Mason 1990; Gritzinger 1990; Hobart 1993). Others focus on the work of anthropologists in the final phases of the process—project evaluation and assessment (Appleby 1988; Poulin, Appleby, and Cao 1987; Chambers 1989; Rickson, Western, and Burdge 1990; Morton 1990). A few voices describe and analyze the actual role of the anthropologist at the implementation stage (Swagman 1990; Morris 1991; Hopkins 1990). These studies generally focus on the relationship between local and national interests. Few studies, other than those of Gulliver (1985) and Curtis (1985), reveal the complexity of dealing with the third partner in the development process—the donor or international agency. This is a lesser, but nevertheless important, theme running through the chapter—the persistence of cross-interests and clashes that dogged the project. National and local interests were bridged through continuous personal contact, discussion, and exchange of information. The concerns of the international agency, however, were difficult to integrate, personal contact and visits were nonexistent, and exchange was limited to written cables, faxes, and, occasionally, letters.

Planning the Interventions

On May 23, 1981, the project officially commenced. During these first few weeks I held a series of informal discussions with the Ministers of Social Affairs and Labor, Health, and Education. These sessions revealed to me the extraordinary concern all three Ministers shared in seeing basic health and education services extended to the nomadic pastoral communities of Oman as soon as possible.[1] And although the original idea shaping the project had been to refrain from active program implementation until a clearer understanding of the community's needs had been garnered, it seemed difficult, if not disingenuous, to refuse to undertake practical work on the grounds of disturbing the neutrality of fieldwork participant observation.[2]

Upon the direct request of the national government, I revised the program of work to incorporate a mobile primary health care component as part of the initial year's field research. In addition, I promised to look into the education needs of the community with a view to tackling that  issue as soon as possible. This revision in the formal program of work, with primary health care as the ongoing service to accompany or justify anthropological fieldwork, meant considerable changes in the first few months' activities. A staff primary health training program was given top priority, in view of the nearly incomprehensible remoteness and isolation of the forty-thousand-square-kilometer fieldsite as well as its extremes of temperature (between ten and fifty degrees centigrade). The Ministry of Health offered to lend the project the services of an American Peace Corps couple who had served as English teachers in a small Omani village. Their spoken Omani Arabic was good and their enthusiasm for the project goals was unlimited. The Sultan of Oman's Armed Forces Medical Services organized an intensive six-week primary health care and first aid course for us, as none of us had had any previous health training.

During these early days of the project the Minister of Health requested that we attempt to undertake the immunization of children against the six World Health Organization target diseases (Diphtheria, Pertussis, Tetanus, Poliomyelitis, Tuberculosis, and Measles) whenever possible. Again the Medical Services offered the loan of a British state registered nurse and midwife for one week each month throughout the course of the project to assist in primary health care delivery and immunization. It was assumed that the experience gained by the nurse would later be put to good use in the annual hearts and minds program Medical Services carried out in the remoter regions of the country.

In the first few weeks of the project's official life, national government enthusiasm and cooperation was particularly strong. The Minister of Health personally authorized the withdrawal from Ministry stores of enough supplies of medicines, drugs, and dressings to run a mobile clinic for two years as well as unrestricted access to whatever quantity of vaccines might be required. As we still had no idea of the size of the local pastoral population, the stores director gave us supplies adequate for a hypothetical population of ten thousand—a figure he assumed would be more than adequate.

As before, the UN field office in Muscat remained a clearing house for correspondence between UN headquarters and myself. A letter of welcome into the UN system carried with it specific instructions as to who could be addressed directly for what kind of request or problem. A report listing the achievements of the first fourteen days of the project was duly submitted to headquarters along with the anticipated program of work, which had so recently been revised. It was reviewed "with interest"—a phrase that was to appear repeatedly in the cable traffic from New York. As the anticipated program had already received the tacit approval of the national government, there was little objection that UN headquarters could make. UNDP's stated objective is one that explicitly aims to carry out government policy—unlike organizations such as the World Bank or International Monetary Fund, which often seek to reform policy.

The first assessment to be made from headquarters came from the Middle East Section of DTCD, acknowledging the team's activities in "preparatory arrangements." It was to be a fairly typical example of most of the correspondence from New York. The cable went on to say that "it appears that you have focused on the health aspect of the project objectives. We are hopeful that you will soon *pay adequate attention* to some of the other objectives of the project" (emphasis mine). Perhaps no one in the section had had the time to carefully read the background material and justifications that we were sending to headquarters. But our impression in the field was of a headquarters that was not listening, that was too busy trying to second-guess our next step, in an attempt, perhaps, to appear efficient and responsible. We had the feeling that our close working relationship with the national government was considered inappropriate and that international headquarters was where approval for local project action should emanate from. Even later in the course of the project, the local pastoral population and its particular set of needs and problems did not seem to be of primary importance to UN headquarters. What was still of foremost concern was the "ideal" reality that was drafted on paper in project documents, anticipated programs of work, and progress reports. A struggle continued throughout the project's life to establish a hierarchy of priorities, of lines of authority, and of reporting and responsibility within the larger system that made up the development process. The national government and the pastoral population were to form a subsystem of their own, with the project personnel intimately involved in translating "real" requirements, needs, problems, and restraints from one group to the other in a kind of survival agenda. Hence a relationship of antagonism between the project staff and the international agencies became inevitable.

The revised program of work the national government had requested was the simultaneous extension of primary health care to the pastoral population from the earliest stage of the fieldwork along with a directed interest into the education needs of the population. Thus primary health care, which had originally been considered as simply a justification or vehicle to gain the trust of the population, became the main thrust of the project's activities. Not only was it extremely useful in establishing the value of the project in the eyes of the local population, it was also valuable in itself. For although we were working from an empty slate—nothing was known of the population, its size, its infant and child mortality rates, the effect of epidemics such as measles and whooping cough (Pertussis)—travelers' reports suggested that the health situation was serious.

Implementing the Project

Once our primary health care training had been completed in Muscat, we moved the five hundred kilometers to the Haima tribal center. We had been provided with two vehicles by the Ministry of Social Affairs and Labor, one a new four-wheel-drive Land Rover and the other an old flatbed truck that was to be used to carry our weekly supplies of water, food, and camping equipment.

On September 7, 1981, we moved into a small two-bedroomed villa lent to us by the Ministry of Education as a base station and a resupply point for water, food, and medicines. One HF radio had been donated to the project by the national oil company and was installed in the new vehicle. Another had been loaned to the project and was set up at the villa/base station. The intent had been to use these radios on a daily basis to establish our location during our weekly four-day trips into the Jiddat itself. Our problem, however, was that the team still consisted of only three people—the local counterparts had yet to be hired and there were no base station personnel with whom to keep in contact. The only other HF radios at Haima at that time were at the police station and at the office of the representative of the Ministry of Interior, the Wali. Neither office was able to guarantee that their operators would be available to receive a daily routine check of location from us during our weekly trips. Their HF radios were used for routine administrative work between Muscat and Haima or for handling emergencies. A regular radio call simply to give a map location as a precaution for the team's safety was, to them, a perplexing novelty.

During this initial setting up period, we paid our respects to the Wali and asked for his assistance. Only with his consent could anything be undertaken. The office of the Wali of Haima was, for all intents and purposes, more powerful than that of the tribal leader. Thus, our request for assistance in selecting and hiring two Harasiis tribesmen—one to serve as driver of the flatbed vehicle and the other to be our physical and cultural guide—had to be made to him. He undertook to call upon the tribal leaders (*rushada'*) to locate the appropriate personnel.

The Harasiis tribe divides itself into seven lineages (of which more detail is given in chapter 4). Each of these subgroups selects two respected and experienced men to serve as their representatives to the advisory council of the traditional leader, the Sheikh, and to the modern government's figure of authority, the Wali. When decisions need to be taken that affect the entire tribe, these men meet together with the Sheikh or the Wali—or more often with both of them—in the offices of the Ministry of Interior at Haima. Part of the Wali's staff consists of fourteen Harasiis guards, or *askars*, two selected from each of the tribe's seven lineages by the rushada.'

News and information, we quickly discovered, spread like wildfire in the Jiddat. The request for assistance in hiring local tribal staff had been presented to the Wali during the evening of our first day at Haima. By the next morning the request was general knowledge and a meeting was held by the Wali with the tribal leaders present at the time to confirm the selection of a driver for the project. Jamal was chosen, a young man who was to prove his mechanical worth many times over. Though he could only present his thumbprint as an identifying signature for any written document, he could pull apart a carburetor in blowing sand and repair it with no more tools and spare parts than a screwdriver and the foil paper of a packet of cigarettes.

The selection of a guide proved more problematic, and twice during the first few days team members were called back into the Wali's office to explain the project and the particular set of requirements for the guide. We were to reiterate that we needed a guide not only to places within the Jiddat but also to the society and the culture—someone who could interpret the Harasiis way of life to us as well as our project to the members of the tribe. As the various tribal elders were to say, any Harasiis man could guide us to the locations on the desert, but rare would be the man who could meet our other requirements. On the third day of deliberation, the Wali informed the team that the special person for our work had been found and would be at Haima in five days time. He was, the Wali told us, an unsurpassable guide and tracker, a man of maturity and responsibility to whom we could entrust our lives, and, moreover, someone who understood the needs of his people and would make sure that we saw and understood all there was to know. The description of the man was almost too good to be true.

Much to our surprise, there was no attempt to undermine or denigrate the man's reputation in the intervening week before he appeared to be interviewed. A unanimous consensus had been reached by the council on the person we needed and that decision seemed to have been respected to a man. Although many of them were desperate to find jobs, not one suggested that he or someone else would be better suited for the work. The choice of the tribal council proved to be fortunate indeed and Hamad was to prove himself to be the key to the success of our research effort. His last wage-earning experience had been as a police driver in Nizwa early in the 1970s and he had been frequently called upon to act as a guide for various mapping and geological survey teams and hunting parties. He was universally respected by his fellow tribesmen and renowned for his tracking abilities as well as his natural conservatism. Hamad was not yet old enough to be considered a tribal elder but not so young as to have begun to lose the intimate knowledge and awareness of the desert that many of the younger men—more accustomed to cars than camels—were beginning to do. He knew the desert omnisciently, because he had actually traveled it most of his life on foot or camelback. His recall of names, however, was weak, something that Jamal, the driver, made up for. Jamal had first seen a motor vehicle at the age of six, and had learned the desert from the cabin of a vehicle. He used the vehicle to travel and visit often, and this had enabled him to acquire a more widely based knowledge of names than the guide. Together they were a team ideally suited for our requirements.

The Ministry of Social Affairs and Labor personnel department had made it quite clear that the selection of tribesmen to work with the project would have to be made by the Wali of Haima and his tribal advisers. They emphasized, however, that anyone found to be unsatisfactory could be fired, following a simple formula—three written notices of warning of dissatisfaction with the man's work performance, followed by a terminal dismissal. The attitude in the Ministry and in the Wali's office, to a more limited extent, was that these tribesmen did not like to work. We were told that it would not be long before we would have to hire a new team. To their surprise, this proved not to be the case. This experience was to be referred to often in later years when government and private company personnel offices hesitated to employ local tribesmen because of their reputation of being unable to respect Western standards of time and production effort. Our argument was that if you give a man a job with no work—such as an installation guard in the middle of nowhere—he soon becomes lonely and bored. But if you give him a job requiring skills that he possessed, he would work. This logic, backed up by the project's actual employment experience, was to be of use throughout the later 1980s in helping local tribesmen get jobs previously held by expatriate unskilled laborers.

Hamad, our guide, seemed to straddle the two generations. He was respected by both the older, more conservative, elements of the tribe as well as the youth who admired his great desert survival skills. Thus he was able to involve the project team in the lives of a wide range of families—from the older more established three-generational units of as many as nineteen or twenty people to the young families of six to eight people recently branched from the main limb. In all cases he undertook to explain the project and its aims. He agreed to have his family be one of the project's in-depth case studies, more in order to set an example than from any real desire to be so scrutinized. This gesture, from one known to be particularly conservative and secretive, was, we were later to learn, a key to the relative reliability of the data we were to collect from the other selected households.

Once the local project team had been selected, and hiring formalities completed, Hamad and Jamal had to make two round-trips at their own expense—one of one thousand kilometers for the fingerprinting of employment papers in Muscat and another of eight hundred kilometers to thumbprint police clearance papers in Nizwa. These distances illustrate the remoteness and isolation of the Harasiis community. In 1981 it was still up to this population to reach the government rather than up to the government to reach them.

During the early weeks spent ironing out administrative difficulties at the Haima tribal center, the project team was the focus of much curiosity and some genuine interest. In a place miles from nowhere, where excitement is a car pulling into the only gas station for three hundred kilometers in any direction, our presence provided—at least in the early days—a form of entertainment, amusement, and even a place for light refreshment for the mainly Harasiis men and boys that passed through Haima either to refuel their vehicles or fill their water barrels. Making use of this attention, the team began formal interviewing of the tribal representatives as and when they came to visit the base station. The project's dual objectives were explained, along with the team's intent to spend four days out of every week in the desert with the Harasiis families for a minimum of nine months. This intent was met with great skepticism. The tribe's only previous experience of a government survey had been conducted a year earlier and had lasted four days in total. Although that survey was not intended to be comprehensive, the tribesmen had assumed that the four-day effort—which they ridiculed—was being accepted in the capital as a definitive statement of their needs.[3]

The Harasiis seemed to acknowledge that their way of life was alien to that of "city people," but they also assumed that a nontribesman would be unable to accept the physical hardship they proudly considered part of their culture. When pressed to define these hardships, our informants listed drinking warm, brackish water, sleeping under the stars, and only washing as was required for prayer. Their previous experience with nontribesmen had been limited to urban Omanis, Egyptians, and Indians, and this list reflected their observations of them. A different body of myth surrounded the English, as two explorers had passed through their territory during the twentieth century and left strong impressions

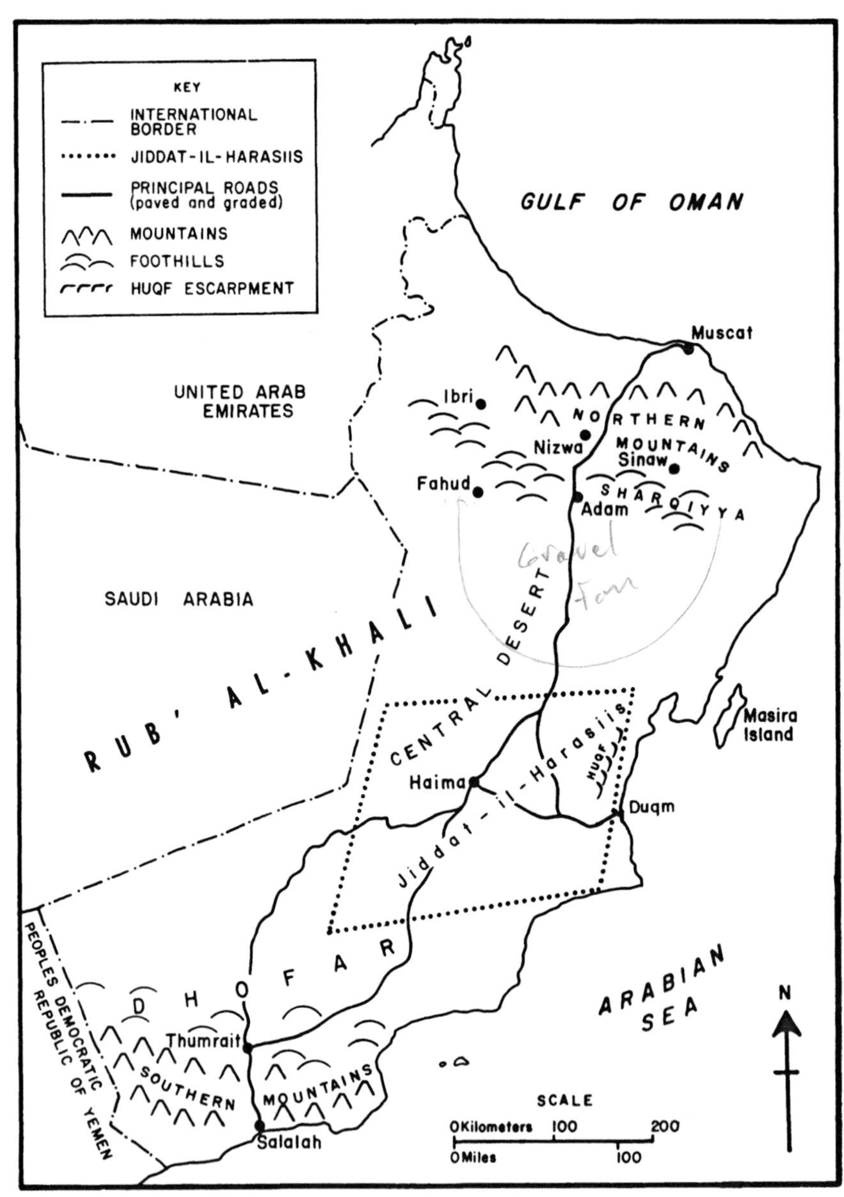

MAP 4 Sultanate of Oman and Jiddat-il-Harasiis

behind them—Bertram Thomas and Wilfred Thesiger. These two men had become legends in their own time, for they had ridden camels, drunk brackish water, and camped under the stars.

During these early weeks the project team was able to interview most of the tribal rushada', the guards employed by the Wali's office, and the other Harasiis men employed at Haima (two in the health clinic, two at the gas station, and a further two at a mechanical workshop where only the pumping of air and the repair of tire punctures could be undertaken). All the other employees at Haima, of which there were forty or more, were either from Sri Lanka or the Indian subcontinent—excluding the Omani police force at the border station.

So long as the base station front door was unlocked, Harasiis men, and occasionally women, were inside visiting one or another of the team. Although each team member had been assigned a particular focus for interviewing in the field, the assumption had been made that this active data collection would not take place until the team was on the road. This assumption was incorrect, and in the course of the early interviews and discussions at the base station a rough estimate of the population size was formed along with a sketchy idea of its wide dispersal over the Jiddat.

From the information that we had gathered, we estimated that there were about 150 families in the Jiddat and that there was a cluster of families in two areas—Rima and Al-Ajaiz (see maps 4 and 5). The triangle formed by Haima at the top and Rima and Al-Ajaiz at the base roughly represented more heavily populated areas of the Jiddat. The distance between all three points was roughly four hundred kilometers. The central part of this triangle was said to be practically devoid of human population—the tribal center of Haima, which was built on an extensive salt flat, was itself also empty of human settlement except for the government personnel there. Given this picture of the Jiddat, we decided to concentrate efforts on alternative weeks on either the western side of this triangle—the Rima area—or the eastern side—the Al-Ajaiz area. A number of questionnaires (sociodemographic), surveys, and in-depth interview schedules (household composition and economics, herd size and composition, mother and child care, and child birth histories) had been prepared earlier in cooperation with the Directorate of Statistics in the National Development Council. The hope was that some of the data collected by these methods would be of use to the Council in the future. The more traditional anthropological field technique of participant observation that the three-team members would be using would be of little use

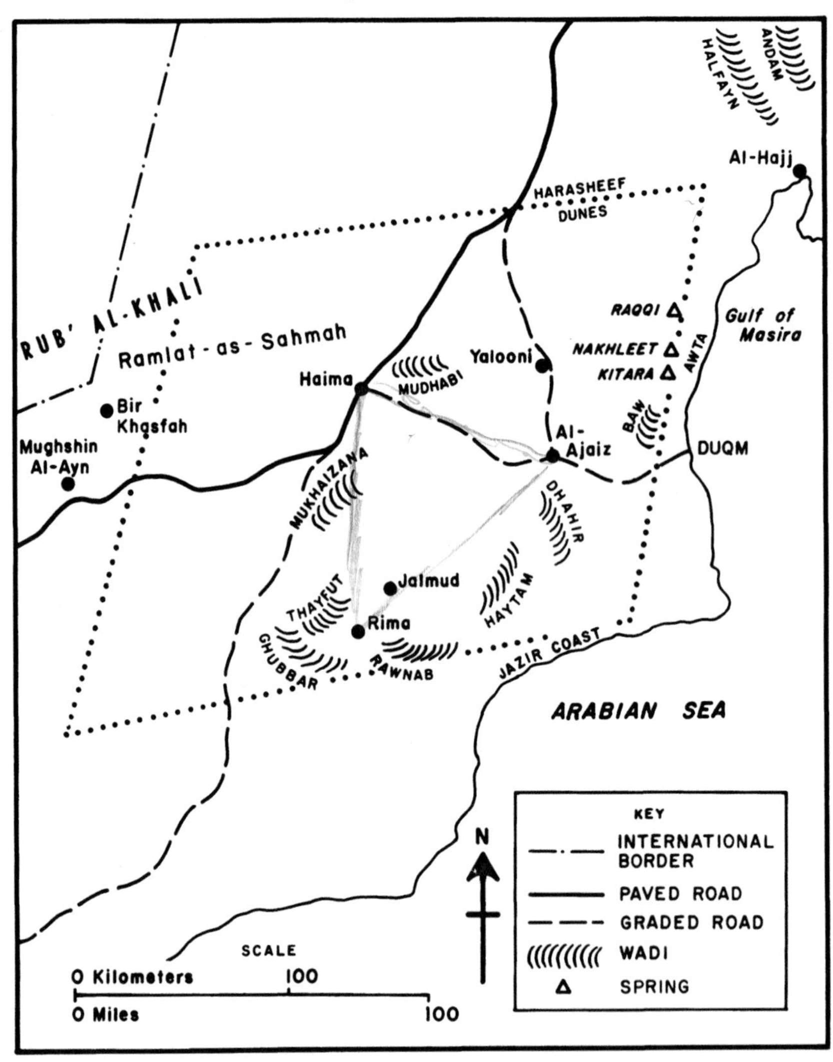

MAP 5 Detail of the Jiddat-il-Harasiis

to the Directorate of Statistics but would underpin the conclusions presented in the project's reports.

At the end of September intensive field activity commenced, and each week the team moved out from the Haima station into either the Rima or the Al-Ajaiz area. Initially only participant observation and a general survey schedule was completed on each family as a preliminary to basic health care delivery. Once we had established the number of visits that could roughly be completed in a week, we were ready to initiate in-depth surveying of some households. A strategy was devised for a random sampling of 10 percent of this mobile population. To complete the information required from each family would take one initial overnight stay and three further visits. Since we were unable to pull household names at random for the sample, we decided to reverse the usual technique. We could visit as many as ten families in one week's field trip. Thus, we assigned these families numbers in the order we came across them. We then selected numbers between one and ten at random, and those families that had been assigned the same number became part of our interviewing sample. We continued in this fashion for a number of weeks, until our sample included fifteen families. This was later increased to seventeen to reflect the change in our estimate of the population size.

Our preliminary assessment of the needs and problems of the population after the first two months of fieldwork fell into the following categories:

1. *Health* Initial assessment of one survey showed that for every projected one thousand live births, eight hundred had reached one year of age but only five hundred had reached puberty. Modern health care, which simply did not reach this population, was a most strikingly vital priority.

2. *Shelter* The winter months on the Jiddat were particularly cold and the majority of the population suffered from colds and chest infections during this time of year. As these highly mobile people had no form of shelter other than the shade they could create by spreading blankets over the fairly common acacia trees, a government-sponsored program or subsidized distribution of tents was a fairly urgent requirement.

3. *Education* Other than two young boys, the entire population on the Jiddat was illiterate. In 1980 an attempt was made to run a school at Haima, and two Egyptian teachers arrived. They spent the whole of the academic year on their own, without any students, since boarding facili-

ties were unavailable. The issue of educating the youth was one most frequently raised by the population. Their underlying assumption was that without education the next generation would have no success in gaining employment. Assistance in setting up a boarding school at Haima was an important task for the project.

4. *Water* There were only four wells in the Jiddat—an area the size of Scotland. A program of controlled well digging was desperately needed.

5. *Animal Husbandry* Animal husbandry of camels, goat, and a few sheep was the population's primary source of livelihood. The cyclical five to six years of drought followed by a year or two of good rain seemed to keep the herds in a weakened state and veterinary services were urgently required.

6. *Government Contact* There was no formal means of communication between the Harasiis tribal population and the government other than through the Ministry of Interior's office. A more direct link was required, and discussions needed to be initiated to open an office of the Ministry of Social Affairs in Haima to deal with the social, economic, or welfare needs of the population.

7. *Weaving* This craft was still being practiced by the Harasiis. But the blankets, camel saddles, and assorted bags that they produced were rapidly becoming obsolete—being replaced by commercially produced goods. As an income-generating activity, weaving had some potential, but the subject needed to be studied further.

At this point in the life of the project, my relationship with UN headquarters began to lose some of its intensely heated nature. Partially this was because the local population, after months of preparation, had finally become a tangible focus. An empathy connected the project team with the Harasiis population. The administrative and bureaucratic issues that continued to be raised by telex and cable from New York dimmed before the reality of the profound hardship that the population accepted as their way of life. Furthermore, there was little additional help to be expected from New York. UN headquarters and, through them, the local field office had set up the machinery to design and develop a project, but its implementation depended upon the continued interest and goodwill of the national government. And it would be the Omani government that would have to carry the burden of financing whatever practical programs it decided to carry out.

The monthly meetings with the Ministers concerned with the progress of the project became our administrative and intellectual focus. It was at these meetings that a link was forged between the national government and the local population. After the initial month's fieldwork, a strategy was put forward at the ministerial meetings to organize activities at the Haima tribal center so that each service implemented by the project for the government would have a mobile component. During the same period the Ministry involved would establish a permanent base at Haima to serve what we hoped would be an increasingly larger number of tribespeople attracted there for its facilities.

Mobile primary health care had already been selected as the project's first activity. But now, after our brief contact with the Harasiis tribe and with the tribal center, we felt that the health clinic, already established at Haima since 1980, needed to be encouraged to work with us. In this way the confidence of the population could gradually be gained and the Harasiis tribe would be increasingly drawn to Haima to make use of the permanent clinic. I outlined similar programs for the Ministry of Social Affairs—the establishment of an office at Haima as well as a mobile team to see to the needs of the population. We asked the Ministry of Agriculture and Fisheries to consider opening a veterinary office there with vehicle support to conduct regular mobile work among the widely dispersed population. Finally, we proposed to the Ministry of Education that a mobile educational effort be put into effect until a boarding school at Haima could be set up.

This strategy found a warm reception in the Ministry of Health, which already had the experience of running a mobile health care program in Dhofar five years earlier. For the other ministries the concept was new and difficult to absorb. The problem seemed to be in understanding that the population of the Jiddat did not actually live in small villages but in households that moved every few weeks or months depending upon the availability of water, graze, and browse. These Ministry officials insisted on regarding Haima as a village and seemed to feel that any government services established there should be able to function as they would in any remote village in the Sultanate. Establishing a service was completely separated from the more difficult problem of having it adequately utilized.

A wide cultural gap between the national administrators and bureaucrats and the nomadic pastoral population of the Jiddat-il-Harasiis was manifesting itself. The issue of a boarding school, for example, was particularly difficult. Oman had a tradition of boarding schools in the Jebel Akhdar, where the large number of remote and practically inaccessible mountain villages made the establishment of boarding schools a necessity. At Haima the Ministry of Education, being under the impression that the local population was within easy reach, considered boarding unnecessary. Presenting the facts that some of the school population might have to travel as much as four hours each way every day to reach the school did not seem to have much impact on administrators and planners in the Ministry. It was only when, upon opening a day school in 1980, none of the 127 boys or 25 girls who had been registered by the office of the Wali appeared that the Ministry decided to review the situation. By the time the project team became involved in discussing an educational strategy for the Jiddat, the in-house ministerial suggestion of bussing the children into Haima was seriously under consideration. We were able to convince the Ministry of the shortcomings of such a venture, given the huge distances that would need to be covered and the almost total lack of paved roads. However, we were unable to convince these same decision makers of the feasibility of temporary mobile schools until a permanent dormitory could be built. A compromise was entertained, and then accepted, to set up a temporary dormitory in the former army barracks near Haima, which had been standing empty ever since the modern tribal center had opened nearly a year earlier.

Having established—in theory—the importance of a permanent base with a mobile outreach program for the Haima center, we turned to the Ministry of Health, which already had a permanent presence there. The team felt that to initiate an immunization effort for children and women against the six World Health Organization target diseases without the cooperation of the health clinic at Haima would be foolish. Whatever success the project team might have during the coming year would have to be carried on by the clinic in later years. The Ministry officials in Muscat agreed, as did the regional officer at Nizwa. The medical officer-in-charge at Haima, a young and talented Sri Lankan doctor, however, did not. Unlike the local government officials in Muscat, he understood the highly mobile and dispersed nature of the Harasiis tribe's lifestyle. After a period of intense discussion, it became obvious he was afraid that the immunization effort would fail because it would be impossible to find children for the repeat doses of vaccine the program required. After some thought he put forward a proposal he felt he could accept, which was the photographing of each child so as to be able to identify him or her for the second and third doses of vaccine. Our initially flippant response was that it would be impossible to identify the women anyway,

Three generations of women: unmarried girl, young married woman, and elderly mother. Their dresses, cut from the same bolt of cloth, reaffirms their close kinship relationship.

as they all wore a full face mask made of indigo-dyed cloth that left open to view only two small oval slits around the eyes. The more serious problem, which we tried to handle with greater sensitivity, was the doctor's poor conception of the way of life of the Harasiis. Assuming them to be totally and randomly nomadic, he could not understand how there could be any guarantee of ever finding a family a second time.

After this experience we decided that basic cultural information needed to be put forward to the mainly Indian and Sri Lankan medical staff at the clinic before embarking on a health care delivery system for the Harasiis tribe. Thus a short period of formal discussion and exchange of ideas was initiated with the medical team. For the first time the project's universalized goal of extending health education along with primary health care was put forward. The clinic staff felt that once an element of trust was established, the local population was going to have to work with the mobile teams in order to get a good coverage of vaccines to the population. To do so they would have to grasp some elements of the theory behind immunization. Since measles and whooping cough as well as poliomyelitis regularly swept through the Jiddat and claimed the lives of a number of children and adults, we felt that there was a good chance of getting the population to cooperate—at least long enough to recognize for themselves the benefit of the vaccination program.

Eventually the doctors at the Haima clinic agreed and an immunization schedule was carefully laid out, with a mobile team from the clinic working the western Jiddat at the same time as the project team worked the eastern part.[4] Throughout each field trip the project members engaged in discussions with the local population about the immunization effort. The need for repeated vaccines may not have been understood, but the population was surprisingly willing to meet regularly at predetermined sites (usually named trees) on set days for the vaccination effort as well as for the opportunity to visit with friends and family. These gatherings rapidly took on a festive gaiety.[5] Women and young girls wore their finest gold and silver, while the men and boys, often seated in their own separate area, proudly displayed their possessions—generally rifles and cartridge belts. The only sad or tearful faces were among the young children clutching their mothers in the tight circle around the nurse as she administered the inoculations. At the close of the first immunization effort for the six WHO target diseases, the joint Ministry of Health/UN project rate of full vaccine coverage was 85 percent—an exceptionally high rate in any environment.

This local response to the health care drive was perhaps a reaction to the previous dearth of government activity in the desert. Although people had little to lose by cooperating and no competitive activity to distract them, the positive local response was certainly a reflection of the care, effort, and thought that both mobile teams took to explain the importance of full immunization coverage. It was up to the family to cooperate in order to have full coverage, and the majority chose to do so. During this period the number of outpatients at the Haima clinic began to climb, and the staff found that children were occasionally being brought into Haima for their vaccines when the mobile teams had missed them or passed them by. This was—to us—a great breakthrough, and in subsequent years newborn infants and their mothers were also brought into Haima to receive their vaccines.

During the second year of the project, measles claimed only one life. A newly delivered Harsiis mother and child contracted measles at the

Nizwa hospital. The mother died of complications and the child recovered. News of this rapidly spread among the population and served as a powerful reminder of the benefit of the vaccines. This one isolated outbreak of the disease was unheard of in the past. So great had been their fear of contracting measles that the community used to isolate any family where it was present. Whether or not the full Western conceptualization of immunization theory was understood mattered little. What did matter to the population was that the government, with the assistance of the project team, had asked for their cooperation, promising that it would be for their benefit. That promise seemed to materialize in the second year and to lay the groundwork for a rapid rise in the expectations of the population.

During the delivery of primary health care and the immunization of women and children, we were actively involved in eliciting information from the community on their own perceptions of their needs. Our preliminary assessments that these needs fell into the seven major categories listed earlier were confirmed. The most consistently voiced concerns, however, revolved about their need for shelter, schooling for their youth, water delivery, and the requirements of many Harasiis for cash welfare assistance. The latter, a countrywide program of cash payments to the old, disabled, widowed, and otherwise incapacitated that was run by the Ministry of Social Affairs and Labor, was already in existence.

Whereas individuals in the rural population of Oman had, for most of the last decade, approached the responsible ministries with their requests, the Harasiis population had made little effort in that direction. Doubtless, the extreme remoteness and isolation of the tribe was a major factor, but this was not a wholly satisfying answer, because other communities, for example in the mountains of northern Oman, were also desperately isolated. Yet they seemed to be able, time and again, to represent themselves and put their needs to the government at Muscat. The overriding factor may have been related to the worldview of many Harasiis tribesmen. Although the community has never been totally self-sufficient—no pastoral community ever is—its contact with villages of the border areas between the desert and the well-irrigated villages of the Jebel Akhdar was very limited. The authority of the central government had only been successfully extended to that border region two decades earlier. And the concept of free government services for the people had not been absorbed.

The issues put forward by the men and women of the Harasiis tribe were discussed at length by us and the Ministers and their advisers. The project team made a number of requests: an annual distribution of canvas cloth or tents; the establishment of a permanent dormitory for boys and the consideration of a similar unit for girls; the establishment of a social affairs office at Haima to undertake, among other things, a study of the deserving welfare recipients in the Jiddat; the reorganization of the present system of water delivery by tanker; and veterinary and marketing assistance for the population's livestock.

The Omani government responded, and over the following seven months a large number of programs were executed at Haima or on the Jiddat-il-Harasiis. These were implemented in no particular order and, in some cases, entirely independent of the previous intervention of the project team. For example, a water tanker was given to the Harasiis tribe by the Sultan along with a monthly salary of 450 Omani rials for its operator.[6]

The Ministry of Water and Electricity, keenly aware of the shortcomings of water delivery in the area, asked us to make recommendations as to its distribution to the nomadic households. Various schemes were proposed, but, more important, Harasiis tribesmen began to represent their own views to these offices. Eventually an elaborate system of distribution, based on the construction of a number of sites that chemically rid the well water of impurities and salts (reverse osmosis plants), the setting up of large storage tanks at predetermined sites, and the running of a fleet of tankers was organized and coordinated by the Ministry of Water and Electricity in the Jiddat.

During this same period subsidized animal feed was made available to the Harasiis tribe. Shortly thereafter, the Ministry of Social Affairs and Labor approved the opening of an office in Haima and the search for counterpart personnel commenced. A welfare commission was sent from the same Ministry to look into the situation. By March of 1982 construction of a dormitory for the Haima school had begun, and five hundred tents were sent to Haima for the project team to distribute along with the help of the Wali's office and the regional social affairs officers from Nizwa. An animal immunization effort was also well underway, and rumor had it that a veterinary surgeon would soon be based at Haima, since a portable cabin-cum-office had already arrived.

The flurry of activity and events in Haima during 1982 were viewed, by many of the Harasiis, as a direct result of the intervention of the project team. Although we knew better and tried to dispel the association that was becoming widespread, it was with limited success. With each delivery of a service came a request for more of the same. In their view they had, in a very short time, experienced an unusual sequence of assistance from the government. Requests for further drilling of water wells came to our attention, another school closer to Rima was also demanded, jobs, livestock marketing assistance, further subsidizing of animal feed—these requests and much more became part of the set of desires, if not wishful expectations, held by many of the Harasiis tribe.[7]

By the autumn of 1982 the Ministry of Social Affairs and Labor had opened its office at Haima and we commenced a handover and training period with our government counterparts. Funding for the project was due to run out in December of that year—though a request for another four months' support was still pending. It was intended that the boarding school would open in December and the veterinary surgeon was also expected imminently. With the prognosis for any further UN input poor, the project team felt any continuity of effort would have to come from the counterpart personnel. The brief period of life left to the project was hardly sufficient for a handover, let alone a period of training—at least not as the project had been organized and run. Nevertheless, an attempt was made to encourage the local social affairs team to take the initiative, to move regularly out into the desert visiting families, discussing their problems, encouraging community efforts at self-help, and, most important, liaising with the other ministries in order to deliver services that crossed Ministry borders.

By the time the project officially closed in June of 1983, the social affairs office at Haima was running well. The officers were regularly visiting the widely scattered Harasiis households and requests for assistance were still coming into the Haima office and being forwarded to the capital. The enthusiasm and near-euphoria that had been generated the previous year still captured the imagination of many tribespeople. But, as the months passed and no further assistance or new government effort was forthcoming from the capital, that energy and excitement faded, and soon Haima began to wear the expression of any sleepy, small establishment in the rural countryside.

The general decline in the level of commitment and output from the various government offices at Haima was inevitable. With only an overlap of six months between the international project team and the local counterpart, and with no further follow-up or supervision, it was surprising how much was continued. The disappearance of the project team from the scene left a void—not so much in the desert, where a physical presence remained in the counterpart social affairs office and its officers, but in the ministerial offices in the capital. With no one to take up the "cause," and to remind the national government of the needs of the Haima center, other, more pressing, issues soon pushed the affairs of a remote pastoral population into the background.

The major link between Haima and the capital was an HF radio, which, although open most of the time at Haima, was not effectively staffed in Muscat. For perhaps a year following the close of the project, the Haima office and the active tribal spokesmen waited for a response from the capital. When nothing was forthcoming, the people began to act, sometimes as individuals and sometimes as groups. At first in isolated visits and later on a frequent, if irregular, basis, Harasiis tribesmen began to make the trip to Muscat to petition for welfare assistance, for tents, for water delivery, and for other services.

At about the same time the social affairs office at Haima sent a message to me: "Have you forgotten us?" Though no longer officially employed, I was still accessible to those that made the effort to locate me in the capital area. I tried, however, to remain unobtrusive and silent, especially where government affairs were concerned. The gradual but steady decline of the system that I had helped to establish at Haima eventually convinced me to act. In 1984 I approached the Minister of Social Affairs on a private basis and, with his concurrence, undertook a yearly week-long "evaluation" of the situation in the Jiddat-il-Harasiis. Every year, from 1984 until the end of the decade, I returned from these short trips into the Jiddat with a report for the Minister on the needs, complaints, and other outstanding affairs regarding that population. These reports I simply submitted to the office of the Minister, as I had no formal authority to undertake any action. In several instances, I later learned, shortcomings indicated in these reports were addressed.

The transformation of the unique outreach organization of the social affairs office of Haima was also inevitable. The role of its staff was very much one of liaison and linkage between the other Ministry offices working at Haima and the far-flung population they served. But their successes depended upon a solid backup in the capital area. For example, the Ministry of Social Affairs and the Ministry of Health traditionally cooperated to provide medical assistance to the physically or socially disabled. Proper channels existed within the two ministries for ensuring that such assistance took place. In Haima one of the earliest tests of this cooperation was in providing a young student at the boarding school—a poliomyelitis victim—with a wheelchair to cross the long distances between the school, residence, café, and store and with a pair of crutches for his regular needs in small confined areas. Both were provided for the student by the Ministry of Health, and the Ministry of Social Affairs paid the bill. Once the project closed, the link in the capital area disappeared. Either because the process was too complicated or because the social affairs officer at Haima did not feel inclined to take the trouble, a request to replace the wheelchair when it broke was refused by the Haima office. The school headmaster, an expatriate, felt that he could not help if the social affairs office would not. The distance between the Haima tribal center and the next highest authority in Nizwa was over three hundred kilometers—too great a divide for anyone to bridge. Finally, in desperation, the boy's father—at great personal expense—had a three-wheeled motorbike built in the United Arab Emirates to replace the broken wheelchair.

The two years the project had been in operation had not been sufficient to effect an institutional change in the way an outpost was run. In the case described above, the senior officer at Haima had no supervision, and no fear of being challenged. His idiosyncratic decision regarding the poliomyelitis welfare case could not be called into question by any of the local population. Had it been, it would have simply become a case of his word against theirs. The cultural gap between the nomadic pastoral population and the government officers would have come to the fore. The burden of proof would have rested with the local population, and it would have been very difficult if not impossible to show that the government employee had shirked his duty. Interministerial cooperation functioned for the twenty-one months of the project when there had been an adviser outside of the system—myself—present to liaise with each of the various government offices. For it to have continued after the close of the project would have required the creation of a position in each Ministry with the authority to liaise with other ministries over matters that concerned the Haima center. As it was, some cooperation continued as long as those government bureaucrats who had worked with the project team were still in office. But as they were replaced or sent elsewhere, the special personal links that had been established during the lifetime of the project slowly died.[8]

The objective of the project had been to study the needs of a nomadic pastoral community in Oman and suggest recommendations to meet those needs. In fact, it did much more. It implemented and further encouraged the government to take the special problems of a marginal and isolated community into account. One must ask, *Did the fact of an international development project such as* OMA/80/WO1 *actually make any difference?* Even the most outspoken critic would have to answer yes. More than anything else, in terms of the sustainability of development, the project presence in the region served to hasten the local population's understanding of what government services were available to them. As late as 1980, when I first visited the region with a medical doctor, the overwhelming response we received to our offers of help was an uncompromising query as to why the government in Muscat was interested in them. The population's conception of their identity was basically tribal, and the broader concept of national identity was only to develop in step with their understanding of the services that a nation-state provided its citizens. Upon offering to immunize the infants against tuberculosis, a widespread disease in the southern region of the country, the most frequent questions were: How much will it cost? Why is it free? Why does the Sultan want to provide it? (Answer: "Because he wants to help his people live a better life").

The brief period of the project's active interaction with Harasiis households helped to raise peoples' expectations of what could be done for them and by them. In the intervening years since the project closed, the members of the Harasiis population have learned to take development into their own hands, and although their efforts often fail, gradually and slowly they are succeeding in pushing for change and forcing the government to recognize their demands as individuals and as a social group.[9] Just as resolutely, they are introducing technical and physical improvements into their life and thus raising their standard of living.

The role of the anthropologist throughout this period constantly changed. Initially it was as interpreter to the UN and the national government of the local population's assumed special set of requirements. During the running of the project, the anthropologist—sometimes wearing the robes of an administrator and bureaucrat—served as a catalyst for change within the local population and in the national government ministries. By the time the project had drawn to a close, the anthropologist had become a spokesperson and, later, an activist for suitable and relevant development in the desert regions of Oman.

The local UN field office had a mixed role in the course of the project's lifetime. Initially the personal support of the Resident Representative swept the project into being. But it was to live without a home base, a technical "backup" unit in UN headquarters, an adequate budget, or a clear division of responsibility and authority over the logistics of running and sustaining a development effort. This vulnerability was most clearly evident when the Resident Representative in Muscat was changed during the closing months of the project. The new incumbent's lack of interest combined with the weak formal links with the UN headquarters meant that any national request to continue the project—however feasible that might have been locally—was unlikely.

The UN headquarters also had a checkered interest in the project, which partially reflected the different interpretations it received from the Resident Representatives in Muscat. Initially a great deal of interest was generated through the offices of the local field mission. But once the project had begun on the wrong foot, administratively and financially, the interest at headquarters became negative. The cable traffic took on a stern, disciplinarian tone, with bureaucrats constantly expressing concern that the project was not accomplishing its work program and fear that it might be sidetracked. As a project funded totally "in-house," there was little enthusiasm to do more than ensure that what money had been allocated was being effectively utilized in the specified period of time.

In the final months of the project—a period when negotiations are generally held between the UN headquarters and the national government for either an extension or a period of follow-up—the offices in New York were silent. Although it was not their responsibility to initiate such discussion, it was usual for headquarters to ask the field office to ascertain if such an interest existed and then to follow it up. During this closing period I initiated a request for a tripartite review. Such a meeting between the national government, project representative, and UN headquarters was far more than a common closing formality. It often became the arena to review priority issues, to set out the outlines of any future work, and/or to extend the existing mission. It also gave the national government the opportunity to discuss project findings and recommendations prior to their finalization in New York. I had hoped to use this forum to draw the national government's attention to the set of recommendations I was submitting, which went beyond supporting the continuation of the existing programs in the fields of health, education, and welfare. I had set out a series of recommendations that directly tackled the problems the Harasiis faced in their mode of production—animal husbandry. I wanted to gauge government reaction before finalizing the report. Unfortunately my request for the review was dismissed as unnecessary by the Resident Representative in Muscat. The project recommendations and final report were sent to New York headquarters without ever being previewed at the national level. A full year elapsed before the authorized report was sent back to Muscat. Then, with a new Resident Representative in Muscat, it was widely distributed with a covering letter to government offices.[10]

Given a different set of personalities, the project might have continued and entered another phase. Whatever might have been, the completion of the project marked the close of only one chapter in the process of development among the nomadic pastoral population of the deserts of Oman.

4

Employment on the Side:

The Changing Nature of Pastoralism in the Jiddat-il-Harasiis

With the accession of Sultan Qaboos bin Saiid in 1970 and the opening up of the country for development, dramatic changes occurred in all sectors. In the desert areas, oil exploration and later exploitation burst forth. For the Harasiis tribesmen wage labor suddenly became available on the margins of their territory in desert areas inhabited by other tribes. By the mid-1980s a series of oil finds on the Jiddat itself meant that paid employment now existed locally for nearly any adult male who sought work.

This chapter briefly describes the Harasiis tribe as it was before the discovery of oil and as it has come to be after significant petroleum exploration, government conservation, and national development efforts within the borders of the Jiddat-il-Harasiis. It also shows how individual households adapted to the ensuing disturbance in their way of life and how a new balance is now being achieved.

The Ecological Setting

The Jiddat-il-Harasiis separates northern Oman from its southern region (see map 4). Its eastern boundary is the Huqf escarpment, which drops, sometimes by as much as one hundred meters, into the Awta lowlands. To the north, the Jiddat gradually changes into the gravel fan of the northern mountains, and, to the northwest, it just touches the southern finger of the Rub' al-Khali sand dunes. Its western boundary is marked by a gradual transition into the rolling plains that herald the southern mountains. The Jiddat itself is particularly flat, with very few ridges or outcrops of more than ten meters. It is divided into three distinct geomorphological parts: a northern, a central, and a western region. Its most conspicuous features are the scattered sand-filled depressions, called *haylat,* which vary in size from one to twenty-five hectares.

Stanley Price (1989:75–81), the first project manager for the oryx reintroduction scheme at Wadi Yalooni, describes the region's central climatic and vegetation characteristics in some detail. The Jiddat displays the extremes associated with most deserts, although its proximity to the Arabian Sea mitigates some of its intensity. June is the hottest month, with an average shade maximum of 43.4°C, and with daily extremes of 47°C or 48°C. The coolest months are December, January, and February, with monthly maximums of 26°C to 27°C, and with an average minimum of 11.4°C in January. In addition to these monthly changes, the temperature on the Jiddat varies by 15–20°C on every day of the year.

Relative humidity can vary between less than 10 percent and 100 percent in the course of twenty-four hours. Between March and October the wind comes from due south, and during this period a sea breeze almost daily causes air temperatures to drop as much as 10°C in ten minutes, while relative humidity rapidly increases. If this breeze drops to below eight knots after midnight, the moist cool air condenses and forms a fog bank at ground level.

Data does not exist on the amount or spatial distribution of rain on the Jiddat-il-Harasiis as a whole. Records at Yalooni, however, do give a good picture of conditions throughout the area. The yearly average rainfall at Yalooni between 1980 and 1986 was 44 mm. There was no rain at all in 1980, 1984, 1985, and 1986. The heaviest monthly rainfall of 143 mm was recorded in April 1983. In general rainstorms are intense but highly localized; thus, for example, Yalooni received rain in 1981, 1982, and 1983, but other parts of the Jiddat did not. From the records kept at Yalooni, a rainfall pattern seems to emerge. Rain tends to fall in late winter and spring but has been known to fall in summer as well.

The vegetation cover of the Jiddat is determined as much by the mean annual rainfall of 50 mm as by the amount of water available from the fogs. For a desert, the density of trees on some parts of the Jiddat is remarkable. The most widespread tree is the *Acacia tortilis,* found mainly in the central part of the Jiddat where it can resemble an open parkland. In sandy depressions and in all haylats *Acacia ehrenbergiana* is common. Where deeper sand accumulations occur, single trees of *Prosopis cineraria* sometimes grow, occasionally reaching fifteen to twenty meters in height. The northern part of the Jiddat is nearly treeless, apart from a few scattered *Acacia ehrenbergiana,* and the western part has no *Acacia tortilis,* but *Prosopis cineria* grows there in groves in areas of low-lying sand accumulations.

Fog moisture is the main reason for the existence of trees on the Jiddat, in view of its low rainfall. These trees show some green leaf at all times of the year. During March, April, and September—when air temperatures are moderate and fogs are common—most perennial herbs and grasses respond to the moisture. Hence growth is stimulated and grasses flower during these two growing seasons.

The most common and widespread grass is *Stipagrostis sp.*, which occurs throughout the Jiddat except in haylats, where perennial grasses are found. The most common perennial grasses are *Lasiurus hirsutus* and *Cymbopogon schoenanthus.* Perennial scrubs include *Rhazya stricta* and *Heliotropium kotschyi.* Annual grasses that appear after rains include *Aristida adscensionis* and *Aristida mutabilis.* The Jiddat shows a marked regional variation in species composition, which is a reflection of its three geomorphological subdivisions as well as fog moisture gradients.[1]

The Territorial and Tribal Scene

The well-developed vegetation of the Jiddat is the habitat of the Harasiis tribe. These pastoralists appear to have been originally a Dhofari people (Thomas 1929, 1937), and they continue to speak a modern south Arabian language known as Harsuusi (Johnstone 1977). According to Harasiis oral tradition, the original section of the tribe was Beit Afarri, living in Wadi Kadrit, between Salalah and Hadramaut. Over the past few hundred years the Harasiis have gradually pushed—and been pushed—northeast into the Jiddat (see map 5). As they moved into the various wadis that mark the natural geographic borders of the Jiddat, they have come up against other pastoral tribes—the Jeneba to the east along the Jazir Coast and the Wahiba to the north in the Wadi Halfayn (see map 2). Unable to push further, the Harasiis today are mainly concentrated on the desert plateau itself, although in the summer they are often found uncomfortably sharing the Awta and the Jazir Coast with the Jeneba tribe (Chatty 1983).

Their traditional economy is based on the raising of camels and goats by natural graze for the production of milk rather than meat. At the core of their way of life is migration determined by a combination of seasonal and ecological variables in the location of pasture and water. Survival of both herds and herders makes movement from deficit to surplus areas

The early morning fog, which sustains vegetation on the Jiddat despite the less than 50 mm annual rainfall. A *National Geographic* photographer capturing the camel feeding routine on film.

vital. As with any pastoral group, the Harasiis seek to control a territory that contains sufficient resources to sustain communal life. They tend to live in the haylats and wadis where there are trees under which to shelter and where graze for their animals is more plentiful. They determine their territorial frontiers loosely as running along the floor of the Wadi Rawnab to the south and east of Rima, along the middle of Wadi Haytam to the northeast, up to the general region of the Harashiif dunes to the north, and across to the Ramlat-as-Sahmah to the west. They share borders with the Jeneba to the east, with the Wahiba and Duru to the north, and with the Beit Kathir to the south.

These borders are in constant flux. Over the past three or four decades the seasonal availability of pasture and water has undergone a pronounced geographic shift from southwest to northeast, requiring readjustment of relations between these four nomadic pastoral tribes. In the 1950s, 1960s, and 1970s various texts and oral traditions placed the Harasiis territory as extending from the Jiddat-il-Harasiis westward to near Mughshin-al-Ayn and Bir Khasfah, where they were said to have watering agreements with the Mahra and Bataharah. Since that time there has been a slow move eastward. Thus, during the 1980s and early 1990s disputes have tended to focus on water rights along the borders shared with the Jeneba in the Wadi Rawnab, Wadi Halfayn, and Wadi Baw.

The Harasiis tribe organizes itself into seven lineages or subgroups called beit: Beit Aksit, Beit Mutaira, Beit Barho, Beit Sha'ala, Beit Aloob, Beit Afarri, and Beit Katherayn. These seven lineages are divided into two factions, one headed by the Beit Aksit and the other by the Beit Mutaira. The leadership of the tribe as a whole lies with the Beit Aksit, whose ancestral forbear is acknowledged to have united the disparate units into one tribe about 150 years ago. Each lineage generally recognizes or appoints two spokesmen who act on its behalf. These men, called *rashiid* (pl. rushada'), represent the lineage in discussions or meetings concerning the welfare of tribal members.

The search for pasture and water is the underlying principle of organization for the Harasiis way of life. To a large extent the coordination of this movement lies with the rushada' of the separate lineages. Effort is always made to ensure that one particular grazing land does not become overcrowded or that another plentiful area is ignored. Thus the relaying of information on the state of pasture and other ecological features is an important function of the rushada' and tribal elders. First among these rushada' is the Sheikh. Though he traditionally enjoyed many privileges, today his most important duty is the regular representation of the tribe at the Haima Tribal Administrative Center.

The Historical Past: Traditional Subsistence

The Harasiis tribe is made up of approximately 2,500 people, of which close to 2,000 are found on the Jiddat-il-Harasiis at any one time.[2] Households are generally extended family units, the average family being composed of nine members. At the core of the household is the nuclear family of husband, wife, and children. Generally two or three adult relatives of one degree or another make up the rest of the household. At one time it will be a grandparent, at another a cousin or in-law, or even more distant relative. On average, a household keeps a hundred goats and a few sheep, which are the responsibility of the women and older girls. The average household also has twenty-five camels, of which five or six are generally kept near the homestead—these are the heavily pregnant or lactating ones. The remainder of the camels are left *mafkook*—free to graze in the open desert. Their whereabouts are very carefully monitored, and an elaborate camel information exchange system operates among all the tribesmen. When they meet, tribesmen first exchange news about the condition of pastures, then the whereabouts of various mafkook camels, and finally news items of various family members. Homesteads are generally moved a significant distance three or four times a year. A serious husbandman, though, will shift his homestead a few kilometers every few weeks to ensure that the family herd of goats and sheep does not destroy what graze exists around the campsite.

In the past access to water for the Harasiis was extremely limited. Tribal tradition has it that they never drank water but lived almost entirely on the consumption of camel and goat milk from their herds. This cultural explanation quite accurately reflects a geographic truth. Until the 1960s there was no sweet water source on the Jiddat. The only source of water in an area of forty thousand square kilometers was found along the Awta, the lowlands of the Huqf escarpment lying just along the coast of Oman from Duqm north toward Al-Hajj. There a series of springs were found (Raqqi, Nakhleet, Baw). These heavily mineralized springs yielded water that was (and still is) barely potable, even under the best of conditions. However, the unique features of a heavy early morning fog frequently provided the herds with sufficient moisture for their needs. These herds then supplied the human population with enough milk for their nutritional and physiological requirements.

The Harasiis herds were bred and selectively culled for their milk-giving features as well as their hardiness in the face of the extreme aridity. Goats were once exclusively the white, short-haired Somali goat, which could withstand long periods without water and still yield abundant milk (one to three kilograms per day per goat). Camels were also bred for their milk-yielding capabilities and careful genealogical records were memorized. Camels and goats were grouped as "daughters" of highly appreciated strains. Both the camel and the goat were well adapted to the traditional migration pattern of the Harasiis tribe. The relatively cool winters were spent on the Jiddat itself, where water was nonexistent, and the summers were spent in the Awta, where the herds had some access to the brackish spring water of the region.

Traditionally herds were divided and managed in keeping with their milk-yielding state. Goats that bred three times in two years tended to be either pregnant or lactating and were permanently kept near the household. They were milked each morning before being taken out to a

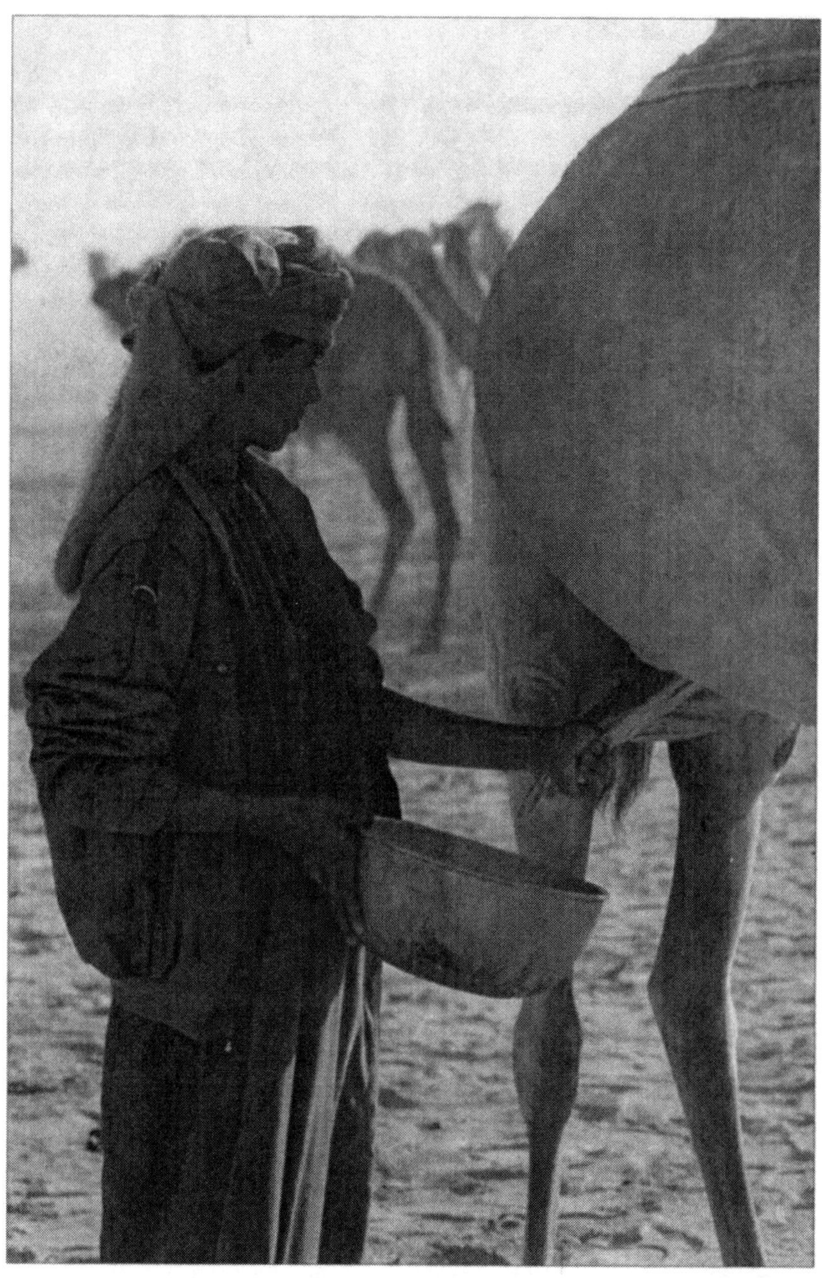

Camel milk is highly prized and is believed to give greater strength than goat's milk. Only men or older boys are permitted to milk camels, which, as a rule, can only be owned by men.

nearby pasture by an available female household member—generally an elderly woman, though as often an older female child—and again in the evening upon their return to the camp. The camel herd was split into an active or soon-to-be active milk-producing section and a fallow section. Camels tended to breed only once in a two-year period—they have a pregnancy of nearly a year and a lactation stage of roughly eleven months. The heavily pregnant and lactating camels—about 25 percent of the total camel holding—were kept near the homestead and allowed to browse close by. They were milked by any male household member in the morning and evening, but on a far less regular basis than was the case for goats. Camels kept near the homestead were still regarded the responsibility of the male household members, as was the fallow, or mafkook, herd. These were watched over by a young adult male member of the household. Thus households tended to be "in milk" throughout most of the annual cycle, although the quantity and type of milk—camel or goat—tended to fluctuate tremendously.

The division of labor within a household was such that few young households had enough members to look after both fallow and lactating herds. Households tended to manage their lactating herds on their own and to join forces with other kinsmen in looking after the mafkook herds. Arrangements within a lineage, and often between mature brothers or cousins, tended to bring together three or four herds of fallow camels under the care of one adult male who had no other responsibility than to follow the combined herd, sometimes numbering as many as one hundred head. Many Harasiis claim that the larger the camel herd, the easier it is to manage.

Traditional household subsistence entailed frequent supplemental contributions to the cooking pot. Though milk was an important part of the diet of the Harasiis, hunting, particularly in winter, added substantially to a household's well-being. The Harasiis ocassionally hunted gazelle and Arabian oryx. The meat of one gazelle was sufficient for three or four days, whereas the meat of the much larger oryx would last one household for at least a month. The meat was not eaten on the day of the kill but hung in strips from the branches of trees to dry. If no gazelle or oryx was available, then a roasted hare or sometimes even a hedgehog might be added to the cooking pot. In the summer months, when most homesteads were sheltered along the Awta and Jazir Coast, some trading was carried out for fresh and dried fish (sardines and shark in particular) with the neighboring, and often contentious, Jeneba tribe.

During this season men and women often braided palm leaf fronds (*sa'af*) from the local wild date trees into food mats, bowls, baskets, and a variety of other vessels for future sale.

Basic to the organization of all pastoral people is the existence of sedentary communities in adjacent areas and access to their agricultural products. For the Harasiis tribe relations of interdependence have long bound them to the sedentary communities along the Sharqiyya foothills. Harasiis men frequently trekked as much as fifteen days on camel back to reach these agricultural centers, surviving on a diet of dried fish and dates. Often they herded their goats along with them for auction in the village marketplace, carried palm frond mats, bowls and baskets for sale and pots, trays and other metal items for repair at the local coppersmith.

For generations this relationship, largely uncomplicated by external factors, bound the Harasiis of Central Oman to the villages of the Sharqiyya foothills—particularly Adam and Sinaw—in an economic partnership. The cash economy of the village was reinforced by the continual influx of "capital on the hoof." Transactions were completed and money changed hands. Significantly though, when the final purchases were made, the bulk of the money had simply moved from one end of the market to another—from the animal buyer's pocket to the merchant's till. For the Harasiis, the relationship with the villages reinforced not a cash, but a subsistence economy. For example, the individual Harasiis tribesman may have sold two goats for forty Maria Theresa thalars, and then spent this exact amount on flour, coffee, tea, dates, sugar, and cloth for his family.[3] His long treks to the village market-place were not motivated by a possible profit but simply by the short supply of basic household necessities.

The Recent Past: From the 1954 Duqm Landing

In 1954 an exploratory party of the national oil company, Petroleum Development (Oman) Limited (hereafter PDO), landed at Duqm, set up a base camp, and made its way from the southern coast of Oman across the Jiddat-il-Harasiis, into the central desert of Oman. Graphically describing that long march, Neil McLeod Innes wrote that "not only did they see no car tracks, there were no tracks of men or of camels and not even the footprints of birds alighting or running on the sands. There was no sign of life at all. They were about a hundred miles from the Rub' al-Khali (Empty Quarter) but they might as well have been crossing it, so empty of all life was the landscape for the greater part of their course"

(Innes 1987:87). The many stories the Harasiis have about that crossing make one realize that the column was certainly seen, but that its Harasiis observers went totally unnoticed. Once at Fahud, contact was made with the Sheikhs of the Duru tribe who agreed to allow PDO to prospect for oil in their territory.

The death of the spiritual leader of interior Oman, Imam Mohammed bin Abdullah Al-Khalili, earlier in the year had removed one opposition force facing the oil survey teams. However, Talib, the brother of the newly elected Imam Ghalib bin Ali Al-Hinai, was determined that if oil were found in this part of inner Oman it should be exploited for his brother and his followers and not for the benefit of Sultan Saiid bin Taimur. To this end Talib sent an armed force to seize the Duru date plantations at Ibri, which were an important source of income for the tribe. The Duru responded by sending guides to Duqm to lead back the PDO surveying party and—more important—its escort of Muscat troops. Eventually, in October 1954, the Muscat troops and the Duru moved on Ibri and expelled Talib's men from the town (PDO 1970:129).

With the commencement of active oil exploration, the fortunes of the nomadic pastoral tribes of the central desert of Oman fell increasingly out of their own control. For example, in the case of the Duru, once the leadership had agreed to allow the oil company to prospect in their territory they found themselves pawns in a traditional power struggle between the Imam's forces and the Sultan's. When that battle had been settled successfully and the PDO surveying party in Jebel Fahud commenced its work, problems of an entirely new nature presented themselves to the Duru. The oil company needed to establish a system for labor requirements and supervision in order to effectively exploit the oil promise of the area. Though tribal leaders were accustomed to acting as mediators on behalf of their tribespeople, PDO's requirements were novel and at times threatening. Initially jealousies divided the Duru political structure, and section leaders took to claiming exclusive rights to providing labor for the company. Eventually the oil company took precedence, and traditional Duru tribal hierarchies were put aside for more accommodating individual associations.

The Harasiis tribe was to face very similar political upheaval to the Duru. In 1958 PDO began to prepare a new drilling location in the middle of the Jiddat-il-Harasiis at Haima. The company feared that Jeneba tribesmen might claim the region as their own, even though Haima was far from any disputable border. After consultation with Sultan Saiid bin Taimur,

PDO decided to search for a labor supervisor from within the Harasiis tribe. A leader of the Beit Mutaira, Salim bin Huweila, was appointed. After some labor unrest, both Salim and the traditional tribal leader, Sheikh Shergi of Beit Aksit, were sent to Salalah to confer with the Sultan. There they were to remain for six months, until the unrest in the Jiddat had died down. Over the next decade PDO played one man off against the other. When Salim became too demanding or too difficult, they would turn to Sheikh Shergi. When Sheikh Shergi made "outrageous" requests—generally for water—they would ask that the Sultan allow them to return to dealing with Salim. Finally, in 1968, Sultan Saiid bin Taimur, angry with Sheikh Shergi, removed him from office and appointed Salim bin Huweila as the "new" Sheikh of the Harasiis (PDO 1974:3).

This arrangement was never acceptable to the tribesmen, nor, of course, to Sheikh Shergi, who bided his time. In 1972, two years after his accession, Sultan Qaboos bin Saiid reinstated Sheikh Shergi as the "official" tribal leader. The decade of oil company and government interference in the Harasiis's tribal political organization had come to a close, but not without considerable loss of confidence in their authority figures.

Economically, however, the Harasiis tribe fared far better. From the moment oil exploration teams came ashore at Duqm in 1954, a new universe opened up for them. Each of the oil company activities resulted in new employment opportunities, and the tribesmen quickly adapted to the routine—if not always the discipline—of the company. As more and more men took jobs as guides, drivers, guards, and unskilled laborers, their salaries became an increasingly important factor in the economic interplay between the desert and the village. In many cases a man's salary began to replace animal revenues as the main source of purchasing power. Animal sales declined and herd size began to increase. This process was checked eventually by a long period of drought and the very low carrying capacity of the Jiddat.

The activities of the oil exploration teams, the development of permanent camps, the setting up of rigs, the opening up of water wells, and, later, petroleum exploitation were accompanied by tremendous infrastructural changes. Tracks came to be replaced by graded roads and eventually, in 1981, a tarmacked highway was opened, running through the center of the Jiddat and connecting the north and south of Oman for the first time. Fifteen-day journeys across the desert by camel became mere memories. In 1974 the first Harasiis-owned half-ton truck appeared on the Jiddat. Within five years nearly every Harasiis household had one truck, if not more. In our in-depth economic survey of a 10 percent random sample of the population, which we carried out in 1981 and 1982, only one household head did not own a vehicle. His three adult sons, however, each had a vehicle and alternated with one another to procure water, animal feed supplements, and comestibles for their father's household and to transport his livestock to market. Journeys to town centers were no longer measured by days, but by hours: six to Nizwa, eight to Muscat, seven to Salalah.

Probably the most profoundly altered factor in Harasiis life was access to water. Before 1954 water was only available on the Awta. The practice of collecting water from the heavy morning fog was universal, and water consumption was kept to a minimum. Blankets were spread under trees and the branches were shaken. Then the blankets would be wrung out and the water collected in bowls. The traditional Harasiis goat, a short-haired white animal, needed no water in winter and very little in summer. During the 1960s black long-haired goats, native to northern Oman, began to appear among Harasiis herds. This was probably the result of successive migrations north to Wadi Halfayn and Wadi Andam during droughts on the Jiddat. These black-haired goats were more marketable in northern Oman, where their meat was appreciated. They were, however, less suited to the aridity of the Jiddat and required greater quantities of water.

Over the last fifty years the Harasiis have been pushed back from the coastal regions by the Jeneba tribe and now are fairly restricted to the Jiddat itself. Fortunately their access to water has not been entirely cut off. Almost as if in response to the urgent need of the Harasiis, the oil company arrived on the Jiddat in the mid-1950s and drilled water wells at Haima and al-Ajaiz. Pressure from the tribal leadership and the government resulted in these wells being left in operation and maintained after the exploration teams moved. By the 1960s the al-Ajaiz well served as a migratory magnet for many Harasiis families and their herds of the more water dependent long-haired black goat. By the mid-1970s, when the truck had become firmly established, families began to move further afield with their herds. Three times a week, and sometimes five, the household head would make a trip to the nearest well to bring water back for his family and herds. The average household required fourteen drums holding 40 gallons of water in winter and twenty-one drums in summer per week. Using half-ton pickup trucks—which only carry four drums at a time, each with a capacity to hold 209 liters—a man bringing water for his family and herds might drive five hundred kilometers a week for water.

There are several water wells located on borders the Harasiis share with other pastoral tribes—for example, the two wells at Ghubbar, southwest of Rima, which are shared with the Mahra, and the well at Rawnab, which is shared with the Jeneba. But until 1984 this area had only one uncontested source of sweet water and another of brackish water. Since then several reverse osmosis plants have been built by the government at points like Wadi Mudhabi, Wadi Haytam, and Wadi Dhahir for the pastoral tribes to use.

Almost as significant as the oil company presence—and their associated subcontractors—were two further developments in the Jiddat-il-Harasiis. These were the government project to reintroduce the Arabian oryx into the wild and the plan to extend social services to the pastoralists of the central desert of Oman.

The Arabian oryx, a traditional game animal for pastoral tribes in Oman, did not come under serious threat of extinction until after the Second World War, when modern rifles and four-wheel-drive vehicles turned them into "sitting targets." Throughout the 1950s and 1960s parties regularly journeyed into the Jiddat-il-Harasiis to hunt these graceful creatures. By 1972 the oryx became extinct in Oman when the last-known herd on the Jiddat was slaughtered by a hunting party. Their extinction was a sad loss to the country and to the Harasiis tribe, who had been unable to stop the extermination of an animal they respected and depended upon for supplemental protein to their diet.

Three years later Sultan Qaboos bin Saiid began the process of restoring the oryx to Oman as part of its natural heritage. Experts pinpointed Haylat Yalooni in the middle of the Jiddat as the most auspicious site for the reintroduction project. Yalooni was one of the largest haylats on the Jiddat, and its browse, shade, and shelter made it a very important area of permanent resources for the tribe. In order to reintroduce the oryx successfully onto the Jiddat, an agreement was reached between the national government and the tribal rushada' specifying that no Harasiis families would camp in that Acacia-Prosopis woodland and associated perennial grasslands of Haylat Yalooni. Completion of the oryx project camp in 1979 made it the only settlement of any significance for three hundred kilometers. With motor vehicles well established on the Jiddat, the Harasiis had been obliged to travel three hundred kilometers north-east to Adam to buy gasoline or to have a split water tank welded. But this changed, as the Yalooni camp quickly became a place where some Harasiis could seek assistance over minor problems. It also became an important source of employment, with 15 percent of the male household heads holding jobs either at the camp or related to its maintenance. Few tribesmen working on the oryx project were not at some time or another faced with news of emergencies or major problems at their home. And the senior staff of the oryx project had (and still has) to devote significant energy to managing and adjusting staff establishment to meet these pastoral crises.

Pastoralists, in particular, are resourceful and quick to see the advantages of any situation. In the case of the oryx project, however, the advantages were not initially clear. As long as there was no drought pushing them to use areas that their elders had agreed to leave aside, they were willing to cooperate. Many Harasiis expressed their excitement to us at seeing the oryx return to the Jiddat and being able to view them from behind their five-kilometer fenced enclosure. A short time later, when they were released into the wild, the Harasiis were to play an important part as project rangers, tracking the oryx as they moved about freely on the Jiddat. Good relations with the Harasiis were a key feature in the ongoing success of the project. Most families cooperated with the staff, and the Harasiis came to perceive the benefits to them from the project as far outweighing any costs represented by their loss of the fertile (in their terms) Haylat Yalooni.

Before 1983 Haima was a subdistrict of the Adam office of the Ministry of Interior. But in 1983 it became the capital of a newly created regional administrative unit and its Wali, appointed to look after the problems, petitions, and requests of the community, reported directly to Muscat. The government services put into effect at Haima in the early 1980s largely expanded and improved throughout the 1980s and 1990s. Permanent and mobile health services had been established in 1981, and plans for a substantial hospital were drawn up. In 1987 the Haima Hospital was officially opened with fifty beds, three physicians, and a medical support staff of twelve. The boarding school, which opened in 1982 with 51 boys, had 120 boys and 9 girls enrolled in 1992. The Ministry of Social Affairs office, which opened in 1982, continued to operate, mainly handling welfare requests for the aged, widowed, orphaned, and disabled. The Ministry of Water and Electricity, which had operated a number of water tankers that irregularly delivered water in 1981 and 1982 to homesteads scattered throughout the Jiddat, improved its service. In 1985 it shifted its emphasis to the establishment of reverse osmosis plants at strategic points throughout the Jiddat. And finally the Ministry of Agriculture and Fisheries veterinary office, which opened in 1982, continued to operate, although its services were mainly curative.

These government services, fully established and running smoothly by the mid-1980s, also provided the Harasiis population with numerous opportunities for employment. Each government office employed a minimum of two guards, or askars. Some, like the Ministry of Interior, employed two from each tribal lineage (fourteen jobs). Drivers, clerks, and liaison officers were also required by most government offices. In addition, the police border patrol station required one, if not two, members of each lineage to work in their units. Thus official employment with the government on the Jiddat grew from nil to a minimum of forty positions at Haima itself in the space of five years. Nearly 20 percent of all male Harasiis household heads held down jobs at the Haima Tribal Administrative Center by 1987. This trend has continued, and with the creation of Haima as one of two regional centers of Al-Wusta Province in 1991 even more job opportunities are expected to come on line throughout the present decade.

Parallel with this government-affiliated growth has been a locally initiated entrepreneurship at Haima. The petrol station—the first to be opened between Adam and Thumrait (a distance of over six hundred kilometers)—is owned by a Harasiis tribesman, as is the cold store, school candy store, general store, and café. A garage that repairs punctures and does some minor vehicle work—although most Harasiis tribesmen manage to repair their vehicles without access to proper tools or parts—is owned by another Harasiis tribesman. Several more tribesmen use the café as an office to arrange for long-term leasing of their large trucks to various companies working in the Jiddat. Tribesmen owning date palms—25 percent of tribal households have some date garden holdings—often make the necessary arrangements from Haima for the care of their northern gardens. Perhaps more significantly, credit arrangements, which were once conducted with nontribal merchants in Adam, Sinaw, and occasionally Nizwa, are beginning to focus on the local Harasiis entrepreneurs, who are increasingly taking on the roles of creditors, particularly as formerly town-based credit facilities are beginning to dry up because of regular, long-term defaulting.

The national oil company presence and associated opportunities for wage labor within the borders of the Jiddat-il-Harasiis, the establishment of the base for the project to reintroduce the oryx and last, the creation of the tribal administrative center in Haima, have all served to irreversibly "pluck" the Harasiis from the classic subsistence pastoral system they had followed for decades, if not centuries. Today the Harasiis are rapidly becoming a part of a modern twentieth-century service- and commodity-oriented market where wage labor is the key to survival.

The Hypothetical Average Household

The "average" family, to emerge from our detailed economic survey of seventeen households in 1981–1982, had become a major user of an assortment of consumer goods. This family typically consisted of three adults and six children ranging in ages from newly born to early adolescence. By 1982 it owned two late-model half-ton pickup trucks, generally of Japanese make. Nearly half of all the driving was carried out to provide the family and herds with water.

Typically this would mean a minimum of five trips a week from household to well and back again in summer and about three trips a week in winter. If the family was camped near Wadi Yalooni, for instance, the drive to the nearest well, the high salt content Al-Ajaiz, would be forty kilometers each way. While a journey to the Haima sweet water well would mean a drive ninety kilometers each way. With only one trip a week for family drinking water (one trip to Haima), the household head bringing water for his family and herds would drive five hundred kilometers a week in summer and nearly three hundred kilometers a week in winter.

The household herd of one hundred goats and twenty-five camels presented an annual feed expenditure of nearly RO 2,300 per year in 1982, bringing yearly feed costs per head to nearly RO 15. In many ways 1982 was a "typical" year, if any year can be given such a label in the arid southeast corner of Arabia. February 1982 saw the heaviest rainfall in seven years in parts of the Jiddat, ending—if only temporarily—a serious drought. Hence figures taken from respondents before the rains reflect the great amount of processed feed pellets that were being purchased to sustain the herds in the near absence of natural graze—as much as RO 23 per head per year. At about the same time the national government permitted a limited subsidized sale of animal feed to relieve the burden the drought was creating. Figures taken after these two dramatic events show very limited expenditure for feed, a mere RO 6 per head per year.

Income from the herds was limited. When there was no paid income,

TABLE 1
Household Economic Survey Employment Status 1981–1982

Respondent	Position	Salary/Month
A	—	—
B	Internal Security Department	265
C	Guide	194
D	Well Operator	100
E	Company Guard	100
F	Entrepreneur	500+
G	Rasheed	30
H	—	—
I	Company Liasion	600
J	Well Guard	120
K	—	—
L	Yalooni Ranger	160
M	PDO/Yalooni Ranger	400/200*
N	Rasheed	30
O	Yalooni Ranger	223
P	Internal Security Department	265
Q	Shiekh	100+
Average		RO 234**

*Two men are earning salaries in this household.
**One RO (Rial Omani) equals U.S. $2.58.

this typical family would sell five goats a month; otherwise sale of livestock took place only when necessary to make purchases. The figure of five goats a month would, at the village auctions, bring in an income between RO 250 and RO 300. By 1982 this family would regularly spend RO18 on comestibles: flour, sugar, rice, tea, coffee, dates, spices, herbs, canned tomatoes, milk, meat, and occasionally fruit. The other major expense for the family after animal feed costs was the expenditure required to keep the two vehicles running. The typical family generally had a monthly income of about RO 200 and further benefits from the employer. When employment was with the national oil company, there were monthly food allowances, which significantly reduced the household's expenditure, as well as preferential delivery of water by oil company water tankers. When employment was with the white oryx project at Yalooni, there was an allowance—generally of a full tank of petrol at the end of each month's patrol rotation. When employment was with the Ministry of Interior or the Royal Oman Police, there would be substantial assistance in delivery of water to the households. Each child in boarding school received RO 10 per month from the Ministry of Education.

TABLE 2

Household Economic Survey Employment Status 1991–1992

Respondent	Position	Salary/Month
A	—	—
B	Police Border Ranger	350
C	Guide	380/250*
D	Well Operator	100
E	Government Representative	250
F	Entrepreneur	500+
G	Rasheed/PDO	50/180*
H	—	—
I	Company Liasion/PDO	900/180*
J	Well Guard	138
K	—	—
L	Yalooni Ranger	160
M	PDO/Yalooni Ranger	600/200*
N	Rasheed	50
O	Yalooni Ranger	350
P	Retired/Police	48/220*
Q	Shiekh	200+
Average		RO 300**

*Two men are earning salaries in this household.
**One RO (Rial Omani) equals U.S. $2.58.

However, even with these extremely generous gestures on the part of the various employers in the Jiddat, the average family in 1982 no longer operated a kind of balanced barter/subsistence economy where livestock capital was traded off to meet expenditures and debts were purely of a social or political nature. By 1982—and the trend has continued—a system of debt management had come into effect. Rather than managing its herds to cover its needs and expenditures, the typical family now tended to take out loans in order to cover the animal feed costs and the expenses of running two vehicles. The assumption was always that come a period of good rains they would no longer need to pay for feed, as pasture would be abundant. The herds, grazing on such natural feed, would then be in a state to bring in a good price at the village auctions and in such a manner the family's debts could be wiped out. With the continued drought (it was ten years before there was to be substantial, widespread rain on the Jiddat in March and April of 1992), debts accumulated with the buildup of interest on outstanding loans, the continual need to feed the herds, and the lack of good marketing opportunities either at Haima or at the end of a three hundred-kilometer trek to Nizwa, Sinaw, or Adam.

Fortunately, perhaps, credit is never extended indefinitely, and sources of borrowing have dried up over the last few years, except from within the tribe. Toyota, Nissan, and other car dealers are no longer willing to sell cars on installment plans to Omanis with an address south of Adam, hence to any pastoral tribesman. Village market creditors have also stopped extending credit, as they have reached their ceilings. What seemed like an ever-increasing spiral of debt in 1982 has been abruptly cut off at a number of points, allowing some elements of sanity to be reimposed on the typical Harasiis household budget. By the 1990s a system had been put in place whereby debts were being collected on a monthly basis from the pay packets of certain household heads.

Household Subsistence and Wage Labor

From our in-depth household survey of 10 percent of the Harasiis population, we were able to extract certain trends regarding employment in general on the Jiddat. Of the sampled households, nearly 54 percent received salaries from the government, close to 30 percent received wages from private companies, and less than 10 percent were self-employed. More than 80 percent of the respondents had some sort of income beyond that generated by the occasional sale of animals (table 1). Equally important was the fact that this employment was all restricted geographically to the Jiddat-il-Harasiis. Ten years later these respondents exhibited the same commitment to wage labor to supplement household subsistence. By 1992 the original sample households had matured, and often more than one individual in each unit had some form of regular employment (table 2). It was still the case in the 1990s that no one needed to migrate out of familiar territory to seek work.

Furthermore, following the pattern established during the oil company's earlier years, the terms of employment were fairly flexible. The company itself rotated men two weeks on duty followed by two weeks off duty. The Yalooni project tended to permit ten days off after every twenty days on duty. Government jobs were more restrictive, but still permitted sufficient time away to keep tabs on the needs of individual households. By the close of the 1980s virtually any adult Harasiis male who sought work locally at Haima or on the Jiddat would find it.

Available jobs tended to fall into two categories: those requiring the man to remain in one fixed place, such as well and installation guards or askars (Omani labor laws required that each company working in the desert hire two local tribal askars), and those requiring the man to be mobile, patrolling or ranging over the desert in four-wheel-drive vehicles usually fitted with HF radios or other navigational devices. These categories of employment fit in exceptionally well with traditional Harasiis organization of male labor. One way or another, whether fixed in one place or roaming on the desert, the wage-earning Harasiis male is able to receive or visit other tribesmen and exchange hospitality and information about pasture, herds, and households—even if only too briefly. Such visiting- and information-gathering networks are important aspects of the individual male's status in the constantly changing social and political world of the Harasiis tribe.

These local jobs hardly disturb men's important visiting patterns, and households throughout the Jiddat are all watched over even if, at times, from afar. What tends to be reduced when household heads are employed is their immediate accessibility to the family and its herds.

The traditional division of labor in pastoral society generally places men as managers of the larger herd animals and women as managers of the smaller domestic animals. Men tend to manage the household procurement needs for purchased food, animal supplements, and water supplies. Women are responsible for the subsistence herd of goats and lactating camels, while the older boys and men tend to be away looking after the fallow mafkook herd of camels. Men are responsible for milking the camels, while women are responsible for milking the goats and sheep.[4] Furthermore, among the Harasiis men are responsible for procuring water for the family and the herd. When a household head is employed and physically away from his homestead for two weeks out of four, for example, he can still manage his family responsibilities. The tendency today is to arrange with another kinsman—sometimes also employed, but on a different duty roster—to bring water, food, or animal feed concentrates to the homestead during his days off and also to milk the family's camels when there are no resident older boys or men present.

Once the employment patterns of adult Harasiis males had settled into a predictability of sorts, the division of labor in the household began to blur. Women took to making some household management decisions along with their more traditional work. In the past few years women have begun to take a more active part in decisions concerning procuring of water and dry feed concentrates for the subsistence herd. Now it is the "temporary" female household head who will ask a kinsman or visiting tribesman to make a journey across the Jiddat to bring back water for the household. As often as not she will also select a number of young male kids and have them taken to market—three hundred to four hundred kilometers to the north—for auction in order to supply the household with whatever comestibles or animal feed is lacking.

Harasiis households today still manage their herds for milk. Subsistence remains the key to the organization of the homestead and the herds. And although wage labor is an important reality, traditional patterns of economic production have not broken down. For example, milking camels was once strictly a male preserve, and, in fact, it still is, for only when no male is available will a woman do the milking herself. Given the arrangements between kinsmen described above, this is rarely necessary. The herd keeps the family well-fed,[5] and the income from wage employment covers "new" necessities. Running and maintaining a vehicle is an expensive undertaking that cannot easily be managed in a household where subsistence is the only mode of operation. The average yearly cost for gasoline alone to the typical Harasiis household was RO 1,244 (about $3,210), representing almost the same sum as the annual bill for village-purchased comestibles and just under the entire yearly salary of a well guard. Nearly half of all driving was for the family's and herd's water requirements. The transformation in lifestyle cannot be measured easily. With wage labor and motor transport, the parameters of daily existence have expanded. More visiting for men and for women, increased entertaining, greater variety of comestibles, better access to information—all point to a broadening of the universe of the Harasiis and to a rise in expectations as well. Employment has taken some of the hardship out of life on the Jiddat-il-Harasiis, but the herds still keep the homesteads going.

In most regions of the world, pastoralists tend to invest their "surplus" capital back into their herds. Not normally having other forms of investment—like property or real estate—the pastoralist generally ploughs his surplus earnings into his "capital on the hoof." This trend was first observed among the pastoralists of Southern Persia, where, until a threshold situation was reached, households preferred to invest in their herds (Barth 1961:103–4). The limits to growth were set by the manpower available within a family or household. In Dhofar in southern Oman, a similar trend has operated over the last ten years. Now, however, the enormously inflated camel and cattle holdings of those pastoralists are threatening to irreversibly damage the once unique grazing lands of Dhofar (Chatty, Zaroug, and Osman 1991; Janzen 1986, 1990). So severe and rapid is this overstocking that the government is considering an emergency "off-take" of camels and cattle and the imposition of herd number maximums.

Yet, in contrast, in 1982 Harasiis households where men were employed full-time—64 percent of the households—had on average 35 percent fewer camels and 25 percent fewer goats than did households with no outside salary. These same households showed a surprisingly low incidence of sales of livestock, due perhaps to the demands of full-time employment as well as the distances between producer and market—a one thousand kilometer round-trip. These households tended to prepare festive meals more frequently—a trend that has continued in the 1990s. Thus, even though employment seems to have inhibited the regular sales of livestock, herd numbers have not risen. Most families insist this is due to the fact that they have to entertain far more regularly than in the past. One Harasiis tribesman employed at a PDO camp said that his family's goat herd numbers dropped from 150 to less than 100 in the first year of his employment because he had to look after so many expatriate visitors from the nearby oil camp. Without herd growth there is little fear of accelerated graze depletion, as witnessed in the south of the country. Thus paid employment has had a beneficial effect on graze in the Jiddat.

Among the Harasiis monthly salaries tend to be used to improve the relative level of comfort of the household. Much of the cash income is used for running the half-ton pickup trucks, the Bedford lorries, and the water tankers that are increasingly part and parcel of every home. Household heads in our sample calculated that their annual expenditure for spare parts, particularly tires, was RO 285 (about $753), and for gasoline was RO 1,244 (about $3,210)—an average total of RO 125 (about $322) per month. In many cases that sum represented nearly 70 percent of a household's monthly income. But trucks make it possible to reverse the standard operating principle among most pastoralists of bringing the animal to water. Now water is brought to the herd whenever possible, and in that fashion the household can cut down on the frequency of its major moves. The former average of fifteen to sixteen moves a year has dropped to approximately three or four (with continuous adjustments of a few kilometers at every site as the subsistence herd eats its way through the surrounding pasture). Such a reduction in the number of moves has been accompanied by an increase in consumer goods. The physical campsite, which once consisted of no more than a few woven storage bags and goatskin water sacks tied up on a tree branch, now has a much more substantial look and feel to it with its wire enclosures, tin chests, petroleum barrels (storing food and water), sacks of clothing, food and gas bottles scattered about.

Obviously the decreasing size of camel and goat herds is directly related to the fact that a large percentage of the male household heads are employed full-time and spend two out of every four weeks away from the household camp. Nevertheless, only men herd the fallow camel herd. Why, one must then ask, have the goat numbers also dropped by as much as 25 percent when it is the women who own and are responsible for them? The answer lies in the nature of the relationship between men and women and is dealt with in greater detail in chapter 7. Briefly, the family name, its honor, is dependent upon the behavior of all its adult members. Hospitality and the requirement to offer a ritually slaughtered animal for all important occasions (the visit of an expatriate employer is still defined as important) is rigidly followed. The goat offered for slaughter may technically belong to the woman, but the honor that accrues from the act is shared by the married couple.

Insuring Against Loss

Pastoralists all over the world tend to increase their herd numbers whenever possible as a way of protecting themselves against sudden loss from drought, epidemic, and other natural disasters. Yet the myth persists, even today, that pastoralists keep large herds primarily to achieve high social status in their society. Certainly the social value of cattle and camel, and even sheep and goat, is important. But other factors are more important. Unreliable rainfall, for example—a fact of life for most pastoralists—leads to great fluctuations in the availability of water and graze. For a pastoral household, keeping a margin against the risk of having part of the herd killed from drought or epidemic is a necessity. The number of animals required to maintain long-term continuous production is much larger than the number of animals utilized at a given period of time.

Furthermore many Western experts assume that meat production is the primary goal of livestock rearing. For a pastoralist, the primary goal is to produce milk for subsistence use. Pastoral livestock operations are not fundamentally capitalistic undertakings, although that often becomes a secondary concern (Chatty 1986). The primary aims are to provide a regular supply of food for the family that can enable both physical and social survival through recurrent and prolonged droughts.

Given the above, how does one explain Harasiis pastoral behavior today, which correlates wage labor with reduced herd size? If the Harasiis are no longer investing in their herds to the same extent as a decade earlier, have they found another fashion in which to insure themselves against loss? It may have been that in the recent past—in the 1960s—when water wells were suddenly opened by the oil company on the Jiddat, animal numbers for both goat and camel were artificially inflated by the sudden ease with which water became available. As long as the male household head was prepared to drive as much as five hundred kilometers a week to bring the required amount of water to the herd, the household thrived. At an average driving speed of twenty-five or thirty kilometers an hour over the rock and gravel Jiddat plain, that would mean a minimum of twenty hours spent driving each week. So long as time was relative and freely disposed of there was no conflict of interest.

Today, however, the time factor cannot be easily dismissed, particularly as the majority of male household heads have limited "free time." Thus herd sizes have to be adjusted to the amount of time a man has available to procure water for his herds when there is no natural source available from rainfall, fog precipitation, or standing pools after rainstorms. Today, perhaps, insurance or protection of herd loss from drought or epidemic lies in the salary that is available at the end of each month. Although the Harasiis are no longer as free and mobile to bring water to their herds—thus the drop in numbers of animals—their monthly salary acts as an insurance with which they can replenish any sudden loss of herd numbers. The Harasiis pastoralists appear to have successfully merged local wage labor with subsistence animal husbandry and, for the time being at least, they seem to have the best of two worlds—the traditional and the modern.

5

The Modern Harasiis Household:

The Traditional and the Innovative

Everywhere in the world families and households show similarities and differences; within any particular environment or locality certain universals of daily existence can generally be found. Life in the Jiddat-il-Harasiis provides numerous opportunities for such generalizations. This is partially due to the extremes of the physical environment, which make meeting the basic requirements of life—food, water, and shelter—a fundamental task for all its inhabitants. The still-relative simplicity of the material culture of the population also serves to make generalizations fairly straightforward.

The Harasiis household in the 1990s blends traditional and innovative patterns in an effort to best meet the requirements of existence in a harsh and unpredictable environment. The once prevalent uniformity of response to the demands of the physical universe is slowly giving way to specialized households. Some households today are attempting to combine full-time employment with subsistence animal husbandry, while others are altering their husbandry practices to derive a viable income from their herds. These two models represent the extremes on a continuum, from full-time husbandry to full-time employment, that characterizes the modern Harasiis household. Very few households in the 1990s fall into the full-time husbandry category; most come closer to a full-time employment and subsistence husbandry classification. In this chapter I will first describe the basic patterns of adaptation found on the Jiddat. Then I will focus on the two models of adaptation—different ends of one continuum—found among Harasiis households today. Finally I will provide an economic analysis of pastoralism and the newfound local employment opportunities of the 1990s.

The basic necessities of life—food, water, and shelter—have set certain patterns of activities into operation among the Harasiis. Until the introduction of motorized transport in the mid-1970s, the seasonal pattern of activities and the division of labor within a Harasiis family were fairly straightforward. The need for water and pasture for the herds rigidly governed the choices available to the family, and movement of households tended to take place every few weeks.

Each ecological niche had something special to offer. In the past the Jiddat in winter generally offered good shelter, with numerous trees in its many haylats and wadis. It also provided many opportunities to supplement the family's diet with gazelle, oryx, and other game. This was a season of relative plenty. It was also during the latter part of this period that the goat herds kidded and milk was abundant. Consequently families tended to move less frequently in winter, as food was sufficient, shelter was adequate, and water was not as urgently required as at other times of the year. The division of labor within the family was clear-cut. The women and the girls cared for the goats and the men and older boys cared for the camels. The camel herd was split into a pregnant or lactating herd. The five or six lactating camels—generally 20 per cent of the total herd—were kept at the homestead, while the fallow herd was let loose into the desert. For the responsible man or older boy, maintaining a healthy fallow herd required constant motion and vigil. Camels tend to spread out as they browse, and much effort was required to keep a check on one's own herd as well as the location of others' camels. The continuous traveling of some of the adult male household heads meant that information gathering and exchange was also undertaken as an essential element of survival. To know where the rains had fallen and where pasture was next going to appear was as important as knowing the whereabouts of all your camels and, sometimes, those of other families. The more information one had, the better one's chances of survival.

The women and girls were particularly busy in winter caring for the herd of goats and the few lactating camels. The women, more than the men, were tied to particular routines. They had the task of milking the goats early each day before taking them out to graze on nearby pasture. Generally an elderly woman or an older female child stayed with the herd throughout the day, returning to the homestead in late afternoon when the goats would be milked again. Later in the winter season when the goats had kidded, there was the additional work of monitoring the amount of milk the young kids took so that the family's milk supply was not threatened and the young kids received enough to survive.

Summer spent on the Jiddat was a rare occurrence. The extreme heat and the total absence of a source of water drove the Harasiis either to the coastal areas or to the north. Along the Jazir Coast and in the Awta were a number of brackish water wells, and the herds of exclusively short-haired white goat and camel would be driven there every week or so as required. Households camped in these areas for longer stretches than was usual in winter. The wild date groves of the Awta provided some food for the herds as did the dried sardine fish (*ooma*) they bartered for or bought from the Jeneba tribe that also shared the region with them. Fresh fish formed part of the diet of the Harasiis as well during this time of year, and it was not unusual for an adult male to cast a net and bring in a small catch for the family's immediate consumption.

Some households chose to move north into the Wadi Halfayn and even further north close to Adam, where a number of families had date groves. These families generally chose to leave the fallow camel herd behind with an adult male family member in one of the major wadis leading to the sea from the Jiddat-il-Harasiis. The rest of the family and the herd of goat would set up household near its date holdings, where water, food, and shelter were accessible. For the next few months they looked after the herds, milking the goat and camel for their nutritional requirements. The women and older girls often spent what spare moments they had braiding the palm leaf fronds into bowls, covers, and assorted containers for their own use and possible future sale. The young male kids that still remained would be sold in the village market to buy supplies for the coming winter months—flour, sugar, tea, coffee, rice, cloth, and sometimes dates. As only 25 percent of Harasiis households owned their own date groves, the majority of the families had to purchase dates.

As summer came to a close and temperatures dropped, families moved back onto the Jiddat and households that had split over the summer months were reunited. These seasonal patterns of migration and work were only interrupted for two events: weddings and the month-long religious fast of Ramadan. The first disrupted the typical pattern of activity in a household for generally a period of one week, as the majority of the invited household members participated in the celebrations. A skeleton crew generally remained at the household to look after the herd of goat—an adult female or older female child and an adult male or older male child could generally carry on for a week or so without too much trouble. The second event, the month of Ramadan, totally disrupted routine and the sometimes monotonous rhythm of daily life. As the Islamic calendar is thirteen days shorter than the Gregorian calendar, the monthlong period of fasting occurs at a slightly different period of time each year. Progressively, over a period of about twenty-five years, it covers all the seasons. Fasting from sunrise until sunset during this holy month was a very arduous religious duty for the Harasiis. And, as such, no single household could carry out its regular chores without help. Thus households always camped together in groups of three, and sometimes four, families—often the group of camel-sharing brothers or cousins. The campsite would be chosen for the ease of access to water for the herds and the amount of shelter that could be created. Sites in the Wadi Rawnab, Ghubbarah, and Awta were the most popular. Here the special evening meals at the end of the daylong fast would be prepared in rotation, each family taking its turn every third or fourth day. The men also shared the work of bringing the animals to water as required. Days could be spent—on the whole—in prayer, rest, and sleep, while the evenings and nights became the time for food, prayer, and social interaction.

The Truck and the Household

In the mid-1970s, as discussed briefly in earlier chapters, trucks began to appear as part and parcel of the Harasiis tribe's everyday existence. And, although daily patterns of activity remained unchanged, the truck very quickly altered the order of importance of the basic necessities to their life. Water was still as critically vital, but with trucks their access to it became more tangible, and therefore any temporary inaccessibility to water became a less serious problem. Within five years the pattern of driving the herds of goat and camel to water all but ceased, and water was brought to the herds instead.

As the importance of being near a water source—particularly in summer—dwindled, the pattern of seasonal movement gradually changed. The once lifesaving flight from the Jiddat during the summer months became less urgent. First a few and gradually, over a period of ten years, most Harasiis households chose to remain on the Jiddat winter and summer, only leaving their *dar* (territory) for the coast or the north when there was no available pasture for their herds. This squeeze back into the Jiddat took place at the same time as other larger and politically more active tribes—mainly the Mahra and the Jeneba—were expanding their borders and claiming formerly contested areas as exclusively their own. The less

Camels are often moved great distances by truck, either to take advantage of good pasture or as part of a general move of an entire household.

use the Harasiis households made of the brackish wells along the coast and in the Awta, the more impoverished their claims to the areas became.

By 1982 the average family had not one, but two trucks; one almost always a half-ton pickup truck, used exclusively for carrying water from the nearest well to the homestead, and the other—a direct replacement of the camel—used to carry the male household head from place to place as he required. Although the truck initially appeared to directly replace some of the functions of the camel, it was to have a profound impact on many aspects of everyday life. Where water had formerly been the main consideration for managing their regular migrations, food or pasture for the herds became of paramount importance. Where the disputes of the past had centered on the rights to use certain water wells, now disagreements tended to focus on the rights to certain pasture. Concepts of time and distance were to change along with ideas of shelter and migration. Eventually the Harasiis conception of economic self-reliance and the importance of wage labor was to be altered, as the truck and other motor vehicles brought them into frequent contact with the rapidly changing communities of the rest of Oman.[1] The rapid acceptance of a device that covered in one hour what a camel took an entire day to do obviously transformed many aspects of life. Journeys of fifteen days to a village marketplace and back suddenly took only a couple of days. And after 1981, when the first tarmacked road connecting Nizwa to Salalah was completed, such trips were accomplished in one day. These changes in travel times quickly affected the Harasiis concept of space, or the dimensions of their universe as well as the relative value of time.[2] The world suddenly appeared physically smaller, and what happened in the capital area now had some relevance to their lives. Visiting between kin and nonkin flourished, and the exchange and gathering of information became even more important to the individual, politically and economically. And as more men took on paid employment, their time assumed a monetary aspect.

The simplicity of the Harasiis concept of shelter gradually gave way to a more encumbered—and more comfortable—type of structure. Up to the late 1970s, and into the early 1980s, shelter for the Harasiis was wherever shade could be created for the family and the herd. Since the Jiddat has an unusually large number of trees for a desert, the Harasiis did not make tents—as other pastoralists in the Middle East do—but relied on finding a tree over which a blanket, and, in the 1980s, a stretch of tarpaulin, could be thrown. The material effects of a household, before the mid-1970s, were limited quite obviously to what could be carried by the camels during their fairly frequent moves.

By the early 1980s the typical Harasiis household had several alternative types of shelter available to it. In the winter months the household could purchase tarpaulin and tents—often army surplus—from the market towns in the north of Oman or from the United Arab Emirates. These would be pitched or thrown over a tree to create shade and warmth for the family. The women generally pulled woven lengths of goat hair (*filly*) around any stationary vehicle to give protection to their goats, particularly the newborn. A typical main winter homestead in the 1980s would have two tents—or one tent and another shelter devised with chain-link fencing and tarpaulin—one for the nuclear family and a second for the additional adults of the group. There would be the shelter for the goat herd and a unit for storage of foods, animal feed, and other household items such as clothes, blankets, water bags, and water. For some this consisted simply of a series of discarded petroleum and chemical barrels. For others more elaborate storage systems were devised—sometimes the

The entire contents of a household (storage barrels, blankets, and assorted containers) are packed up and put on a truck on moving day. Most of the herd of goats walk to the next campsite, but the young newborn are packed onto the truck as well.

flatbed of an engineless Bedford truck, sometimes a series of metal sheeting trunks, or a discarded wooden crate. Whatever the storage container, it was still moveable or towable, and not fixed to one place. In summer these main households had a less compact feel to them. The clutter of possessions was still the same, but the sleeping quarters and rest areas were more dispersed, a tree and three or four wooden stakes sometimes formed the support for large stretches of tarpaulin-created shade.

In both summer and winter temporary households were also set up. Their appearance was generally what can best be called marginal. When a family moved to a new site to take advantage of a good but very limited pasture, it often left some of its recently acquired baggage of household goods behind as an indication that it planned to return shortly. Thus it was not unusual to come across a series of barrels and a few bags tied onto lower branches of a tree. During seasons when there had been brief but scattered showers and therefore widely dispersed areas of limited pasture, the Jiddat would be heavily dotted with these unoccupied camps. To the untrained eye these vacant homesteads could be mistaken for the litter left behind after a camp had been abandoned. What did this recent phenomenon of empty homesteads reflect? To a degree, these units were symbolic representations of a household's continuous presence. They served as a sign to any newcomers looking for a campsite that the area had been previously claimed and not yet given up.

With motor transport, families could move camp almost as fast as news itself traveled, so physically staking a claim to a campsite became an important way of letting others know a household's whereabouts. Leaving possessions behind no longer meant losing them or arduous journeys of several days or more to retrieve them. On one occasion during our early survey work, the flatbed truck that carried our supplies of food, water, and camping equipment broke down. Jamal managed to repair the vehicle, but its engine still cut out regularly, causing us frequent and regular delays. Eventually he asked whether we could make a small detour to collect "something" belonging to him. We agreed, and traveled a few more hours until we reached what looked like an abandoned campsite. It was one of his father's temporarily empty households. He rummaged about in one of the barrels until he found what he was looking for—a used carburetor. Half an hour later he had successfully installed this piece in the flatbed truck's engine and we were able to continue our journey with no further delays.

There was almost a novelty value to the assortment of accumulated possessions the Harasiis had so recently acquired. Nothing was of a permanent, private nature and individuals freely gave away and exchanged items.[3] A storage barrel at one household could show up at another a few days later. Blankets and mats moved from one household to another. Hunting knives, cartridge belts, jackets, wristwatches all changed hands frequently. When I would comment on this loose exchange of items, the Harasiis would tell me that they could give them all up tomorrow. The ease with which individuals were willing to part with these modern material items made it easy to imagine a household returning to the simpler and less encumbered past of a decade earlier if conditions of life required it.

Changing Survival Skills

In the nearly twenty years since truck transport appeared on the Jiddat, a distinction has manifested itself among the male population between those who have walked the Jiddat and those who have driven over it. Our guide Hamad and our driver Jamal represented these two groups. The depth of knowledge and intimacy each type of experience develops or instills is different, and that distinction is clearly emerging. The dividing line between these two groups seems to fall at about the age of twenty. Men over that age are apparently in the category of those who grew up in the days where survival meant knowing the desert intimately, as can only happen when one has literally walked it on foot or ridden it on camelback. Young men today—those around twenty years of age or younger—did not have this opportunity. As young boys when motor vehicles were first introduced into the desert, they spent much of their time in the cabin of trucks. Their knowledge of the Jiddat is less intimate, but more widespread; they have probably covered greater areas in the desert and the agricultural regions bordering onto their homeland. In many ways this younger generation is better adapted to cope with the changes that are occurring and will continue to transform life for the tribe. At the same time, it is a more vulnerable generation, one already more dependent on laborsaving devices and at the mercy of the desert should one of the newly introduced technologies fail them.[4]

The distinction between these two generations is most obvious when tracking skills are tested. To become a good tracker, in Harasiis belief, requires skill and art. It is both an acquired and an achieved craft. To the Harasiis it is both an inborn and learned skill. Early during our fieldwork in 1981, it became obvious that a camel, gazelle, or, when required, an oryx could be tracked with great skill by the generation in their thirties and forties. The younger group of men in their late teens could not, as a rule, follow animal tracks with the same ease, but could identify and follow a car track out of a maze of tens of hundreds of tracks. Thus Hamad in his thirties exhibited astonishing tracking skills, never failing to find a household or animal when he wanted to. Jamal in his twenties could not lead us anywhere, but could follow car tracks over any terrain and was nearly always able to identify the vehicle. Each generation has developed the skills that are most relevant to its life. What is unfortunate is that some of the younger generation are not building upon the survival skills of their elders, but merely developing those they find important or interesting. In the harsh and extreme environment of the Jiddat, a motor vehicle breakdown in an isolated location could spell death for someone who no longer had the skills to deal with the environment without the mediation of a modern technological device.

In the last few years a balance seems to have been struck for a few youths. Some of the younger generation are acquiring an intimate knowledge of the desert and following in the footsteps—as well as tire tracks—of the older generation. The motor vehicle is a part of their life, but so too is a firsthand knowledge of the desert. This small group appears to have been selected to carry on the traditional care of the family herds. In a sizeable number of the families originally surveyed in 1981, one such youth has remained in each homestead helping to care for the herds. In nearly all cases these youths were aware of the decision their parents were making about their future. In many cases a boy was chosen because he showed an aptitude for animal husbandry. In a few cases the selection was based on a boy's unwillingness or disinterest in modern education. The rest of the boys in a family who were considered old enough were sent to the boarding school at Haima, and only return to the homestead two days a week when they help out as best as they can. Some of these schoolboys show promise in animal husbandry as well and do take an active part in helping their families with the household herds.

The Truck and Wage Labor

By the early 1980s most Harasiis families had come to regard their trucks as necessities. Their traditional self-reliance and simplicity of life had been replaced by a more comfortable form of existence a bit removed from the cutting edge for survival. The cost of this was a reduction in their economic independence and a corresponding bondage to wage labor.[5] Although the truck brought about dramatic increases in the distances that could be covered and the resources that could be tapped (water, pasture, comestibles, and other supplies), it was at great capital expenditure and use of human resources in its own right. A truck would only move when there was sufficient gasoline to run it. Until 1985 there was only one gas station for the entire Jiddat (after 1985 there were three). As late as 1992 tires and other spare parts were still only available at Nizwa or Adam, requiring a journey of at least three hours one-way. The only repair that could actually be undertaken in the Jiddat itself was tire puncture repair at Haima, and even that was sporadic. All these services and purchases required immediate cash payment—a full tank of gas cost RO 8 (about $20), and a barrel to take back to the homestead RO 24 (about $60). Although a number of goats would on occasion be sold to cover an unexpected expenditure, most of the costs of keeping trucks and other vehicles were defrayed by taking on temporary paid jobs.

With motorized transport, household heads and other adult males found themselves able to range further and faster than ever before. The needs of the family for water, shelter, and food should, theoretically, have been met much more rapidly, and the adult male population should have found itself with correspondingly more free time at its disposal. However, with the need to do temporary wage laboring in order to support these new devices in their midst and, furthermore, with the tendency in the 1980s to remain on the Jiddat throughout the summer months and bring in water for the herds and the family, the adult male population found very little free time to spend with the family. What time was released by these laborsaving devices was eaten up trying to acquire the capital to keep them running. And what energy was gained by reducing the number of migrations during the hot summer months was expended in providing the family with its increased requirements for water and, sometimes, dry fodder.

Pastoralism on Wheels: The Full-Time Husbandman

Between 1981 and 1982 we focused our attention on seventeen Harasiis households for in-depth interviewing and limited participant observation. Of these, two stood out. These were households at one end or another of the continuum of adaptation. One household head was a full-time husbandman and the other was employed full-time at the government administrative center at Haima. All the other households fell within the broad range created by these two examples.

Hilaal was a full-time animal husbandman. He was unemployed, or, rather, self-employed. He held no part-time jobs and received no government stipend. He relied solely on his ability to manage, cull, and care for his large herds to provide for his family and maintain his three vehicles. He was, by Harasiis standards, a very well-off man. Although his good fortune was in large measure due to his own efforts, his resources were many and the number of people available to help from within the extended family was significant.

In 1982, when he became part of our survey, Hilaal was married and had five children ranging in age from a newborn baby girl to an adolescent boy. This eldest son was a great help to the household, taking full charge of looking after the camels in his father's absence and generally assisting him as would any "apprentice" in the West. His younger son, tragically strickened with poliomyelitis three years earlier, was unable to walk and had to be carried from place to place.[6] Two younger daughters, about six and four years of age, were just beginning to take an active part in the care of the family herd of goats, regularly helping with the hand- or bottle-feeding of the young kids. Hilaal's wife was a very hard worker, known throughout the Jiddat for her weaving skill and her culinary excellence. However, she suffered badly from asthma, and was often away for long periods of time receiving medical attention either at Haima, Nizwa, or sometimes in the United Arab Emirates. Laziness was despised in a woman, and such a woman—Hilaal's half-sister and longtime house guest, for example—was often the butt of jokes. Fortunately for the family, Hilaal's widowed mother lived with them and she was often the pivotal figure at the homestead. Between her and her oldest grandson, the homestead would be looked after for weeks at a time in the absence of Hilaal, and sometimes his wife as well.

Hilaal, his wife, and his mother technically each owned their own herds: Hilaal's camel herd, his mother's goat herd, and his wife's goat herd. Individually their holdings were large, approximately 120 goats for each woman and 40 camels for Hilaal. Should either the mother or wife have decided to leave the homestead permanently, they would have been correct to take their herds with them. In reality the managing of the herds was very much a family affair. In practice, the actual ownership of an animal came into question only when selling or slaughtering was required. At all other times the bounty and by-products of the herds were shared by all the family and other close kin.

The relative wealth of the family was reflected in the accumulated possessions. Besides two half-ton pickup trucks, Hilaal had also acquired an old Bedford truck that he used to store twenty-eight barrels of water. When he needed more water for the family and the herds, he would tow this engineless vehicle to the nearest well and back again. The family also owned a trailer in which all the food goods, blankets, clothing, and other possessions were stored. It was one of the first families to own a cooker run on bottled gas and to experiment with chain-link fencing and soldered hinged entrance doors for the winter shelter.

A further source of wealth for Hilaal lay in the well he had hired Awamir specialists to dig in a region of sand dunes close to the Rub' al-

Khali. Begun ten years earlier, during a time when he was employed by the Omani Army as a guide to a British seconded officer, Hilaal had used his position and salary to have this well dug and to set up a series of fields to grow dates as well as a limited assortment of vegetables. At some point after his retirement from the army, the well failed and the fields died—though the Harasiis version is that marauding tribesmen from across the border in Saudi Arabia attacked the fields and filled in the well with sand. By 1982 Hilaal was busy again directing a renewed effort to open the well, this time installing a mechanical pump. These efforts cost him close to RO 3,000, and after petitioning the government, assistance was provided in the form of a monthly salary for a well guard to keep watch over the well and pump.

The activity associated with reestablishing a well and looking after his holdings of camels was, fortunately, shared. Hilaal and his brother, Humaid, pooled their manpower resources and jointly looked after their herds of camel. As the only two sons of their father, their herds had probably been one until very recently—women rarely inherit camels. Humaid's three sons regularly helped look after the camel herds of the two households, along with Hilaal's older son, freeing Hilaal and his brother to carry on with all the related and time-consuming activities required in such a nomadic pastoral existence.

Working together with his brother, his sons and nephews, the fallow herd of about eighty camels was well looked after. However, after 1982 when the boarding school at Haima opened, a new division of labor among the male members of Hilaal and Humaid's household was required. Hilaal sent his youngest son, the nine-year-old poliomyelitis victim, to the boarding school and Humaid put two of his three sons there as well. Each brother has been left with one son to take on part of the responsibilities of the care of the camel herds. In Hilaal's case the choice of the youngest son for schooling was fortuitous and inevitable. For Humaid the choice was more difficult. All three boys wanted to try out the school, but Humaid could not afford to let them all go. He chose to keep the middle boy at home to help him with the herd, letting the oldest and the youngest go off to Haima. The loss in manpower is strongly felt, and during the weekends at home all the boys work very hard in bringing in the supplies (e.g., sufficient water and dry feed) for the coming week. Both men have recognized the importance of educating the next generation and have been able to avail themselves of this government service without unduly neglecting their herd. If motorized trans-

port and other innovations had not been available in the Jiddat, that would probably not have been possible. Both men seem to appreciate that the Jiddat will only provide a living for a limited number of people and that some of the coming generation will have to work if not outside the Jiddat then outside the scope of full-time animal husbandry. And only with education will the future generation have the opportunity to make choices for themselves.

The amount of time that Hilaal must spend away from the homestead serves as a good indicator of the energy that is required to maintain a healthy and productive herd and household. First, he spent considerable time each week towing the old Bedford shell of a vehicle to and from the nearest well to keep the family and herds in water. At some times in the year, water needed to be taken out to wherever the jointly owned fallow camel herds were grazing—this was often the job of Hilaal's son or of one of his nephews. Second, providing supplementary feed pellets from Muscat required gathering a number of young male kids for sale at the distant town auctions in Nizwa, Adam, or Sinaw and a further trip into Muscat to buy the feed directly from the Omani flour mill. This exercise in itself frequently took five or six days and was generally combined with a number of visits to places and people with some relation to the family's well-being—creditors in Adam, kin at the date gardens south of Adam in Adaba, and so on. The work at the well needed to be supervised, and Hilaal frequently lent his facilities there—a camel trough—to other pastoralists to use. On such occasions he attempted to be present to supervise the working of the motorized pump. The overall impression was one of constant movement. The days spent at the homestead in a month were often but a handful.

At the homestead itself, information was constantly being filtered back as to Hilaal's whereabouts. When the physical site needed to be shifted a few kilometers to gain better access to pasture for the goats—the household herd of goats tended to exhaust the pasture adjacent to the homestead every few weeks—Hilaal would return and supervise the activity. But as his son grew older, Hilaal tended to let him take over. Any serious health problem in the family—particularly his wife's—brought Hilaal back to the family unit to escort her to the nearest or most appropriate medical center.

At all times, whether away or at the homestead, Hilaal was constantly gathering information. He was keeping tabs on the whereabouts of his camels and those of other families. He was collecting information on the state of pasture throughout the Jiddat—and in the adjacent regions. And he was keeping track of the movements of other families, both of the Harasiis and other tribes who were making use of either pasture or wells in the area. As the Jiddat was along the major trade path from south to north and back again, any movement of goods, particularly camels, from the south required some support as it crossed the area. Hilaal was both in the position to know of such movement and to offer the assistance that might be required. Such help was often tallied into political and economic gain. The wider one's circle of political or social debtors, the further one could cast one's net when seeking loans for bad times, or when attempting an expensive project.

The installation of a motorized water pump at Hilaal's well was a fine example of manipulation, and contained all the above-named elements. He would not have been able to provide all the cash required to dig out the well and install the machinery without help. That help came through the calling in of past favors to fellow tribesmen and those from elsewhere who had benefited from his assistance at some other time.

Without complete freedom to respond to the regular and the unexpected events surrounding him, his family, and his herds, Hilaal would not have been able to flourish as he has. He is the master of his own time and as such he uses it totally to look after his own interests and those of his brother. Such concentrated effort on the welfare of his family and his herd allows him little time "at home," but does guarantee that he can provide for the entire group's well-being, including the running of three vehicles and a water pump without taking on wage labor of any sort.

Pastoralism on Wheels: The Full-time Employee

At the other end of the continuum between full-time animal husbandry and full-time work is Hamad, a man in his early forties employed full-time as a guide with a government office in Haima and required to be present at that office from 7:30 A.M. until 2:00 P.M. (official government working hours) five days a week. To manage, cull, and care for his herds and to provide for his family as well as maintain his three vehicles (two trucks and a small water bowser) takes up every minute he can spare from his nonworking hours. He is, by Harasiis standards, just comfortably well-off. However, his economic survival is, in large measure, due to the continuous support he receives from his brothers as well as from the labor available to him from within his immediate family.

In 1982 Hamad was married and had six children ranging in age from a one-year-old daughter to an adolescent girl. The four intermediate children were boys. The eldest child was a great help to her mother and took full charge of the goat herds. After helping to milk them in the mornings, she would take them out to pasture and return with them later in the day. Thus her mother was freed to look after the immediate needs of the younger children at the homestead. The oldest male child, a preadolescent boy of about ten, took on many of the tasks his father would have carried out had he been home to do so. This child often drove a family truck to the nearest well to collect water for the family and herds, as long as the distance was not very great. He also took care of the five or six lactating or pregnant camels that were kept at the homestead.

Hamad's manpower resources were larger than this immediate nuclear family. And although there was no one permanent adult kinsman living with the family, there was generally one or another of Hamad's younger brothers staying with his wife and children during his weeklong absences. For Hamad was very much a paterfamilias for his four younger brothers. As a young adolescent, his own father had been killed in a blood feud over rights to a particular water well. Hamad had, from that moment, taken charge of the family and herds. After taking revenge, he set about managing his father's large herd of camels and helping his mother with her own sizeable holding of the traditional Harasiis short-haired white goat. For the next six years he managed the family holdings as one unit operating out of one homestead. Several years after his own marriage and after the birth of several children, he split off from his mother's homestead and set up his own. Three of his younger brothers continued to live with the mother and the other two used Hamad's new household as their base. These five brothers maintained their interests in their camel holdings jointly. And between them the large fallow camel herd was always well looked after. One brother was given total charge of herding these one hundred head of camel whenever possible, or just keeping tabs on them and arranging for the provision of water when it was required. The other brothers took on an assortment of short-term and temporary wage jobs as well guards, seismic crew workers, and drivers. Whatever the work situation, one brother always returned to the mother's dwelling to help with the lactating camels and another tended to call in at Hamad's home when he was away in the week.

Hamad's wife was a very hard-working woman and a careful, penny-wise housewife—though that tightness was often attributed to Hamad himself. Her herd of goats was not particularly large, numbering about ninety at any one time. The household depended upon this herd for its supply of milk, and sales of the young male kid provided a supplemental income after the steady wages of Hamad. The limited family members available to look after the herds tended to keep animal numbers down. The young male kids were either sold to buy whatever was needed—petrol, tires, spare vehicle parts, supplemental feed pellets, comestibles for the family—or were eaten to honor a guest at the homestead. The herd of goats, however was not regarded as a source of income per se. It tided out the household's budgetary requirements on some occasions or provided them with the means for maintaining their social obligations to visitors, friends, and travelers.

Hamad's work for the government has created much hardship and stress for the man himself and for his family. Before this employment in 1982, he had only occasionally taken on paid work. From a very young age he had gained a reputation as a skilled guide and tracker, and his services were often requested by the hunting parties that used to come into the Jiddat in the 1960s and early 1970s in search of game, particularly the white oryx. In 1982, and for the following two years when he was working for this project, his work time remained quite flexible, generally running into a four-day on-duty and three day off-duty schedule—not unlike the PDO schedule of two weeks on-duty and two weeks off-duty for local employees. His present formal five-day government schedule and relatively sedentary activity—his services as guide are presently only used one day a week, if that—are difficult for him to accept. He prides himself on his desert survival skills and chafes at being forced to act as a "sentry" (his own word) in front of the government office for most of his official working hours. However difficult the constraints upon him are at present, Hamad will probably persevere until a change of personnel in this government office results in more reasonable "working schedules" similar to that followed by most of the major employers in the Jiddat—the police, the PDO, the white oryx project, and various ministries.

As a government-employed guide, Hamad receives a good salary, competitive with the better-paying employers. He gets fairly generous annual leave (forty-five days a year) and frequent public holidays (about fifteen days annually). He is also entitled to leave every few years to make the Haj—the Muslim pilgrimage to Mecca. Moreover, he will be entitled to a pension of half his salary once he reaches the age of fifty-five. These entitlements in themselves make the constraints and present immobility of his work fairly unimportant. His long-term gain fully compensates for whatever distress he is experiencing now.

On the positive side, his employment at Haima puts him in the physical position of being able to monitor the events at his own household and his mother's. And although he, personally, is not in a position to carry out the vital provisioning for his family, he is at the hub of where all information on the Jiddat comes—Haima—and can direct his brothers and other related kinsmen to carry out the required work. He can monitor the movement of his brothers and is one of the first to receive important information. When a shipment of feed pellets is received at Haima for sale by an enterprising countryman, Hamad is the first to know, the first to make a purchase, and the first to seek out a kinsman to transport the load to the homestead. For all the time that he is forced to be away from the household, Hamad is often able to make up for that absence by having greater access to information vital for the general well-being of his family. And, as often as not, he is able to get information to a brother to carry out some household task or another. The difficulty for Hamad comes when he receives news of a shortage at the homestead—they have run out of water or finished all the feed pellets—and cannot locate a brother or kinsman to take care of that need. Then he is obliged to wait until he is permitted to leave Haima at the end of a working day to take care of the matter himself. When the family is camped more than a two-hour drive away, this presents enormous hardship for him.

Hamad has been able to transform his enforced idleness at Haima into a positive attribute and managed to build an information network for himself on the grounds of his near permanent presence there—rather than through the usual means of constant travel throughout the region. He has become the central "command post" for his family, his brothers, and more distant kin. With his whereabouts fixed, the other members of the family need only guarantee easy access to him. Toward that end, his household, which still requires pasture for its herd of goats, tends to remain within a two-hour drive of Haima. Moreover, the distance from a major graded road to the homestead also tends to be less than half an hour's drive. Other Harasiis households do not make a concerted effort to remain near a graded road, or within a particular driving distance of Haima. By keeping within such "driving times," Hamad has reasonable access to his family and, vice versa, the family can reach him without too long a delay in times of emergency, trouble, or crises. What is sacrificed, on some occasions, is good graze for the household herd of goats. The lactating and pregnant camels are already living basically on dry feed, third-grade wheat chaffings, and other "artificial" foods.

The fallow camel herd is still well looked after, with one brother permanently caring for that unit and each of the other four brothers taking their turns to bring water, feed pellets, or special high-grade feed to the still jointly run large camel herd. And when a camel has strayed, one or another brother sets off in search of the beast. Hamad's children do not all take an active part in herding. Of his four sons, all but the second oldest son are at the boarding school. The middle son takes most of the responsibility for caring for the few lactating camels at the homestead, though he is on occasion sent out to help his uncle with the large fallow herd. The emphasis in Hamad's homestead, as in Hilaal's, is on giving as many of his children as he can spare an opportunity to have a "modern" education. Furthermore, the opportunity to learn English is encouraged. A decade before, the Harasiis tribesmen who could speak some Arabic were the ones able to find employment (however temporary) to supplement their incomes. Today, it is the tribesmen who have some knowledge of English who tend to get the jobs with the potential for promotion and permanence—PDO, for example, will only hire local tribesmen in staff positions if they have some knowledge of the language.

Education for Hamad is the key to the future success of his family, whereas for Hilaal it is a fortuitous event that promises to give his handicapped son a chance of some success in life. For many other Harasiis families—though perhaps not the majority—it is also seen as the key to improving their children's standard of living. Some families are too busy surviving to consider releasing even one set of hands to attend school five days a week. And other household heads seem not to be looking to the future, so busy are they maneuvering and manipulating other tribesmen in their bid to become the leading political brokers and entrepreneurs of their community.

Pastoralism on Wheels: Other Household Adaptations

In between Hamad and Hilaal are a large number of household heads who actively search for permanent work. Many succeed for periods of time, leaving when the requirements of the job seem to demand too great a sacrifice of their highly prized freedom of movement. Others succeed in finding employment that, by its very nature, is temporary, such as the work available between 1983 and 1986 with a number of subcontractors of PDO doing seismic testing for petroleum and gas throughout the Jiddat before their rights to the concession area expired. For many, those three years were boom times, as the work was both mobile and social. The men worked in crews of as many as twenty, and time off-duty was generous—fourteen days on-duty and fifteen days off-duty. Other jobs, such as well and installation guards, are not intended to be temporary, but are so solitary and isolated in space that the employee tends to either quit or be fired for failing to remain at his duty station.

In 1982, 82 percent of our sample had some form of income from other than animal and animal by-product sales. Most received a salary from the government (54 percent), some received a salary from a private company (24 percent), and one respondent was self-employed (see table 4.1). By 1992 the percentage of household heads employed was still the same, but more men were employed, and full-time husbandry was becoming the exception rather than the rule (see table 4.2). Although most families still depended upon their herds of goats for the family's immediate subsistence needs, wages, stipends, and other paid labor provided the ready cash to run the vehicles, buy gas and spare parts, and on occasion purchase other laborsaving devices or sponsor and import expatriate labor from the Indian subcontinent to work at the household. The goat herds remained an important part of the household's economy, and it was through the sales of livestock that most of the comestibles for a household were purchased. A healthy goat herd of one hundred head usually produces a surplus young male population of fifty to sixty kid a year—goats tend to produce three times in a two-year period. The sale of four or five kids a month generally covers the immediate household's needs. And as long as the family is not forced to rely on artificial feed for long periods of time, these sales keep the family in the black.

But paid employment has begun to affect decisions concerning the homestead's regular movement in search of graze for the herd. As families try to balance the requirements of the herd with the requirements of paid employment, they are forced to rely increasingly upon dry feed pellets and other costly feeds when they cannot migrate to take advantage of natural pasture or when there is no pasture during a long drought.

The size of a household's goat herd seems to be carefully watched.

And with the exception of the one household that was totally devoted to raising livestock, the size tends to remain at or below one hundred head of goat. This number seems to be the optimal size for a family, given the constraints on the time of the women in a household. It is also a size that produces sufficient milk for the family's needs and sufficient offspring to provide the family with the occasional goat meal as well as a saleable commodity to regularly purchase the household's food requirements.

It is the size of part of the household's camel holdings that over the last ten years has increased at great expense and great inconvenience to the household. The number of lactating camels kept has not increased noticeably yet. But the number of special reserve camels that are now also kept at the homestead has increased dramatically. These are the camels that the household heads hope will be prized race camels. Many a family head now keeps two or three of these nervous, lean, and skittish animals tied up and often muzzled to prevent them from eating anything other than a very special diet. Camel racing has for long been a very popular sport among the Harasiis and other tribal groups in Oman; religious and national holidays have been marked by the popular camel races. But in the last eight or nine years the cash purse for the winning camel owner has increased enormously. And although there has always been a market for a fine racing camel, recently there has been an enormous increase in the prices that such an animal can bring. In 1982 RO 5,000 was a good price for a racing camel. In 1992 RO 25,000 was an acceptable price—although one exceptional racing camel was bought for RO 60,000 (about $13,000, $65,000, and $156,000 respectively). With such figures becoming commonplace, it is understandable that a Harasiis household head will try to breed a racing camel and when he feels a particular camel has the potential will set aside much of his salary to buy special feed for the animal. The problem today is that so many families are doing just that. And many are using up large chunks of their salaries and even taking out loans to feed and care for these potential "lottery winners."

Ultimately good sense and rational use of available resources will prevail among the Harasiis. Just as the initial impact of motorized transport was one of enthusiastic acceptance and, for many, increasing debt, once a ceiling on credit had been reached individuals were forced to make the necessary adjustments to keep their households going and the cars running. For most family heads that has meant seeking out paid employment, which is available within the Jiddat itself. The current craze to hand-raise and selectively feed particular young camels especially for racing and the enormous expenditure that it entails for most households is just that, a craze. Once a threshold of debt has been reached, many individuals will return to the more sensible former practices. Camels will continue to be raced for sport and for money. And with the huge prices being paid for exceptionally good racing camels, it is unlikely that the Harasiis will stop nurturing some special animals for the several weeks leading up to a race. However, a few household heads are already recognizing a fact that seemed to have eluded them in the past few heady years of soaring racing camel prices—that racers are born and not made by any special diet.

Pastoralism on Wheels: Raising Livestock for Meat

In many ways the Harasiis have been spared the suffering of pastoralists in other more habitable environments such as Dhofar. The extreme aridity of the Jiddat and its very limited water has never permitted the Harasiis to expand the size of their herds dramatically. At the same time, the appearance of numerous employment opportunities has permitted them to improve their standard of living without taking more out of their environment. Unlike the situation in Dhofar, where gross overstocking has resulted in a very rapid degeneration of the rangeland, the Harasiis have eked out a pastoral existence on very little rangeland. And even today there is little sign of degeneration of their pasture land. Although the Harasiis often complain that there is not enough rain, just as there is not enough water, after rainfall when pastures bloom, they do not talk about a worsening of pastures or range conditions as the pastoralists in Dhofar do.

For the Harasiis, paid employment and the limited government-supported water sources have helped them to create a new balance between subsistence herding and wage labor. It now remains to be seen whether they can, with some government support, be helped to improve their herding practices so as to raise goats for greater profit. I have described earlier how the Harasiis have experimented with their goat herds in the past. During recent decades they have imported and cross-bred the black long-haired northern Omani goat into their white short-haired goat herds. Their traditional animal was a very good milking animal, but its meat was considered tough by town and village buyers. The northern

Omani goat did not give much milk, but it had more fat on it and was thus considered tastier by the buying public. Today most Harasiis herds are mixed black and white hybrids—not great milk givers, but tastier to eat. Many Harasiis say that they would like to be able to sell their animals more regularly, but the long drive to the nearest markets (six hundred to eight hundred kilometers round-trip) and the remote likelihood of getting a good price at the animal auctions there discourages them from trying.

Oman, like so many Arab states, must import live meat on the hoof to make up for a shortfall in meat on the local market. Already the national government subsidizes the sale of young cattle (veal) from the Dhofar mountains to the rest of the country in order to control the rapid deterioration of that environment. Certain government agencies (the armed forces) are even required to buy Dhofari veal for their kitchens. In the case of the Harasiis simple encouragement in the form of marketing assistance at Haima or from Haima into the villages and towns of the north would go far in persuading more of the pastoralists to raise some of their animals for meat sales instead of only for milk. Thus a simple government extension and transport program might help to reduce the country's dependence on imported meat and simultaneously assist the Harasiis to help themselves.

6

Entrepreneurship and Marginality:

Harasiis Brokers and the Outside World

The literature on pastoralism is replete with examples of nomad-settler relations. In Northern Arabia, for example, the classic raid/tribute (ghazu/khuwa) relationship was, up until the middle of the twentieth century, the rule rather than the exception. Pastoral tribesmen offered protection to the settlements on the margins of their pasture land and, in exchange, the tribesmen received payment in gold or in kind. Over the past five decades, the political basis of the tribute/raid relationship has come to an end. Today pastoralists tend to enter into relations with settled communities that are grounded in economic realities and fulfill their need to acquire agricultural products.

Within every tribe or pastoral group, there are individuals and families who seem able to truly profit from the new horizons that contact with settled communities brings. These individuals are either already established leaders or bilingual, bicultural, marginal men. In either case these

are the entrepreneurs and political brokers of the tribe. Among the Harasiis two sets of brothers fill these roles. They are the politically active Naili brothers and the entrepreneurial Bakhiit brothers. The relations between the pastoralists and the settled communities that these sets of brothers have developed over the last fifteen years is of particular interest in understanding the ways in which new ideas and innovations have been introduced and accepted by the Harasiis population. Furthermore, individual differences among and between each of these sets of brothers are shown to be important factors in the adaptive strategies being played out in the Jiddat-il-Harasiis.

A number of anthropological works recently have sought to understand the way in which modern industrial technology is adopted by traditional society (Hebdige 1981; Hall 1971; Pelto 1973; Grotsch 1972;

Pfaffenberger 1988). As Pfaffenberger points out, in such studies there is no such thing as "traditional society." Rather, "every human society is a world in the process of becoming, in which people are engaged in the active technological elaboration, appropriation and modification of artifacts as the means of coming to know themselves and of coordinating labor to sustain their lives" (1992:511).

What appears as a "spontaneous change" in any society is often the result of limited but continuous and ongoing experimentation on the part of certain individuals whom I will call brokers.[1] What is perceived by the society as successful, in that it is seen to improve living conditions or the quality of life, is then enthusiastically accepted by the majority. What the community does not perceive as successful, or is regarded as too costly in terms of benefit, then remains an option that is only taken up by the innovative brokers themselves. Most decision making and subsequent change among the Harasiis tribe is based upon rational choices aimed at the steady improvement of the conditions of life.

Tribal leaders who are formally recognized by national government often play only a passive role in this process in that they are generally only the recipients of gifts of food, cash, blankets, trucks, water tankers from the government or another national or multinational agency. This largesse, then, frequently remains within the larger extended family and subsection where leadership is officially seated. Thus such contact tends to be static and of limited potential to change either attitudes or actions. Far more interesting is the effect that the marginal, often bicultural and bilingual members of the tribe have had as the innovators and beneficiaries of the community in general. The technology that these individuals and their families introduced into the Jiddat generally came after a period of close interaction with the settled community.

The Recent Past

When the national oil company landed at Duqm in 1954 and made its way to Fahud, where oil was soon discovered, it was desperate to establish a system of labor recruitment, and sought out the local tribal leadership to nominate the men to be employed by the company. As the role of the tribal leader had never encompassed such absolute power, it was not long before nearly all the minor leaders had approached the oil company claiming to be able to recruit loyal workers for the company. Faced with this confusing cacophony of claimants, the oil company turned away from the traditional leaders and sought out more accommodating, generally already marginalized—but acculturated, in a Western sense—tribesmen.

At the end of the 1950s the Harasiis faced similar political upheaval when the oil company began to drill at Haima, and in the course of this upheaval individual Harasiis were finding that the employment and salaries they received opened new horizons for them. For a short period of time, there was work both at Haima and at Al-Ajaiz for the Harasiis, but by the early 1960s, having found no oil, the company decided to move on. After repeated requests by Sheikh Shergi to the company and to the Sultan in Salalah to leave the water wells open, Sultan Saiid bin Taimur asked the oil company to leave the wells at these two sites uncapped. A few individuals with some spare cash were able to take full advantage of this bonanza. With water suddenly available, they brought the black long-haired northern Omani goat onto the Jiddat.

In 1970 when Sultan Qaboos bin Saiid took over from his father, he overturned a number of the rules that had stymied the development of the country. Among them, he lifted the ban on the importation of private vehicles, and in 1974 the first privately owned half-ton truck was brought into the Jiddat by a Harasiis broker. Six years later nearly every household owned one if not two vehicles.

Harasiis Brokers

The changes briefly outlined above, both planned and unplanned, affected the tribesmen in different ways. Some individuals simply carried on as they had always done and others were at the forefront of the changes of the last two decades. The two particular sets of brothers—the Naili and the Bakhiit brothers—mentioned above are isolated for closer study in this chapter in order to describe some of the changes in more detail. In each set only one brother was part of our in-depth household survey. Thus some of the more detailed information on household economics has had to be extrapolated from the example of the one sibling in each set that we included in our survey. Both sets of brothers fall in the forty-to-fifty age range, and were young children when the first vehicles were brought ashore at Duqm. For many, if not all the members of the tribe, this was the first time that a motor vehicle had ever been seen. It was an event that assumed historic importance to the tribe and today serves as an important time marker along with other events such as the

Jebel Akhdar campaign against the Imam's forces and, obviously, the accession of Sultan Qaboos bin Saiid in 1970.

The Bakhiit Brothers

The Bakhiit brothers are three—Amir, Athaith, and Tomais. One concern that comes through in the literature on technology and social change is the question: What are the characteristics of the individuals who succeed as compared with those who are less successful? An assessment of the causes of individual economic success or failure is beyond the scope of this book, although certain features are raised frequently. These are individual access to information, high activity levels and mobility, and geographic marginality (Pelto 1973; Attwood 1979; Schaniel 1988), as well as bicultural, acculturated, or marginalized families (Hall 1971; Dalton 1973; McClelland 1977). The Bakhiit brothers are bilingual and have had some exposure to another tribal culture. As their mother was a Beit Kathir tribeswoman, they have spent their early childhood speaking Harsuusi as well as Arabic. And though most of their youth was spent on the Jiddat or in the Awta with their father's kin, the brothers had access to their mother's far-ranging network of relatives in southern Oman and parts of the Gulf. It is not particularly surprising then that by the early 1960s Athaith Bakhiit should leave the Jiddat—as a young man of perhaps fifteen—to seek his fortune. He began his career with the Trucial Scouts, which were headquartered in Sharjah (now part of the United Arab Emirates). He was to remain there, working his way through the ranks, mastering English as a third language and being sent for training to the United Kingdom and later on an official visit to the United States. After twenty years he reached the rank of lieutenant colonel in the Abu Dhabi Army, now also part of the United Arab Emirates. Throughout his career Athaith continued to maintain his ties with his brothers on the Jiddat. Though his animal holdings were small, they were looked after by one or other of his brothers, and he made important financial contributions to the sibling group. In 1974 he brought the first private Harasiis-owned vehicle into the Jiddat. The success of that venture need hardly be described here other than to point out once again that within six years it was universally adopted by all but one Harasiis family.

Athaith was to introduce many innovative and modern items into the Jiddat. Some of these were widely accepted and others were not. Those that had an easily recognized beneficial impact on daily life were enthusiastically imitated and widely accepted. Such items as radios, cassette players, commercial tents and tarpaulin, thermos bottles, flashlights, and other household convenience items were quickly adopted, as more families found the income to make similar purchases. Further innovations, such as keeping chickens, were also introduced by Athaith, but the added nutritional benefit of eggs and chickens to the household diet was not as obvious to the Harasiis and few families have gone to the trouble of keeping them.

Tomais also left the Jiddat in his youth and took up employment with the national oil company. After nearly twenty years of service, during which time he also added English to his credits, he retired. Using the savings he had accumulated, he purchased the franchise from Shell Oil and in 1981 opened the first gas station at Haima. For three hundred kilometers in either direction there was no other source of gasoline. In quick succession Tomais was to open a small general store as well as an Indian restaurant and café and, with his brothers, to set up a small trading and transport company. In the early 1980s Tomais was to be actively involved in almost all the commercial enterprises that had a bearing on the Harasiis tribe. Initially his concern was to establish his company and give it a broad diversified base for future growth. Tomais and his brothers were the first—and only—traders to take part in the government-subsidized animal feed effort of 1982.

At this time the government offered to refund half the purchase price of any feed (third-grade wheat chaffings) bought from the government-owned flour mill and sold in the interior to the pastoral tribes suffering from the continued drought. Unlike the other regions of the country, where the government directly sold the animal feed at the subsidized rate, for the Harasiis, only the efforts of an entrepreneur would get the wheat chaffings to the people who needed it. Tomais, and his brothers, had to undertake the full capital outlay for the feed, which they transported the five hundred kilometers from Muscat to Haima and then sold for 60 percent of the full price. Only much later were they to recoup the 50 percent government-promised subsidy. Initially none of the Bakhiit brothers had been particularly interested in this investment. But intense pressure from Harasiis tribesmen who did not have the capital to underwrite the subsidized feed program convinced them to act. Unlike so many investment opportunities in the Sultanate, this one promised a very low rate of return. The brothers realized little more than a 10 percent profit on the operation and even that return was slow in coming, as so many government ventures can be. In a region where 100 percent profit—and sometimes even more—is common, it is not surprising that there were no competing bidders for this venture. However, though the actual monetary profit was small, the Bakhiit brothers were building up  their social and economic credit among the tribesmen. And they knew it.

The Bakhiit brothers have come to take on an increasingly larger role in the development of Haima as a social and economic center for the Harasiis. In part this role is of their own making, but there is also a measure of "reward" in some of the contracts that their company has acquired.

Recently, in 1986, the Ministry of Water and Electricity required a company to grade a road from Haima to a nearby oil installation. A number of local trading companies owned by other Harasiis tribesmen sought the contract. It was awarded to the Bakhiit brothers, in part because their tender was lower than the others, but also, in some measure, for past services rendered. Several years earlier when the Ministry of Water and Electricity had been unable to find a local contractor to transport water to the newly opened boarding school at the rate the government was prepared to pay—almost half the rate offered by the local subcontractors of the oil companies operating in the region—the Bakhiit brothers stepped in rather than see the school opening postponed another year until permanent facilities would be completed. In an area as vast and as sparsely populated as the Jiddat-il-Harasiis, little is private, and the Bakhiit brothers very quickly came to be viewed as local sources of support for the community as a whole.

These brothers have now acquired a reputation as "good" men among their fellow tribesmen. And although now most of their business ventures are purely for profit, an element of community welfare can be interpreted into much of what they do. Many Harasiis tribesmen look to them for assistance when they need help in negotiating with a private agency or with the government representative at Haima, the Wali. The fact that one brother or another can generally be found at Haima and that both Athaith and Tomais are fluent in English and Arabic also contributes to the aura that has developed around them as men of sense and mediation. They are, by virtue of personality and inclination, set to continue to lead the Harasiis tribe into further developments aimed at improving their standards of living and prospects for the future.

The third brother, Amir, remained outside the boundaries of the

Jiddat-il-Harasiis throughout the period of our in-depth field work (1981–1983). He seems to have had responsibility for looking after the small-but-respectable-size herd of camels that were being kept in the Wadi Andam and Wadi Halfayn during that time. He was also responsible for the combined date garden holdings of the brothers. This fruit and vegetable patch of one *donum* (about a half an acre) containing seventy trees was located near Adam.

In spite of this seeming isolation from the mainstream of events and activities in the Jiddat, Amir also took an active role in promoting the general welfare of the tribe. In 1983 I finally came across Amir in the corridors of the Ministry of Social Affairs and Labor, where he was waiting for an opportunity to petition the Minister for a further distribution of tents to the households on the Jiddat. Poor health seems to have played a role in the division of labor among the three brothers. By the late 1970s Amir had lost one leg to disease, and in 1985 he died of cancer. His children, however, continue to be educated at Haima along with the other Bakhiit children. Tomais and Athaith have, at least since the late 1970s, shared the same extended household.

Although it is very difficult to establish precise dates, it appears that Tomais, who had remained in Oman throughout his period of employment with PDO, married first in the early 1970s and had two sons. Initially this household was the focus for the Bakhiit brothers. And although the brothers' camel holdings were looked after by Amir, further to the north of the Jiddat, Tomais's homestead with the goat herds belonging to his wife was the organizing point for the two brothers. In the mid-1970s Athaith married for the first time and Tomais for a second time. The pair of brothers wed sisters who, like them, also had a non-Harasiis mother. By the early 1980s Tomais and Athaith shared the same extended household. Each wife maintained her own shelter—by now a rather sophisticated commercial tent—and the women's father, Mohammed bin Salim, was a regular, long-term visitor to the homestead.

By the early 1980s Tomais's two sons by his first marriage were leaving childhood and becoming important assistants to their father in his various undertakings. In the absence of either Athaith or Tomais at the homestead, these boys would regularly undertake the tasks associated with maintaining healthy herds. One boy or the other regularly made the weekly, and, in summer, the biweekly, trip from the homestead to the nearest source of water for the family and herds. The boys were given the responsibility of seeing that the two young families that made up the homestead did not want for anything. The youngsters constantly shuttled back and forth between Haima (where Tomais spent most of his time) and the camp, carrying food items, animal feed, and other provisions as required by the rest of the household.

Given the combined wealth of Tomais and Athaith, the animal holdings of the household were small. Few of the camels owned by the brothers were kept at the homestead (in 1982 there was only one) and thus there was little work associated with keeping "this racing camel" healthy. The goat herds owned by the sisters were also very small, considering their means. Together they had in the region of one hundred goats. This seems to have been the optimal number for providing the families with the goat milk they preferred and the meat that was occasionally required for guests. The goat herds were maintained simply for the families' subsistence. They were managed so as to be self-replenishing over the annual cycle. They were no longer considered to be income generating. That came from Tomais and Athaith's trading and transport company, their jointly owned gas station, general store, café, and the generous salary—and later Athaith's retirement pension—from the Abu Dhabi Army.

This joint household was well stocked and well cared for, and, even during periods when neither brother was present, seemed to want for nothing. The material possessions were stored in a large Bedford truck. When various items such as sewing machines, radios, cassette players, camel trappings, and saddle blankets were not in use, they were carefully put away on the truck, ready for the next move of the household. Since they kept a small herd and relied on third-grade wheat chaffings during the 1981–1983 period, they moved only three or four times in a year. Even then, the household tended to move between two adjacent wadis—Wadi Yalooni and Wadi bu Mudhabi. Between the two brothers, the household kept four vehicles, two Bedford trucks, a Land Cruiser, and a Toyota Hilux for Athaith's regular commute to Abu Dhabi in the United Arab Emirates. In 1984 the brothers purchased a large camper with air conditioner and generator for use during the difficult monthlong fast of Ramadan.

Both brothers look to the boarding school at Haima as the key to the future success of their children and they are concerned that their children study not only the required Omani Arabic curriculum but English as well. They go to great efforts to keep their sons in school. By 1992 they had a total of five boys at the boarding school, one of whom left at the intermediate level to become a police cadet. In emergencies at the school they are first to come forward and help. In 1984, for example, there was an outbreak of hepatitis. One of the Bakhiit children was stricken, and Athaith quickly removed him along with his siblings and cousins, keeping them in isolation until the child recovered. In 1992 Athaith found himself chairman of the parents' committee, organized to develop afterschool activities to keep the boys "off the streets" after class finished. The Bakhiit brothers behave as though education is the answer to their children's future. They seem to recognize that whatever they themselves achieve for their families during their lifetime will die with them unless the next generation is given the appropriate skills to deal with a rapidly changing multilingual, technologically oriented world.

Since 1984, when Athaith retired from the Abu Dhabi Army and returned to live permanently in the Jiddat, the two brothers have taken it in turn to be either at Haima or at the homestead. It is very rare to find them both at the same place for very long. When one is looking after the joint business venture at Haima—and thus available for the family if so required—the other is actively involved in either promoting more business or developing further plans to improve the quality of their life.

In 1985 the Sultan asked the management at PDO to "make the desert bloom" and so set an example to the tribesmen. After extensive hydrological surveys and tests, a spot at the very edge of what the Harasiis consider their border with the Mahra tribe was selected. Here at Wadi Arah the oil company was able to tap into a large artesian water source and, after a year of experimenting, produced mainly farm vegetables as well as Rhodes grass, which proved to be tremendously successful with the local population for fresh animal fodder. This station was producing forty-five tons of Rhodes grass per hectare per year, enough to feed 120 goats or 10 camels.[2] Tomais and Athaith watched this experiment with great interest.

In 1986 the brothers staked off some land at the mouth of the Wadi bu Mudhabi and paid to have a well dug. At 374 feet they hit water, which tests showed contained four thousand parts per million impurities. Tomais and Athaith's intent had been to set up a farm to produce fresh animal fodder for their own animals and for sale locally in the Jiddat. But the high salt content of this well was a setback, one that a number of other enterprising individuals among the Harasiis had faced before (i.e., Hilaal's well and gardens at Ghubbar, Abid bin Naili and L'Utha' bin Saiid's date garden at the old Haima well).

But unlike earlier efforts that stopped once salty water had been reached, Tomais and Athaith have continued to search for success, and in 1988 were uncovering promising information on the possibility of introducing salt-resistant fodder crops on their "farm." With Athaith recently appointed a member of the State Consultative Council,[3] he was often in the capital area and had access to a wide variety of expertise. Of all the Harasiis tribesmen, Athaith stood the greatest chance of finding the right information to successfully set up an animal fodder operation in the Jiddat. And, as before, many of the Harasiis looked to him and Tomais to take the next innovative step in the development and transformation of life on the Jiddat. By 1989, after numerous setbacks and much expense, they had a working farm and were selling small amounts of clover and other grass locally. Three other enterprising men, Hamdan Naili, Shagaim Naili, and Mohammed bin Thamna also had small farms under development on adjacent strips of land.

The Naili Brothers

The Naili brothers are another set of enterprising siblings in the Jiddat-il-Harasiis. Unlike the Bakhiit team, the Nailis are more numerous and less cohesive. They are Abid, Hamdan, Sa'ad, Shagaim, and Yahya. Of these five brothers only Hamdan and Sa'ad shared a homestead during the period of fieldwork. Abid, Shagaim, and Yahya each maintained distinct units. Their families were spread far and wide over the Jiddat, and it was only through the constant movement of two of the brothers, Shagaim and Hamdan, that this group of brothers presented any form of a united front.

The Naili brothers, as a group, are slightly older than the Bakhiit siblings, and in 1954, when the oil company landed at Duqm, Shagaim was among the handful of Harasiis tribesmen who watched and eventually took part in the setting up of camp. Shagaim, along with Salim bin Huweila, whom he backed against the traditional leader (Sheikh Shergi), quickly demonstrated his willingness and ability to work with the European managers trying to set up oil exploration work in the region. While Salim bin Huweila came to be appointed the labor supervisor for the Jiddat, Shagaim was soon thereafter chosen to be the guide and driver for one of the oil company's liaison officers in the interior. In such a position, Shagaim was to have continuous and long-term contact with the European expatriates in the Jiddat as well as in the capital area. By the early 1980s, when field research for this project began, Shagaim Naili was widely considered to be the Harasiis spokesman by those Europeans working in the capital area.

In many ways, Shagaim and his brothers Sa'ad and Hamdan were the representatives of the Harasiis to the expatriate community. Each of these brothers had struck out on his own and created a special niche for himself. Sa'ad had gone to Saudi Arabia in the late 1950s and 1960s and was reported to have worked for an intelligence agency there. Hamdan joined the internal intelligence unit in Oman and Shagaim moved from PDO to the police force in the early 1970s. Among the tribesmen, however, these brothers were suspected of being spies, and conversation was always very stiff when any of the three entered the scene. The claim of the Naili brothers to the Ministry of Interior that they were of sheikhly lineage and thus entitled to be included in the list of tribal sheikhs who received annual gifts and acknowledgment from the Sultan was regarded with incredulity and resentment by other Harasiis tribesmen.

By the 1980s the Naili brothers had transformed themselves into "marginal men" in the eyes of the rest of the tribe. Each brother had gone his own way and created a special place for himself. This had often been at the expense of others from within the tribe. Unlike the Bakhiit brothers, very little of the benefits that accrued to these brothers trickled down to their fellow tribesmen. The establishment of the oryx reintroduction project at Wadi Yalooni, for example, is regarded by many Harasiis tribesmen as Shagaim's doing. In some ways they are correct, for in 1975 when European experts were searching for a place in the Jiddat-il-Harasiis to set up as the base of the operation, it was Shagaim Naili that they sent for. And although he took his time—three months—to suggest Wadi Yalooni as the site, many Harasiis say he did not consult widely with fellow tribesmen and there was little if any group deliberation. When a meeting of the tribal rushada' was called by the project consultants, it came as a surprise to many of the tribal elders. The formal session asking for their agreement to hand over Wadi Yalooni for the animal reintroduction was held in Muscat. There a consensus was reached, but not without some difficulty.

Fifteen years later some resentment still lingers among Harasiis households—especially during periods of drought—at what they see as a usurpation of their rights for little return, and Shagaim is still remembered as the tribesman most responsible. The fact that he also managed to win the contract to truck water to the project base camp at a rate competitive with the high PDO scale has not helped to eliminate that resentment. Having established himself as a mediator of sorts—between the interior desert and the capital area—he continues to be called upon by deskbound managers who require a service from the interior. When the police force determined to set up a mounted camel corps, Shagaim was called for and put in charge of acquiring the appropriate number of camels. Inevitably he stirred up even stronger feelings of resentment as he moved about the interior buying up animals from the various camel-raising tribes. Although his reputation is growing in urban Omani and expatriate circles in the capital area, among his fellow tribesmen he continues to be regarded with some suspicion and caution.

Abid Naili had, until the early 1980s, far less contact with European experts. Where his brothers moved far afield in their youth, Abid seems to have remained on the Jiddat itself, going to Haima to act as a well guard for PDO. There he and another Harasiis guard, L'Utha bin Saiid, were to plant the first date garden in Haima and set up the first permanent *mihrab* for direction of prayer. It is likely that Abid looked after part of the combined herds of his brothers during their more far-flung adventures. When an opportunity did present itself to work as a guide/driver in a region removed from the Jiddat (Thumrait), Abid did not pursue the post, letting L'Utha take on that responsibility. My suspicion is that he had far too many responsibilities to his brothers and cousins—his wife is his first parallel cousin—to absent himself from the Jiddat for long periods of time. In the late 1970s, when PDO took the decision to build a permanent camp in the southern region of the Jiddat-il-Harasiis, Abid was the first Harasiis tribesman to arrive on the scene. Following on from that, he was appointed the head guard for the temporary camp. And, as each new subcontractor arrived, Abid was appointed as troubleshooter. By 1981, when field work began, Abid had been settled on the same campsite just a few kilometers from the PDO camp for two years. His wife's herds of goats had, according to him, dropped from nearly two hundred to about fifty. His monthly salary—by our calculations—was about RO 600 (about $1,560), which came from holding down four different liaison positions with the various subcontractors of PDO.

Whatever grumbling there may have been about his brother Shagaim among the tribesmen, there was very little discontent associated with Abid. He was regarded as a fair levelheaded arbitrator by his fellow tribesmen and a hard and consistent worker by the oil company and its subcontractors. Harasiis tribesmen were on occasion involved in disputes at this oil camp. Many of these disturbances were intertribal and were brought to Abid to arbitrate. On one occasion a disagreement broke out over how often a water truck should be delivering water to nearby Jeneba and Harasiis families, on another it revolved around who should have the right to the stale day-old bread being thrown out. Sometimes the disagreements were more serious, and revolved about a labor issue or, very occasionally, a petty theft. Abid often took the side of his own tribesmen. What must have required some skill was convincing the European expatriate that the correct judgment lay on the side of the Harasiis claimant as often as he said it did.

Six years later, in 1988, Abid's homestead was still to be found near Rima. His job as a middleman/mediator had become established. He was named deputy to the official government representative at Rima, the Naib Wali. The oil company had, in the intervening years, helped him to stake out a garden plot and set up an irrigation system as well as build a fine two-storied house adjacent to it. Abid may well be the first Harasiis to have had a house built for him. Well-versed in public relations after so many years' contact with Westerners, Abid invited the Ministers traveling with the Sultan on his annual land convoy throughout the country to visit his home. This was done with great flair, the Ministers being flown in by helicopters to see the house that the oil company had assisted a pastoral tribesman to build. As with so many of the enterprising efforts of the Naili brothers, this accomplishment derived less from economic astuteness than political acumen vis-à-vis the non-Harasiis personnel involved with the interior.

Abid expresses great concern over the education of his children. When the decision was taken by the Ministry of Education to build a boarding school in Haima, Abid was understandably disturbed. He did not want to put a three-hour drive between himself and his children if they were to attend that school. He had created an important political and economic position for himself at Rima that would only last as long as he was camped there and immediately available when required. He had also managed to get his oldest son employed at a PDO camp nearby. Although Abid was genuinely interested in seeing that his children had the opportunity to acquire a modern education, when faced with a choice he decided to continue his present course. In 1988 he brought a used portable cabin from the oil company and set it up on his property. The following year Abid was able to convince the Ministry of Education to send two teachers to the makeshift school for the fifteen children—his own offspring and his nephews—who lived with him. In 1992 the Ministry of Education took the decision to build a permanent school at Rima.

The Naili brothers have all carved important niches for themselves within the Jiddat-il-Harasiis. Further afield, they have acquired a political prominence that few Harasiis tribesmen could match. Shagaim is widely regarded in the capital area as the model Harasiis tribesman. He maintains his contact with the oryx project expatriate personnel, who address him as "sheikh." He is most probably still on the payroll of the police force and responsible for a wide range of activities that impinge on the interior desert of Oman. Hamdan holds the post of Head Road Patrol Ranger for the police force and probably maintains his ties with the internal security department. Abid maintains his special place with the oil company and its subcontractors in the interior of the country. By the late 1980s these brothers were operating very much on their own. The activities of each brother complemented the work of the others and information exchange between them must have been an important priority. Although they did—and still do—not have the same cohesive and united front as the Bakhiit brothers, their own successes would be short-lived if they did not support each other to the world outside the Jiddat from which they derive their political strength.

Family Dynamics and Individual Mobility

The Bakhiit and the Naili brothers are not the only sets of male siblings to have struck out in their youth and explored the world outside the Jiddat-il-Harasiis. There is a pattern of leaving the Jiddat, or rather the safety of the extended family, and searching for adventure at a certain point in the life cycle of a male tribesman.

A quick glance at the collected life histories of the household heads of our survey shows that 60 percent of these men, now in their fifties and sixties, left the confines of the Jiddat in their youth. One, Saad Al-Luweyti, was so impressed by Bertram Thomas's march through the Jiddat with his father as guide that he set off to find other Europeans needing guides. Another, Merzooq bin Khalfaan, left to seek his fortune in the United Arab Emirates and beyond. He finally reached the shores of Lebanon before returning to the Jiddat to marry and carry on the husbandry tradition of his father. Many others of that generation had shorter journeys to make because of the sudden increased presence of British seconded officers in Oman, who were quick to hire these sea-

A young girl bottle feeds reconstituted powdered cow's milk to an ophaned young camel.

soned desert survivors as their guides. Such opportunities were then quickly followed by those of the oil company and, by the early 1970s, the Omani government itself.

What seems to be an important, almost a determining, factor as to the acceptable length of absence and distance from the Jiddat is the size and composition of the extended family left behind. When the older generation is still actively involved in the subsistence of the unit, the young male is allowed greater scope. When, however, the household has been struck by the premature death of its head, then fewer if any of the young males seem to be able to go far afield without threatening the well-being of the family. Birth order and size of male sibling group also play a role in determining how many of the youth will be permitted to leave. Thus the Bakhiit and Naili brothers are in some ways no different from earlier generations of Harasiis. Luck, or fate, seems to have determined that these two sets of brothers, among their generation, had the opportunity to move beyond the confines of the Jiddat and build up ties with the settled world on its borders that were the foundation stones of their later entrepreneurial and political activities.

The Survival of Pastoralism

Two concepts that I first grappled with in an earlier work (Chatty 1986) are worth raising here as they have relevance to the Harasiis tribe. The first issue focuses on the dynamics of human population growth. The desert can only carry a limited population of people and subsequently animals. There must always be a mechanism to remove the excess populations. Barth's model (1961) asserted that the excess population was sloughed off from either the extreme of poverty or extreme of wealth. This was later qualified with the introduction of the truck, which offered opportunities for the poor to reenter the system. Today the "excess" is removed in a less haphazard way that bodes well for the future. Extremes of wealth or poverty have never totally precluded a return to pastoralism, as exemplified by the Ruwala (Lancaster 1981), the Basseri (Barth 1961), and, most recently, the Tibetan case (Goldstein and Beall 1991:105–22).

The second issue focuses on government interaction. In my earlier study on the Bedouin in Syria and Lebanon, I maintained that a government attitude of benign neglect helped the nomadic pastoralists plan and orchestrate their own integration into the regional cash economy. In Oman a government policy does exist—to extend social services to the pastoral population but not push them to settle. This benign but not negligent policy, coupled with the sheer remoteness of the population, makes active government interference in their culture unlikely. Thus the Harasiis are likely to have time to find their own particular, and perhaps idiosyncratic, solutions to their problems.

The most promising of the solutions being pursued by the Harasiis today is the manner in which modern education for the young has been accepted by the tribe. In the ten years of its existence, the boarding school at Haima has continued to grow. Now encompassing a secondary school alongside the primary unit, it has in excess of 120 youths in attendance. Throughout the world primary education and sustained economic growth have been shown to go hand in hand, for children are the key to development (Morales-Gomez 1992). The Harasiis have realized this fact and make numerous adjustments to their households in order to place as many children as possible in the boarding school. The selec-

tion is made with care to balance the labor needs of the households with their desire for education. When a child is selected for schooling, his or her entry is delayed by manipulating his age. The official age for school entry is seven years, but Harasiis boys and girls are often a few years older. The reason for this delay is to ensure the children have been sufficiently socialized in the ways of their own culture and are equipped with the survival skills necessary for life on the desert before sending them away to school.

Education gives individuals choices in life. Some of the recently educated Harasiis youth will choose to move out of the desert and find other forms of livelihood made possible by their education. Some will remain in the desert by choice. They will exhibit an unwillingness to give up a way of life that continues to sustain them and with which they are most familiar. In view of the tremendous culture gap, discussed in earlier chapters, between the nomadic pastoralists and the agrarian and urban elements of a society, the key to the future of these peoples lies in the careful education of their children. With care, a balance is now being struck to impart the tools for survival in the desert along with the keys for dealing with a culture not far removed from, and pressing ever closer into, the heart of the desert.

Are the proud, independent attitudes of the Harasiis comparable to those of Athens's fishers? If so, what further inferences may be drawn?

7

Harbingers of Change:

Women and the Quest for Education

21 p

Voluntary change or experimentation with new ideas and technologies presupposes an authority or power usually associated with men. Women are generally regarded as the bearers of time-honored cultural institutions; men as the innovators of modernity.[1] Among the Harasiis tribe, however, the driving force behind some changes springs from women's efforts. Contrary to popular notions that women, the "upholders" of tradition, are the conservative element within society, I will show that Harasiis women, within the framework of their culturally specific gender relations, are able to initiate those changes that they deem most beneficial to themselves and to their families.

Nearly twenty years ago I first wrote about the shifting relations between men and women in nomadic pastoral society. At that time the anthropology of women was coming into being, and discussions of the "universal subordination of women" (Rosaldo and Lamphere 1974) were current. In that context the private, domestic, or informal universe of women was regarded as generally subordinate to the public, extradomestic, or formal universe of men. Power was generally seen to be attached to the public and formal sphere of life, and women were subsequently viewed as powerless and hence subjugated. I felt compelled by my own ethnographic material to challenge that rigid compartmentalization of men and women's worlds (Chatty 1978). I argued that although something resembling such a dichotomy did exist in a number of societies studied by Western anthropologists, in a number of other societies (Thomas 1958; Mead 1935; Turnbull 1962) the distinctions and boundaries between the private and public spheres were difficult to determine. Far from being a universal condition, that dichotomy—a Western distinction—was not everywhere a relevant indicator of women's subordination. Finally, referring to my data from two nomadic pastoral tribes in Northern Arabia, I argued that though sex roles in the society were different, female activities were not viewed as subordinate or less important than male activities. Male and female relations were characterized by complementarity rather than inequality.

Much has been written about women during the intervening two decades. The nascent anthropology of women of the mid-1970s moved into the anthropology of gender in the 1980s, where ever more sophisticated analyses emerged of various concepts related to the relationship between women and men. Questions of power (Sacks 1974), of nature versus nurture (Ortner 1974), and of sex versus gender (Rubin 1975) have led to many powerful and stimulating analytic arguments (Caplan 1987; Strathern 1988; Cornwall and Lindisfarne 1994). Now, during the present "postmodern" era, the perspective of the anthropological observer has come to the fore and the existence of multiple perspectives is more recognized.

Postmodern theory clearly explains much of the bias of early works on nomadic pastoral studies. Until twenty years ago very few female anthropologists had conducted fieldwork alone among nomadic pastoral societies in the Middle East (Sweet 1970; Nelson 1974). The image received from the largely male ethnographers was of societies where women were mostly invisible or shadowy figures whose perceived behavior threatened the honor and hence status of related men. One notable exception was the work of William Lancaster (1981:158). Together with his wife, Fidelity, he found that women played a large part in how society worked and, though not thought of as equal in public expression, were frequently treated as equal in private. My own findings in the field twenty years ago were that male-female relationships were not based on inferiority or superiority but rather on a complementarity of roles and duties within the structure of the domestic unit. To a degree this reflected the different perspective I held as an unmarried young woman who freely moved between the worlds of the older men (and some women) and their gatherings, the younger men and their constant sheep marketing, as well as the young unmarried women whose labors were so important to daily life.

In the intervening period, a few studies by women of women in nomadic pastoral societies have appeared (Tapper 1978, 1991; Pastner 1978; Abu-Lughod 1985, 1986). The focuses of the studies vary, yet they too indicate that women's relations with men in these societies are far more complicated than previous Western portrayals had suggested. My own findings among the Harasiis tribe are based on twelve years of continuous contact and fieldwork. Consecutively over those years my perspective was that of a newly married but still childless fieldworker, a twice pregnant researcher, and a mother with schoolchildren. At the close now of that extended study, I conclude that Harasiis gender relations are not based on a concept of inferiority or superiority but are founded on a complementarity of duties, roles, and needs. Harasiis men and women regard their own positions in society as mutually reinforcing, not opposed or competitive (see Kuper 1975:13). Their difficulties lie in the fact that this relationship is not understood by actors in the wider culture. Local Omani administrators and many national and international experts presume a male control in primary activities related to production as well as secondary ones related to other social activities. With the exception of health services, all government interaction with the tribe is directed at menfolk. Full education services are only provided for boys. This bias has pushed Harasiis women to act in order to see their daughters gain the same opportunities at full-time primary education as their sons.

Features of the Society

The Harasiis tribe is an Arab, Harsuusi-speaking, Muslim community. It is a patrilineal society where descent is traced through the male line. Marriages are primarily monogamous, even serial, and polygyny is rare. Although permitted in Islam, few Harasiis men, until very recently, had the means to support more than one wife and household. The plural marriages that do exist today involve the few men who have the secure cash incomes to afford multiple households. Residence at marriage tends to be matrilocal for the first few years and later neolocal. When the groom's family is seriously short of human resources, however, the bride will leave her natal home to help out in that household. More usually, the groom is expected to come to live with the bride for the first few years or until the new unit can stand on its own. Marriages are arranged by parents, and girls generally are aware of the negotiations several years ahead. The brideprice is paid in cash today, but in the past would have been in kind. Girls are formally married after their first menses, which tends to come in the mid-teens, and that is when they take on the black face mask. In the past, it was not considered appropriate to have the first child until three or four years after marriage. I was told of a case several

Households are often without adult male members for long periods of time. Women and older girls take on most of the daily chores. Older boys are often away with the camel herds or collecting water by truck for the households.

years ago where a marriage had been arranged between a young girl of about twelve and a much older man in his forties who had become quite wealthy and was taking a second wife. The whispering and innuendos over the fact that the young bride gave birth to a child within a year of the marriage were all directed at the older husband, who had been expected to behave in a more appropriate fashion.

Women own property, mainly sheep and goats. They also can inherit camels from their fathers and husbands. This capital is at their disposal. The highest respect is earned by a woman who successfully manages a goat herd, particularly of the white short-haired Somalia variety. Otherwise women's wealth is held in jewelry (or, today, watches, which can be passed on to daughters). It is most often sold or melted down to create new decorative pieces.

Women do not take a formal role in the seated gatherings of men. They do nonetheless participate informally from the background and sidelines and their opinions can inform the discussions. The traditional meetings of tribal elders take place within households, so women are routinely present. The modern formal assemblies held occasionally by the government-appointed representative at Haima do exclude women. But the topics are always discussed beforehand by men and women together, in family camps, so the men go to the formal assemblies representing a consensus of ideas. I recall a particular case where a charge of rape had been leveled at a young Harasiis man. The Wali at Haima called for a meeting of elders to decide what action to take. For weeks prior to the session, tribal elders traveled to different households to discuss the case. Women often joined these circles to add their opinions and to argue until the group reached a consensus.

Decisions related to economic production are likewise not exclusively the prerogative of men. Women do have a say in deciding when to move camp, though they often are not as well-informed as the men about the condition of the pastures in other parts of the Jiddat. The very nature of their daily routine limits the contacts they have with others and thereby the amount of information they have access to or can control. But ecological factors are not the only considerations for moving camp. Proximity to kin, to jobs, to water wells, and to schools are also considered.

Women make requests for household goods, and they often make the "shopping list," but they do not regularly go to market. Occasionally women will attend a town market with a husband or brother to sell some young male goats, but generally only when this can be combined with a hospital visit or some other task. Women have no role in the management of camels, which are owned by men. Even when women inherit camels from fathers or husbands, they are managed entirely by male kinsmen. A few families own date trees in the northern foothills of Oman, but these are registered in the men's names. They are tended by hired laborers and have little impact on the daily lives of either men or women in Harasiis families.

As a woman passes through the different stages of her life cycle, her position and status in the society develop and grow.[2] The young married woman, who often wears a short face mask that might reveal some of her neck and chin, is still regarded as an immature adult and is expected to be quiet and obedient to her parents. Her honor and her modesty are still open to assessment based on how she conducts her life. As she ages and completes her family, her deportment changes. Her sexuality becomes less apparent, her *burqa'* becomes longer and fully covers her face. Her total covering becomes her modesty, and her physical segregation from men is symbolized by this full masking of her "sexual" and "sensual" features. The expression of sexuality is perceived as dangerous and is thus carefully controlled within the bounds of marriage. There it is channeled into a constructive energy that results in children (Mernissi 1975).

As a woman ages and her family grows, her physical appearance becomes more muted, and her voice on issues of the day becomes a more significant part of adult conversation. Men who do not marry and fail to raise a family seem to be excluded from serious discussion (unless it is about camel herding, the traditional role for the unmarried male). Women who do not marry remain a part of their father's households and are treated as immature dependents. Only after men and women marry and have children are they regarded as full adult members in the community. A woman may acquire such high esteem that her children carry her own name. For example, a male child, say, Mohammed, born to a mother called Huweila and a father named Hamad, would be addressed as Mohammed bin Huweila in all but the most formal, official government documents. Harasiis women have power in various spheres of life, and action directed at change can be initiated by women as well as by men. Virtue, generosity, modesty, and hence, honor are attributes of both men and women that can be acquired, augmented, and lost.

In the sections that follow I will present portraits of two women. One

Goats are owned and managed by women. As a rule only women and girls milk goats.

is married to the full-time herdsman and the other is married to the fully employed tribesman that are both discussed in chapter 5. Although they do not reveal the extremes of character and statuses that are found among women in the Harasiis tribe, I choose to focus on them because they complete the picture I have sketched earlier of their husbands and their families. I will then open a discussion of how, in some situations, women can and do take action and exercise power to direct the course of developments within their universe.

Shamma

Shamma bint Shelayweh bin Ali was a married woman with two boys and two girls when I first met her at her campsite in 1981. She was a slim, tall woman of great energy, who nearly matched Hilaal, her husband, in loquaciousness. She was determined and headstrong regarding matters that affected her family or their guests. Whereas Hilaal could sometimes be prevailed upon to bend certain rules of hospitality, Shamma could not. She was a fiercely independent woman, of overflowing generosity, who was the focus for her family despite numerous, serious asthma attacks, which occasionally required her hospitalization. In 1981 she was advised by hospital staff to have no more children, as the next pregnancy might kill her. Everyone around her supported this opinion, but Shamma had other ideas. Over the next decade she successfully delivered herself of two more infants.

Shamma is the eldest of four daughters of a woman, Ghariba, who had been married twice. Ghariba's first marriage had produced a son. When that husband died, she married her present husband. Both of Shamma's parents are from well-respected families, but her mother's, in particular, had a reputation for benevolence and good works. This family, for instance, tried to organize government subsidies for the children left orphaned by car accidents involving Harasiis pilgrims returning from Mecca.

She was a skilled weaver of the filly the Harasiis people use as windbreaks to protect the young of their herds from the cold, the damp, and the winter wind. Shamma was a proud homemaker. Her household was organized as no other. Most households had a few woven bags, blankets, and discarded petroleum barrels scattered around a campsite, but Shamma organized her family's effects into boxes and barrels stored on an open trailer that was attached to an old Bedford flatbed truck. This vehicle served as the water reservoir for the household and it contained twenty-eight barrels of water.

Complementing her husband's curiosity for the new and the modern, Shamma quickly mastered the new gadgets he brought back from his numerous trips to the towns of northern Oman. The gas bottle for cooking first found a place in her "kitchen" in 1982. That was several years before gas became a common source of fuel for heating water or cooking food. At about the same time, Hilaal brought home chain-link fencing and set it up to define sleeping compounds and cooking units. A few years later this development was refined by the addition of a door with a bolt action closure. This was Shamma's idea, and she was particularly delighted as it made entry and exit far easier and was more secure than the previous "door," which was a simple overlapping of the two ends of the chain-link fencing.[3] Discarded steel cabinets, large wooden packing crates, and temporary shelving (among other paraphernalia of modern urban life and bureaucracy) always found a place. Steel cabinets became kitchen storage units. These replaced the earlier petroleum company cast-off barrels. Wooden packing crates became more than adequate shelters for the young kids and lambs, and shelves that goats could not devour replaced tree limbs as storage areas. These incursions of modernization and change always seemed to find a home first in Shamma's household.

Even food and its preparation was changed by Hilaal and Shamma's curiosity and invention. As women rarely visited towns to shop for food, they had to rely on men to bring groceries to the household—this is a pattern common throughout Oman and much of the Middle East. In Shamma's case, this was carried out with imagination and flair. The household never seemed to run out of its supply of coffee, cardamom, tea, sugar, flour, rice, limes, onions, tomato paste, canned chicken curry, and a wide variety of spices and herbs. When Shamma was at home and cooked, she imaginatively incorporated various spices along with limes, lemons, and tomatoes into her basic rice dish. She was known to be able to produce rice in the middle of a sand storm with not a bit of grit. Her meals had such charm that my notes were filled with references to the "finest Italian kitchen in the Jiddat." This appreciation of her cooking was so widespread among the Harasiis that our guide and driver regularly manipulated our surveying work so that we ended up at her home for an evening meal.

Much of this innovation came as a direct result of Hilaal's travels back and forth between northern Oman and the Jiddat while he was making arrangements first to get a well dug, then to create a vegetable and palm garden adjacent to it, and in later years to keep it in running order. Some also came about as an indirect result of Shamma's travels. At various times in the last decade, she had gone to Abu Dhabi, a metropolis dedicated to the new, the shiny, and the modern, seeking a cure—or at least relief—from her asthma. During these visits, which often lasted a month or two, she purchased gold jewelry, bright eye-catching fabric as well as the spices and herbs she used in her cooking. She wore the jewelry at out-of-the-ordinary occasions or appropriate festivities, and she cut the cloth into floor-length bodice fitting dresses. She delighted in wearing these brightly colored dresses—purple and white being two favorites—and often neglected to don the black gauze outer dress worn by most mature Harasiis women.[4]

Shamma was a woman of uncommon verve and creativity in an environment that offered little material. But her strength of character, and the independence of spirit that marked her—and many other women of the Harasiis tribe—were not clear to me until several years into fieldwork. Shamma and her mother-in-law, Buta, were often left alone with the children to run the household and manage the herds of goat and sheep. Hilaal was away a great deal of the time on his never-ending quest to keep his well pump working, to keep the family in water, to manage his herd of camels, and to keep the family provisioned. But the household was still one unit, nevertheless.

Following several years of drought, Shamma and Buta decided they could no longer remain in the particular region Hilaal favored for the camels. Good graze that would benefit the goats and sheep was reported in the southern part of the Jiddat. In the spring of 1988 they decided to split the household into two smaller units. Buta and Shamma, along with the six-year-old daughter and eighteen-month-old toddler, took their goat and sheep herds south to Wadi Mukhaizana. Hilaal went 150 kilometers north to Khamkham with the herds of his and his brother's camels. He kept with him the two, by now, young adolescent daughters. Each household functioned independently of the other. Shamma and Buta managed their herds and the household with no help except for that of the six-year-old girl. They fed, watered, milked, and when necessary hand-nursed their flock. They took turns taking the herds out to pasture and bringing them back in. They spent hours searching for missing goats. When there was time, they cut the wool and worked it on a spindle to make yarn. They decided which animals to send for sale in the market towns of northern Oman and what provisions they needed. The only link they had with Hilaal's household was through Rashid, the oldest teenage son. Although based in his father's camp, he regularly drove a water truck between the two encampments to provide them with water and convey messages or directives concerning the family and its herds. I asked other families about this arrangement and found that Shamma and Buta were admired for their actions. Although not often undertaken, it was a course of action that Harasiis men and women regarded as sometimes necessary for the well-being of the family herds.

By 1993 the household had been reconsolidated into one for several years and remained in the general region of Hilaal's well. Rashid had married his uncle's daughter in 1990 and spent most of his time at his uncle's household, where he had just become a father. Shamma and Hilaal's oldest daughter had also married one of her uncle's sons, but remained at her parent's household as was customary. She had just become a mother. Two unmarried adolescent girls and one seven-year-old girl also lived at the campsite. Though Shamma and Hilaal had registered their daughters for schooling long before, they saw no way of making it possible now. They felt their adolescent daughters were too old and their last-born daughter still too young. The son, Saiid, had remained in the boarding school at Haima and had only one more year to do before graduating with the equivalent of a high school diploma. Both his mother and his father appreciated that he had no life before him except as a literate civil servant. At first both parents thought that the poliomyelitis Saiid had contracted as a seven- or eight-year-old child could be overcome, and Shamma had taken the physiotherapy instructions from the hospital in Muscat very seriously. Eventually she realized that they were not going to be able to reverse the effects of the disease. Far from abandoning him at the boarding school, they showered him with presents and eventually bought him a three-wheeled motorcycle when his government-issued wheelchair proved incapable of traversing the soft sand and gravel that separated the dormitory from the school. He was a regular weekend member of the household, but he could not and was not expected to be a great help with chores.

The household was short of labor. Both Buta and Shamma had large herds of goats and sheep that required one or the other woman to be out much of the day watching over them. Hilaal was very busy with the combined herd belonging to his brother, his nephews, and his sons. Hired foreign camel herders had been observed for a number of years on the Jiddat, so it was not particularly surprising when Hilaal engaged two Baluchistani laborers, one to look after his well and keep its diesel pump running and the other to help with his camel herds as well as Shamma and Buta's goat and sheep herds.

Previously these workers spent most of their time solitarily with the camel herds and were rarely seen around the family units. But here at Shamma's home they were very present and even became part of the ceremonially and symbolically important ritual of slaughtering an animal to mark an important event or celebration. Shamma was particularly proud of her family's reputation for generosity to guests and always set out to top her previous efforts. In this fashion she and Hilaal were perfectly suited. Whenever she had guests, but had no menfolk present, she took great pains to prepare unusual and tasty food, partially to substitute for her inability to have a beast ritually slaughtered and prepared for a feast. As only men were permitted to slit an animal's throat—in the approved Islamic halal tradition—she could not offer the supreme compliment of a goat to visiting guests.[5] This had always bothered her. With hired male laborers present at the homestead, Shamma could now entertain fully.

In January 1994, in the course of returning to Muscat, I stopped off to see her and the family for what I knew would probably be the last visit I would make with my family. Hilaal was away, as was her daughter's husband. Shamma was unwell and weakened by a recent asthma attack, among other complaints. The subject of a ritual meal came up. Shamma insisted that we share one and I—as had been my policy for nearly a decade—refused unless it was to mark an important celebration. This was not to be a long visit but only a brief stop to see everyone, with promises of a long visit in the near future. Shamma reminded me that the year before I had also called in briefly and, because Hilaal had been away and I had been in a hurry, she had given me a sweet dish of vermicilli that she had cooked with sugar and cinnamon to mark the occasion. This time she insisted we would share a goat, since she had the Baluchistani laborers to slaughter and cook the animal for us.[6] I refused as a matter of principle, and this led to a battle of words and wits unequaled during our previous twelve years' friendship. Shamma insisted that I could not leave her home without her being allowed to honor us. I riposted that the honor was ours in being able to see her and share coffee with her. This was an occasion for coffee. We exchanged words with great vehemence, feigned and real anger, and finally a little humor and good will. Not until I reminded her that I had years before crossed the line between guest and stranger, and had often stayed with her and Hilaal without sharing a ritual meal, did Shamma agree to let us go with only the sharing of dates, coffee, and tea. She accepted this, but with a disappointment that everyone could feel. Her own pride and her pride in her family's reputation had not been well served on this occasion. On future visits I do not expect she will yield. Hilaal would, but not Shamma.

Teshoona

Teshoona bint L'Utha bin Said had been married for nearly twelve years and had had six children when I first met her at her home in 1981. She was slim, delicate, and tiny—the top of her head reaching to my shoulders. Physically she had a presence matching that of Hamad, her husband, in its quiet, contained dignity. Both moved and acted with a feline grace that hinted at suppressed strength and emotion. She was generous but, one could say, not to a fault. This social label applied to her husband as well, and was recognized throughout the tribe as a household trait. I had always suspected, in fact, that the traces of parsimoniousness that I had picked up from Hamad were actually attributable to Teshoona's influence. Although I rarely solicited Harasiis opinions of each other, I recall that I occasionally commented on the lack of food in Teshoona's household for guests. This was always met with a smile and a statement that suggested this was not unusual for her. Such behavior would make perfect sense among Bedouin tribes of Northern Arabia, where the popular adage is that men should be generous and spend all their property in honor of a guest, but women should be thrifty and guard the family's wealth (Marx 1987:162).

Teshoona was the oldest daughter of a much respected tribal leader, a rashiid. Her mother died when she was a child. Her father had remarried and had six children by his second wife. When the government-appointed administrator at Haima wanted a respected elder to supervise the setting up of dormitory facilities at Haima, it was Teshoona's father whom they approached. And when he and his second wife made the pilgrimage to Mecca, it was Teshoona who looked after these younger siblings instead of a member of their mother's family. The Harasiis often spoke in admiration of Teshoona as "her father's daughter."

Teshoona is a careful homemaker. She sews all her children's clothing and her husband's white summer gowns as well as his heavy brown or gray winter ones. She is conservative in her own dress, and wears only dark colors—black, blue, or brown. Her burqa' is very long and covers her face as well as her upper neck. Her head and hair are always covered by black scarves. Earrings or necklaces never show under these fabrics. She wears *sirwaal*, long baggy trousers that are finished at the ankle with a stiff, tight band of brightly colored embroidered designs. She continues to wear the black gauze outer slip long after other Harasiis women have stopped. Teshoona, as do most women of the Harasiis, breast-feeds her infants and toddlers for two and sometimes three years. In order to provide access to their nipples women cut slits into the fabric in order to be able to pull out a breast without removing any apparel. As feeding is "on demand," it is often that Teshoona, and other women, are totally covered from head to foot while a breast remains exposed after having just satisfied a hungry child.

Dress as a badge of honor varies from culture to culture. Among the Harasiis tribe it was obvious that modesty of dress for men and women followed the traditional Islamic precepts to cover head, hair, and one's wealth. With these notions strictly observed, I dismissed any thoughts of wearing long shirts and trousers or jeans, as had been my fashion in earlier fieldwork.[7] I devised a dress that was a cross between a Syrian Bedouin woman's gown and an Egyptian farmer's jalabiyya—something of a loose tentlike dress with numerous pockets and two six-inch slits, one at each side, to give me extra breadth should I need to leap or run. Each dress had a matching finished piece of cloth a meter square to use as a head cloth. Thus outfitted, I commenced fieldwork.

I met Teshoona a month into fieldwork, in September 1981. I had already established the routine that both Hamad, our guide, and Jamal, our driver, myself, and David and Liz (the American Peace Corps couple on loan to the project) spent four days each week visiting families, sometimes joining their camps for a night and at other times camping alone. In our third week of this pattern of surveying the population, we called on Teshoona, intending to stay the night. At some point that afternoon, I was standing up, talking with Hamad, when I felt a tug on my gown. Thinking it was a small child using my dress as a support, I did not immediately look down. But when I slowly realized that the pulling was unrelenting, I glanced down to find Teshoona squatting by my side with needle and thread sewing up the slits that revealed some of my ankles when I walked. Needless to say, this very real action could not be ignored, and I had all my gowns altered accordingly. Liz, on the other hand, chose to adopt the sirwaal as part of her ensemble instead.

In 1981 Teshoona and Hamad's children included an adolescent boy, an unmasked girl of about twelve, three young boys, and an infant daughter of four months. It was a small unit with about ninety head of goat and a few pregnant or lactating camels. Although Hamad's widowed mother had separated from his household with her large herd of white goats, Hamad, as the oldest of her children, remained the focal point for all his male siblings. The unmarried brothers split their time between his household and those of their mother when they were not looking after their combined herd of camels.[8] There were few extra hands about on a regular basis, and to manage the day-to-day running of the household Teshoona had to depend heavily upon the help of her two adolescent children. Her son regularly drove a truck to the nearest well to get water for the family and her daughter helped her to manage the goat herd. When the boarding school in Haima opened in 1981, Hamad decided to send two of his four sons. Although she would miss their help at home,

Teshoona did not object. She was, however, very concerned about her sons' social development and urged her own father—the boys' grandfather—to travel to Haima and help to organize supervision of the boys in the school dormitory.

The household was very much a reflection of its mistress. It was a simple traditional Harasiis home with few innovations and no permanent or mobile shelter. A few blankets were thrown over a tree to make shade, and blankets and mats under the tree created the physical structure. This contained a sewing machine, a few flasks for coffee and tea, some woven storage bags, a few leather and palm frond drinking bowls, several cooking ladles and pots, leather water containers, and a few discarded petroleum barrels. When Hamad was home, there would also be a knife, rifle, and cartridge belt resting in the corner. Everything about the household was simplified and pared down. There were no large reserves of food items. Though she always had milk and yogurt, Teshoona occasionally ran out of rice and other foodstuffs. Her cuisine was very simple and straightforward and lacked any experimentation. In order to manage the household and the family, Teshoona and Hamad had to call in the help of various brothers—especially during Hamad's now regular weekly absences first as the project guide and later as the government-salaried guide for the Ministry of Social Affairs' office at Haima.

She is deeply religious, as is her husband, and although she may not have been taught the "proper" recitation of some verses of the Koran, she fulfills the pillars of Islam in her own eyes. She has made the pilgrimage to Mecca and she prays five times a day with her daughters. By her own account, she only removes her face mask when she sleeps and when she prays.

In 1986 her eldest daughter was married to her paternal first cousin. In the same year her mother-in-law died and the household seems to have been released from an obligation to remain nearby. Teshoona and Hamad shifted their household's movements to the region of soft sand between Haima and the Saudi Arabian border. This move followed very good rains in that area and made it possible for her to keep her goat herds in closer proximity to where the combined camel herd of Hamad and his brothers had been for the past five years. This also meant that her brothers-in-law became regular residents of her household. For Hamad it meant that his commute to work was reduced to between two and three hours a day from the previous three or four.

By the end of the decade, Hamad and Teshoona's household had developed, grown, and become a large three-generational extended family. Teshoona had given birth to two more children, for a total of eight. The interval between each child was about three years. Most probably this was as a result of her continuous on-demand breast feeding of each child for as long as twenty-four to thirty-six months.[9] Her oldest daughter lived at the same encampment with her husband and their two small children. Hamad's two unmarried brothers, who took most responsibility for the camel herds, were also regularly part of the group. The domestic unit was mature, and there were plenty of hands available to help manage the goat and sheep herds as well as to look after the younger children.

Hamad always maintained that he would also send some of his daughters to school, once the government opened a dormitory for girls at Haima. Although it had never expressed a formal plan to do so, many of the Harasiis tribe had assumed this would happen. They registered their daughters with the Ministry of Education without actually enrolling them. Teshoona never expressed any strong opinion as to the value of "modern" education. But after her oldest son completed nine years of schooling, he refused to carry on, saying it was childish. He had been part of the first intake at the school, when boys were being accepted for enrollment up to the age of twelve instead of only at the standard age of seven. He started school at about eleven or twelve and remained there until he became twenty or twenty-one years old. It was then that the police force was recruiting young Harasiis men with a minimum of nine years schooling as border police and approached him and his classmates. Nine of them applied and four were selected.

When Teshoona learned that her son was one of the four, her joy around the campsite was palpable. She had especially worried that the educational experiment would come to nothing. The two previous years had been spent steadfastly refusing to allow this son to "drop out," telling him it would be for his own good, although they did not know how they would be able to keep him in school long enough for him to actually finish the twelve years required to make him eligible for employment with the national oil company.[10] With his youthful beard and deep voice, he had felt too old to remain in school with boys who were much younger.

Girls' Education

Throughout the decade different Harasiis families temporarily living near Haima or employed at the tribal administrative center registered a

Young girls take on the responsibility of looking after the offspring of their mothers' herds of goats. Each animal has a given name. The young kids remain around the campsite during the day. At sunset young girls help to place the young with their lactating mothers for nursing.

daughter or two in the school and petitioned the government to build a female dormitory. These girls remained for one or two years, until their families moved too far away to commute or they emigrated to other countries. In 1991 my own daughter was five and had just completed her first year of primary school. During a family visit that year, Teshoona watched my daughter demonstrate to her daughters how to write their names. She questioned me about the benefit of sending her girls to school. I responded with the argument that both girls and boys had to be prepared to meet the changes taking place so rapidly and that learning to read and write Arabic was the best preparation I knew of. Whatever hesitation she may have had dried up, and Teshoona agreed to let her daughters enroll in school. One was eleven years old and the other was nine. Hamad took them to school each day and returned with them in the late afternoon at the end of his work shift. Sometimes it was a two-hour drive over the desert, at other times it was even longer. That year a total of nine girls registered in the school, and all of them lived a commutable distance from Haima. They also belonged to families whom I regularly visited and encouraged to educate their daughters.

The following year the number of Harasiis girls enrolled at the school exploded. I could not claim any credit for influencing this action, since most of these girls came from families I saw infrequently. Not prepared to wait any longer for the government to build a residence for girls, their families took it upon themselves to do something. A further eighteen girls were enrolled in 1992, most of them from homes too far away to be able to commute daily. As the tribal administrative center at Haima was set on a sabkha, or salt flat, there was too little vegetation to support even one herd of goats. Having made the decision to give their daughters the same education as their sons, a solution had to be found to the problem of distance. That solution lay with the women. Families that wanted to enroll their girls in the school but lived too far away to commute had to split their households. A number of women came to Haima and set up temporary camps in the sands off the main road. Shamma did not come, but her sister did with her own children, as did five other women, bringing their daughters and younger children with them along with a few goats for milk. Their husbands were left behind at the main camp with the herds of camels and the rest of the goats. Some of these "abandoned husbands" held jobs as rangers for the oryx reintroduction project and complained not that their wives had gone off to educate their daughters but that the government hadn't arranged residential education for them.

In order to send her children to school, one woman, Bukhaita, left her husband with his camel herd and traveled two and a half hours north to set up a household a kilometer from Haima complete with goats, chain-link fenced shelters, and supplies of feed for her livestock.[11] With eight children, four of them girls between sixteen and ten years of age, it was a move that made sense to her. Were she to wait any longer, she said, her older girls would miss out completely. As it was they would very shortly be betrothed, masked, and married. Within a few weeks she effectively created a dormitory in the gravel and rock close to Haima. Teshoona's daughters, among others, began to spend weekday nights at her camp rather than make the journey back to the sands north of Haima. In 1993 Bukhaita was told that her two oldest daughters could no longer attend the school. The Egyptian school headmaster explained that it was unbecoming for two such mature girls to be in the same place as adolescent boys. Bukhaita was surprised by this attitude, since neither she nor any Harasiis tribesman considered it inappropriate that their daughters attend the school despite their nubile appearance. The school offered to send a teacher to her household once an afternoon to conduct classes for her daughters. Bukhaita accepted this offer, and enrolled herself in this home education program. At about the same time, two other adult education centers were established, one near the experimental fodder growing station where the Bakhiit brothers' families lived and the other in the Wadi bu Mudhabi, about an hour's drive from the oryx project at Wadi Yalooni.

Although these centers are open to men and women, primarily women and teenage girls attend. One motivating factor is that Arabic is often poorly mastered by the women—the older women hardly speak any Arabic at all. Increasingly women are finding that they need to use Arabic to communicate with doctors, nurses, and orderlies at the regional health centers as well as with the expatriate work force at Haima and in some of their own households. With so little opportunity to learn the language casually, Harasiis women conscientiously attend classes. Many of them are from households where expatriate labor from the Indian subcontinent has recently been introduced. And, thus, women are able to take the time to attend lessons. Most men claim they are still too busy to attend.

Planned development in Oman has hardly touched the deserts and their human populations. Where it has, it carries with it cultural baggage that conflicts with ideas and ideals the Harasiis people hold about women and men. The attitudes that government workers, often expatriate, bring to the desert sometimes undermine the control that women traditionally have over their lives. When they become part of blanket development, these "foreign" ideas tend to dilute, curtail, and reduce women's authority. Consequently, independent, respected, and self-sufficient women of the desert are losing the traditional power they have to take decisions about their own lives.

Development issues that planning sectors of the national government have usually addressed over the past two decades are largely those raised to meet the perceived needs of men in agricultural development, water provisioning, and livestock (camel) overstocking. The traditional woman's domain of goat and sheep production has been recast by planners as a man's sphere of interest. Projects for farming and training, extension services, breed improvement, and fodder crop production are today directed exclusively at men. For decades women have been systematically left out of Western-designed agricultural development plans throughout the developing world (Bossen 1975; Boserup 1971; Rogers 1980). This is one obvious reason for the failure of so many of those plans to achieve their goal of agricultural self-sufficiency. A recent review of development agency work with nomadic pastoral societies (Bonfiglioli 1992:71) shows a Western male bias in project implementation that disempowers women and removes them from primary activities related to production. Development plans in Oman are taking the same direction. Women in these communities are being deprived of the opportunity to improve their lives, while men's traditional roles are being recast to create new areas of activities. This urban, Omani identification of modern development only with men undermines women's place in their society. When and if similar projects reach the desert communities, women there will face the danger of being marginalized. Clearly the modernization and development that served to open nomadic pastoral women's access to market in earlier decades (Chatty 1978; Olmsted 1975) could also impede it if these processes fail to respect the value system of the local community—its ideas, ideals, and beliefs about men and women and their relationship to each other.

Education policy in the Jiddat-il-Harassis is one example. The principle that education should be available for all the citizens of Oman was announced by the Sultan soon after he acceded to power. Its application in the context of the desert, though, has been colored by the cultural values and ideals of people from outside that society. Education in the

Jiddat has been directed at boys, while girls have been merely tolerated. This reflected the experience in many agrarian and urban parts of the country, where families were initially reluctant to send their daughters to school. The Harasiis, however, had no such qualms and made it clear that they would enroll their daughters as soon as a residence was built for the girls. I believe that the government never really planned to build a female dormitory, because such an institution would have been impractical and unthinkable in the mainstream urban and agrarian sectors of Omani culture.[12]

The assumption that Harasiis families would not permit girls to board has been proven to be based on many misunderstandings of the tribe, its men, its women, and, most pointedly, its children. The way government policy was initially interpreted tended to exclude these girls from the benefits of education, and even hinted at a physical segregation of the sexes that the Harasiis themselves never required. The fact that education now fully extends to both girls and boys is a tribute to the spirited efforts of a handful of women and their supportive spouses. Harasiis women, through a concerted cooperative effort to help themselves and their daughters, really have been able to demand formal schooling. At another level this action clearly reveals that women as they view themselves—and as their men regard them—are actors, with the power to determine their own needs and those of their families and the authority to control their lives and those of their children.

8

Looking to the Future:

Pastoralists in Oman and the Middle East

The great expanse of land across the Middle East can be characterized as an unpredictable but invariably harsh and arid environment. Very thinly populated and receiving little rain, it is a landmass that discourages agricultural exploitation. Indeed, its only successful use over the centuries seems to be for animal husbandry or mobile livestock management. Like the pastoral areas of Africa, which Dyson-Hudson discusses at length (1991:219–256), existing local techniques of exploitation are often regarded as minimal if not controversial by national and international experts. Many of these same experts regard local populations as having a poor knowledge of animal breeding. In some cases, academic theories of the 1930s (for example, Herskovits's cattle complex), long rejected by most scholars, are still maintained, as is the common opinion that for these peoples the condition of the livestock is less important than the number. In addition, many "development" experts assume that the pastoral populations in parts of the Middle East, as in Africa, are ruining their physical environment (Dyson-Hudson 1991:219).

Unlike Africa, however, the Middle East has never been the focus of mass international pastoral development assistance.[1] Governments of the Middle East, perhaps because they regarded their pastoral populations as signifiers of internal political problems, sought local rather than international solutions. Accordingly, government policy in the Middle East has been directed at settling these populations either by physical force or by economic enticement. Settlement of nomadic pastoralists has been seen as the only way to control and integrate marginal and problematic populations that did not conform to the modern nation-state aspirations of the newly created republics and kingdoms of the region.

Settlement Efforts in the Middle East

In the northern part of the Arabian Peninsula, and in parts of North Africa, governments have attempted to lure the nomadic pastoralists out of the deserts and arid rangelands to settlement schemes and agricultural pilot projects. These, in large measure, have failed. More forceful approaches have included revoking the traditional communal land holdings of these people. Modern private registration of land has been encouraged, particularly in the marginal areas of the desert that border the agricultural belt, the Fertile Crescent, where dry farming of cereals can be supported in years of good rain. This last approach has had some success from the governmental point of view. At the time of the various cadastral surveys, many tribal and subtribal representatives were able to register themselves as private owners of land that tribesmen had considered to be held in common. Impoverished families who were forced to leave the pastoral way of life through loss of herds or manpower—or both—often found themselves transformed into hired shepherds or, worse, agricultural laborers for their landowning tribal leaders. Even after several generations of uneasy compromise, these families have continued to keep some livestock—generally goat and sheep—and many maintain that they would return to their former pastoral way of life if circumstances made it possible.

In Saudi Arabia and the southern region of the Arabian Peninsula, the situation of the nomadic pastoral populations has been complicated first by the discovery of oil and, more recently, by the tremendous wealth that has come into the hands of these governments. Saudi Arabia has for decades tried to settle its large nomadic pastoral population. Beginning as early as the 1920s, settlement schemes were built to house these populations. Initially the urgency of the projects reflected the government's need to consolidate its hold over the country by controlling its far-flung and highly mobile population. The association of this way of life with a backward, less evolved human state also contributed to government efforts to suppress it. In later decades settlement projects built at tremendous expense were financed locally from oil revenues. Predictably, the schemes failed (e.g., the Wadi al-Sarhan Project, the King Faysal Settlement Project). The nomadic pastoralists, discouraged by attempts to turn them into settled tillers of the soil, flitted away. Some returned to their old way of life; others turned to new endeavors more compatible with pastoralism, such as in the transport industry or in trade. Many an abandoned settlement scheme stands today as a stark reminder of how little understanding there was, and still is, for this way of life.

With the tremendous increase in the profit from petroleum extraction, which the Arabian Gulf States, Saudi Arabia, and the Sultanate of Oman experienced in the early 1970s, came a new approach to the problem. Mass settlement schemes were abandoned in favor of enticements to individual citizens. Control, in a political sense, was attempted by encouraging the individual tribesman to come forward and register himself as a citizen. In return, these governments granted various privileges. In the wealthier states, with very small settled populations, registration carried with it an entitlement to a plot of land, a house, an automobile, and a subsidy for each head of livestock. In other states, registration meant a monthly stipend—generally in the region of the local equivalent of several hundred U.S. dollars—often disguised as a salary for some form of national paramilitary service.

In Oman, where the profits from oil extraction as well as modern statehood have a historical depth of less than twenty-five years, the government policy toward its nomadic pastoral peoples has been equally problematic. Unlike its neighbors to the north and west, Oman's pastoral population has never represented a large percentage of its overall population. Although some of these tribes did take sides in the centuries-old struggle for control of Oman, they were never considered a threat to the central authority of the government. Unlike the Aneza and Shammar tribal confederacies of Northern Arabia, which historically threatened to overrun and take control of large areas of agriculture on the borders of the Ottoman Empire, the nomadic pastoral tribes of Oman could only pose a threat to individual villages.

In the early 1970s a tentative and incomplete effort was made to settle the pastoralists. This step was more of a gesture of largesse on the part of the new Sultan, Qaboos bin Saiid bin Taimur, than an effort to force a people to transform their way of life. A large housing scheme was built to the west of Ibri with the first profits from petroleum extraction. In some ways this project could be seen as a simple effort to "repay" the pastoral tribe on whose traditional grazing area petroleum had first been discovered. The houses were never occupied and now, two decades later, serve as a reminder of the tenacity with which people hold on to their culture and way of life.

Pastoral Development Efforts in Oman

By the early 1980s, with basic social services rapidly and methodically extending further into the rural countryside, Sultan Qaboos issued a number of decrees of vital interest to the remote nomadic pastoral communities. This component of the country's population was to be targeted for development. His wishes, reiterated in a number of speeches, were that the desert regions of Oman were to receive the same care and attention as the villages and towns of the country. This mandate initially became the responsibility of the thoughtful and conscientious Minister of Social Affairs and Labor. With his own intimate experience and understanding of the nomadic pastoral way of life, the Minister took the Sultan's directives to mean that a way was to be found to extend the same social services to these people without forcing them to give up their traditional way of life. Plans were drawn up to create a series of six "tribal administrative centers" throughout the desert areas where the basic social functions comprising health care, education facilities, and welfare services would be available.

By late 1980 the first of these centers was nearing completion at Haima in the Jiddat-il-Harasiis. As described in detail in earlier chapters, the Minister of Social Affairs and Labor recognized the need to learn more about this population and to find ways to draw them to the newly created, but totally artificial, center set on a salt flat right in the middle of nowhere. In May 1981 the first UNDP project aimed at the development needs of a pastoral population in the Arabian Peninsula was initiated. I had been intimately involved in the project's development from conception to implementation.[2] The first year's terms of reference were basically to conduct an "anthropological study of the population" and identify their felt needs and problems to the government. The second year's terms of reference were to recommend, and implement, practical programs that would extend basic social services to this remote and marginal community.

By September of that year the project was well on its way. The team had settled into the government villa allocated to it at Haima. The project's Harasiis driver and, more important, guide had been selected by a committee of tribal elders under the chairmanship of the Wali, the government's representative at Haima. Information on this tribe had been very limited and contradictory and was based on a few reports and notes made at the beginning of the century by explorers such as Bertram

Thomas and, later, Wilfred Thesiger (see Lorimer 1986 [1908]; Miles 1966 [1919]; Thomas 1929, 1937; Thesiger 1950). Some reports claimed the tribe inhabiting the Jiddat-il-Harasiis numbered only "250" arms-bearing men, and others that they numbered 450 men.[3] There were reports that these people were so "primitive" they had no tents and grabbed what shelter they could from the shade of a tree. Others claimed the people lived in such hardship and were so weak that they could not control any wells, springs, or other watering points and hence spent their lives drinking only milk from their herds of camels and goats. My knowledge and field experience in the Syrian desert led me to doubt this "information."

The project team's first visit to a Harasiis family took place in September 1981, shortly after our guide had been appointed. Setting out from Haima across the rock and gravel plain called the Hadab, we traveled for hours, bumping and bouncing over what seemed a featureless terrain. Occasionally we passed a few *Acacia tortilis* bushes. Whenever we came in sight of a *Prosopis cineraria* tree, our guide would stop the vehicle and give us its local name. After nearly three hours of driving we came to an area that seemed to have a few more acacia bushes then we had seen before. This was identified to us as a wadi (a valley). As our eyes began to take in some details, we noticed a tree with a commercial acrylic blanket thrown over it. A goat standing in its shade appeared to be tied to the trunk on a lead of less than two meters. Then we noticed a young hobbled camel nearby becoming increasingly agitated by our presence. A few discarded petroleum barrels lay about on the ground and bags made of cloth and of animal skins could be seen hanging from branches of the tree, out of reach of children or goats. A woman dressed in black with a mask of dyed indigo covering her face and a thick, black muslin scarf wound round her head and neck appeared from the shadows. Only her eyes were visible through her mask and even her hands were obscured by the thin black muslin outer covering. Clinging to her were three young children between the ages of three and nine, while an infant of perhaps six months lay in a portable crib that she carried as she approached us in greeting. The children looked and dressed no differently from children in the rural countryside of Oman; the girls wore colorful dresses with their hair left uncovered and the boys wore light-colored shifts—locally known as *dishdasha.*

At first I took this site to be a temporary camp, with a more permanent and solid encampment belonging to the family being elsewhere.

Finding enough water for camels is a constant worry. A large herd is rarely watered at a homestead or campsite but needs to be taken, instead, to one of the few community wells and camel water troughs (as above) in the Jiddat.

Although our conversation revealed that this was the only homestead for two brothers, their wives and children, I still did not feel that this would come to represent a fairly typical household. However, after moving on and traveling a few more hours until we reached the homestead of our guide, I realized I was wrong.

Our second household was also an encampment of astonishingly few material possessions. Unlike the pastoralists of Northern Arabia, with their elaborate, if at times shabby, goat-haired tents filled with carpets, rugs, pillows, reed section dividers, bags, and boxes, this Harasiis household was stunning in what it seemed to lack. Here, with no large tree to use for shade or shelter, a few wooden poles had been inserted into the sand and gravel. Some blankets were thrown over them to create a small rectangular area of shade from the sun's fierce heat. Temperatures of 45°C to 48°C were not unusual at that time of year. Again, as we had seen earlier, a few goatskin bags, woven palm frond and leather bowls and sacks were thrown over the top of an acacia bush. An acrylic blanket was spread out over the ground and, to the side of the shaded area, were a few large tins, one of corn oil, the other of powdered milk. A woman rose to greet us with two of her children. This was our guide's wife. Having married the year before Sultan Qaboos had acceded to power, we were able to establish some relative dates. Their oldest child, a daughter, was about eleven years old and their youngest child at the time, also a daughter, was about four months old. Three other children were spaced out at three-year intervals. This was a young but established family. Our guide was in his early to mid-thirties and, thus, in his prime, and his wife, perhaps in her late twenties, also displayed a vigorous maturity.

A decade later, in January of 1992, I found myself making another visit to this household. Over the years my visits had changed in character. In the mid-1980s they had been part of an informal, ongoing evaluation of the project and had involved traveling throughout the Jiddat-il-Harasiis with my guide and perhaps a doctor or nurse to offer any medical help the population required. Gradually, as my own family had grown, I began to take them with me, until the last few trips had begun to assume the appearance and feel of a family visit. I continued to collect the follow-up data I wanted on the seventeen households in my initial sample. And, perhaps with more hopelessness than in earlier years, I recorded their grievances, requests, wishes, demands, and suggestions for transmission to any government official willing to hear me out. During the early years, when the project services were being implemented, Harasiis requests were nonspecific (such as the generalized pleas for canvas tents or tarpaulin, for more schools, for more mobile clinics, for more frequent road grading, for better water distribution, for veterinary services, for subsidized animal feed, and for livestock marketing assistance). As the years passed, some of these services were realized, but the people continued to need water, mobile shelter, and livestock marketing assistance. Besides these last three needs, the Harasiis began to express more personalized requests (such as welfare assistance for an elderly kinsman or kinswoman, blankets for ill or infirm individuals they knew of, and special medical care for specific disabled or handicapped persons).

Pastoral Policy and Praxis

Over the ten years I had worked with this population, my priorities and research focus had changed and matured. First my goal had been to learn as much as possible about their way of life, so as to act as something of a cultural translator. Anthropologists and other social analysts, in the words of Dyson-Hudson, "are essentially translators," and anthropology's utility in development aid is in "the conviction that it is both necessary and possible to explain human groups to each other" (1991:253). Not surprisingly, my next few years of involvement had been largely devoted to trying to interpret this population's needs and problems into realities and concepts that both government and the international aid agency could grasp. At times it did seem as though, in taking on the role of cultural broker, I was succeeding in getting a kind of three-way conversation going between the people, the national government, and the international aid agency.

Toward the end of the decade, however, it became apparent that, although a conversation was still taking place and the voice of the community was being heard in translation through my reports and commissioned studies, this was not being transformed into any special government or international development assistance especially designed for the pastoral community. It was as though the official policy decreed by the Sultan, to extend services to the pastoralists of Oman without forcing them to settle, only succeeded in thinly veiling national and regional "expert" opinions that the pastoral way of life was somehow backward and that settling pastoralists was synonymous with development and progress (see Bocco 1990:101). For example, throughout this period I had tried to translate the needs of the pastoralists' to move with their herds into concepts and terms local officials understood. I had also tried to indicate the many ways in which government could assist in raising the living standard of this mobile way of life. Seasonal allocation of tarpaulin, or tents, would go far in improving the kind of shelter these people created for themselves as they moved their animals from grazing and browsing areas.

The futility, the expense, and the folly of building "low-cost" housing had been a particular focus of my interaction. Twice government officials had nearly passed plans to build small permanent modern housing settlements and twice I had been able to show how wasteful and economically unviable it would be. However in 1990 a political decision, following a Ministerial visit to an oil installation, resulted in the order to build twenty three-bedroom town houses on the outskirts of Haima for the pastoral population of the desert. This compound, now completed, has been inhabited by a few nonpastoral families from a rival tribe and is the focus of much contention. There is little likelihood that the modern building site will ever be occupied by Harasiis herding tribesmen on a permanent year-round basis.[4] For a fraction of the cost the government could have provided each family with a good-quality tent annually for the duration of its existence as a discrete unit—around forty-five years. Without any conscious decision to do so, I saw myself slip from cultural translator, to broker, and, finally, to activist. Over this same period of time, a decade during which most families purchased one if not two vehicles and material possessions proliferated, the requirement for a regular cash flow became an urgent preoccupation.

In earlier chapters I have described and analyzed the impact that regular male employment had on the tribe as a whole and on the family itself. During this period, women turned their traditional skills at making camel straps and decorations to the production of car key "switches" and stick shift covers for their husbands and sons.[5] A few more industrious women began to leave samples at the small shop at the Haima gas station for sale to any passer-by or tourist making the long overland journey from Muscat to Salalah. These items sold quickly, and soon I was bringing a few samples to the capital area for sale. The British weaving consultant who had first looked into the possibility of developing a "weaving" component for the project during the early 1980s returned to the area on a permanent basis and quickly became the focus of the women's handicraft efforts. An outlet was found for selling their work at a gift shop in Muscat popular with expatriates. Before long it became clear that the sheer number of women who wanted to participate required more organization than the British weaving consultant or I could offer.

After numerous unsuccessful attempts to interest various ministries in setting up a small project for the female Harasiis population, I decided to pursue the possibility of forming them into a nongovernmental organization (NGO) or voluntary association of traditional craftswomen. If the women and their husbands were interested, and such an association was formed, then international funding could be sought—with government permission—and these women could embark on a more formal and less unpredictable moneymaking venture. Indirectly, I hoped that the current process of marginalization of the women within their own society—through the loss of many of their productive roles—would be slowed down if not halted.

The women and their families were very interested, and a formal application was made to the Ministry of Social Affairs to recognize them as an NGO. At the same time, I prepared a formal request for a two-year grant of nearly RO 45,000 ($120,000) to set the association up on its feet with an office and collection center at Haima, a vehicle, a revolving fund, and a salaried marketing coordinator. In theory the grant would give the group two, possibly three, years to become a self-sufficient income-generating business. The funding request was granted several months later and only awaited the group's formal recognition as an NGO by the Ministry of Social Affairs. More than twelve months later, and after numerous unsuccessful attempts to secure that recognition, I had to decline the grant. The government was only prepared to conceptualize the women and their families as illiterate, both literally and figuratively. I was bluntly told that these people were not yet developed enough to run an independent venture and that government would be better able to set up an in-house craft project for them. Needless to say, the Harasiis people involved in this effort were very disappointed.

What effect has my role as an activist, encouraging Harasiis men and women to organize themselves—to shortcut and streamline the bureaucratic process whenever possible—had on the population? Was there anything I had attempted to do that had any impact upon their daily lives? And did any of my efforts to put forward their case really make any difference at the decision-making level? Were there any changes in their expectations of the government or any other formal associations of authority? In terms of material things, like the boarding school or tent distributions, the answer is probably yes, but in psychological terms, probably not. Although their expectations might have changed and their political consciousness might have been raised, their natural pragmatism and self-reliance was unaffected.

Their continuous adaptation to an exceedingly harsh and unpredictable environment and their firm belief in a strong, just, and beneficent deity presupposes an unshakable independence of spirit and mind. They have taken in the past, and perhaps always will take, every opportunity to plead their case, to ask for assistance, to request help from the larger society on the fringe of their universe. Their pragmatic position has been that sometimes they succeed and sometimes they don't. Grudges have never been held for assistance not given. Although some of their material expectations—mainly centered on their acceptance of the motor vehicle and the way it has transformed daily life—have grown, their cultural integrity remains.

Cultural Foundations: Generosity and Hospitality

The Harasiis tribe's contact with other people and cultures has been minimal, and their exposure to modern Western culture and society limited to what has been imported into the desert by the few intrepid explorers, soldiers, oil workers, and, more recently, a handful of zoologists, anthropologists, physicians, nurses, teachers, and administrators. Without exception, these individuals have been accepted as guests, entertained, and then maintained as friends or discarded as people with no understanding and no "humanity."

The important cultural markers that underpin the society remain and, if anything, have an exaggerated quality about them. These fundamental values, which link their material culture with their moral and belief system, are best described as goals of generosity and hospitality. Among nomadic pastoralists—particularly in the Middle East—these two goals are part of the fabric of the society.[6] It has been put forward by some that Arab society as a whole is based on "Bedouin society." This position, which perhaps draws its inspiration from the theories of Ibn Khaldun and the cyclical nature of nomadic pastoral (bedu) incursions from the desert to the towns, still finds adherents, as, for example, in the recent work of Hourani (1991). Furthermore, Wilkinson has argued that Omani society as a whole is Bedouin (1987). However, as Webster (1991) very ably reveals, this assumption, or myth, that all Omani tribes, or all Arabs, are former Bedouin is based on the assumption that Bedouin are those who have not yet settled. Thus the nomadic pastoralists/settled farmer dichotomy is reduced to an outdated and discredited notion of stages of human development. Such assumptions ignore the easily observable differences in economic behavior and in outlook, goals, and values. It is the existence of herds raised primarily on natural graze and browse that marks the difference between these two ways of life. As Webster and many others, myself included, have tried to convey in their work on nomadic pastoralism, "It is the life of the desert that is both the cause and effect of the characteristic social forms, political systems, symbols and values of the bedouin" (Webster 1991:7).

Among the Harasiis tribe, as well as the other nomadic pastoral communities of Oman and the Middle East, the society's evaluation of its members as good or upstanding is based on an assessment of how they manipulate their material possessions—or, as Barth first analyzed, their capital (1961). Hospitality and generosity, in a society of few material pos-

sessions, requires the utilization of livestock to that end. Where the small herding group is isolated and vulnerable and where the instability of material and personal attachments is pronounced, complementary social and symbolic structures exist that reinforce the benefits of such a precarious existence and give it meaning. These principles of kin solidarity, tribal cohesion for defense, and self-reliance are at various times and occasions described as self-sufficiency, honor, and generosity (cf. Chatty 1986:52; Lancaster 1981:119). Thus generosity and honor become the foundations of the relations of equality and sharing that permeate the society (Webster 1991:7).

Livestock in this context has a dual value, one material and one symbolic. Development planners generally emphasize the former value but not the latter, which in many ways is the more significant for the continued well-being of the society's survival as an integrated community. Livestock are the nomadic pastoralists's means of going without, of asserting their independence and self-sufficiency. Their cash value is recognized; they are sold and bought. Just as important—if not more so—they are essential to the correct entertainment of visitors, upon which a reputation for generosity is built. Hospitality in the form of fresh meat, generally a goat or a sheep, slaughtered by the host from his family's herd, underpins the acquisition of a reputation for generosity. The failure to provide such a meal for a guest, or a friend or business associate at the conclusion of negotiations, undermines the host's standing and renders the agreement questionable. For great feasts or socially significant events like weddings or funerals, or for the visit of an especially important guest, one or more camels will be slaughtered. A comparison of the households of the Harasiis tribe between 1981 and 1991 would show a substantial material development. Households, which earlier in the decade were simple affairs of a few blankets and goatskin bags tied or thrown over an acacia tree with a number of storage barrels of water, perhaps a sewing machine and a cassette player, are today serious, though still mobile, establishments. This material development has unexpectedly been matched by an increasing elaboration of the practices that support their moral economy—the use of livestock to augment and reassert their hospitality and thus their reputation for generosity.

The household of the project's guide is a good example of the way in which certain values important to nomadic pastoralists have been nurtured and perhaps exaggerated during the past ten years. During this decade the family has matured and its membership has grown.

Furthermore, its material presence can no longer be mistaken for a temporary camp. In the winter of 1992 the household consisted of two interlocking, portable metal enclosures totally covered in tarpaulin. These four-by-four-meter living areas were further organized with high shelves upon which children's school satchels were stored along with a briefcase containing important papers for the family, a radio, some clothing, and other valuables that needed to be kept out of reach of the young and the livestock. One enclosure was "home" for the married oldest daughter and her children while, the other belonged to my guide and his family. The third enclosure, created with the same metal fencing, had no roof or overhead covering and served as the kitchen for the homestead. Cooking gas bottles were stored along the outside wall while within several large metal cabinets held supplies of flour, dates, rice, sugar, coffee, tea, and other kitchen sundries.

Between these shelters were an assortment of vehicles. An old and battered Bedford truck that had once been used to haul water to the homestead now served to store water and to shelter the lactating camels and their young from the harsh winter wind. Another vehicle with no license plates, clearly earmarking it for the women and children to drive only off-road, was parked nearby. The household head's own automobile, a registered but only marginally newer version of the women's vehicle, was close by. A wind shelter made up of empty petroleum barrels and woven goat-hair sidings stood about one hundred meters away. Within this enclosure, the household's herd of goat and sheep sheltered from the cold and wind. This homestead could still be packed up within hours and moved by truck to a new site, just as in earlier times when possessions were very limited and transport depended on pack camels.

The flock of goat and sheep was nearly the same size as it had been ten years earlier, and the camel herd was only marginally larger.[7] As before, a guest was entertained generously. But, unlike earlier times, there was no option but to slaughter a goat. On very special occasions, the visitor would be more than generously honored with a meal of fresh meat on arrival and another such meal at an adjacent household the following morning. In the early part of the 1980s some households fed guests the woman's cooking—rice with a meat- or fish-flavored sauce. A choice could be made as to whether a complete gesture of hospitality—in the offering of fresh meat—was required or not. Returning to the analysis offered by Webster (1991), one is left to ponder over the recent emphasis on traditional behavior and gestures. Perhaps the past decade has

seen too much change on the borders of their universe, and the reaction of individuals within the community is naturally to fall back on traditional ideals and values as a way to protect themselves and their family from outside influences. Or perhaps the newfound emphasis on the importance of entertaining is related to the association that hospitality, and accrued generosity, has with the social standing, influence, and, finally, authority the individual household head can muster in his dealings with other tribesmen, government administrators, and creditors.

Associated with this recent emphasis upon gaining and establishing reputation is the economic problem of debt management. With few exceptions, Harasiis herding families regularly carry debts that have been incurred buying third-grade wheat chaffings for their livestock during the long periods of drought in the Jiddat-il-Harasiis.[8] A reputation for generosity built up through hospitality makes the management of such debt more viable. The "generous man" is more likely to get an extension of credit from the local lenders. When those terms are exhausted, the herder must sell off a camel to repay his debts.[9] The herd, then, is an economic and moral asset, but only so long as it is not allowed to grow so large as to be a burden. Unlike other areas of Oman where huge growth in herds has been documented, such as in Dhofar, the Harasiis tribe seems to have struck a balance. Although the large camel herd owner is respected as a good manager, the man with a reputation for generosity, but perhaps possessing a smaller herd, is more highly valued both within the community and among the circle of local decision makers at the tribal administrative center at Haima.

The presentday management of the herd includes the ritual slaughter of small stock (goat and sheep) for entertainment and indirectly increased reputation; the frequent sale of young male stock—mainly goat but some young camels—for daily household requirements; and the occasional sale of large livestock—camels—to clear debts, make large purchases—usually of vehicles or vehicle parts—or mark significant ceremonies such as marriage or death. This animal husbandry can be viewed from two perspectives. First, it underlies the traditional system in which the economic and moral value of the herds is upheld, and, second, it highlights the newly evolved system whereby the reputation for generosity is interpreted into credit terms. The generous man is regarded as the good credit risk and thus is more likely to be able to operate in a debt management cycle that requires the occasional liquidation of surplus assets to meet his obligations.

The Harasiis Tribe and the Omani Development Paradigm

Chapters 2 and 3 considered the process whereby a development project for the nomadic pastoral people of the central desert of Oman was designed, initiated, and implemented. The administrative orphaning of the project, cutting it loose from the full control under which most schemes in large international development agencies operate, was—in hindsight—a blessing. The project was left free to develop along the lines the Harasiis population preferred, with a special emphasis on education. The plight of the population became more widely understood on a national level. But intervention was minimal. For all the philanthropic and well-intended slogans used by development agencies, they are fundamentally organized to promote international business. As Escobar eloquently argues, development strategies from the early 1970s and onward centered on the "modernization and monetization of rural society, and with it the transition from traditional isolation to integration with the national economy" (1991:663). This focus, he concludes, was little more than a reproduction of the world of big business monopolies, "a world organized around production and markets, divided between developed and underdeveloped, traditional and modern, ruled by the politics of aid and multinational corporations, riddled by fears of communism, anchored in a faith in material progress through technology and the exploitation of nature" (Escobar 1991:664). A current catchphrase of many of these agencies is to "make the poor of the world economically productive people." Such phrases are now, in the 1990s, just beginning to be sounded out in government corridors in the Sultanate and applied to its nomadic pastoral people. Administrators are seeing large numbers of these people come forward to request monthly welfare assistance from the government. These officials, in turn, regard the requests as evidence of increased poverty among that sector of the country's population, evidence that requires solutions in order to make these people "economically productive."

The nomadic pastoral population of Oman is increasingly classified by government administrators as a "poor" people that are making no productive contribution to the national economy. They are seen as a drain on the country rather than as an asset. This assessment is not derived from any particular facts or technical study, but rather from the longstanding ambiguous nature of the relations between the urban, settled societies of the towns and cities and the mobile, remote, pastoral peoples of the desert interiors. Hence "income-generating" schemes, among other ideas, are now being considered as a way to turn these "poor" debt-ridden communities in the country into productive contributors to the country's gross national product. Such schemes, which are based more on fancy and wishful thinking, have little chance of making any long-term impact on the pastoral population of the country. This is not to say that government assistance is not required but simply to point out that the implementation of economic development schemes requires a detailed understanding of the population targeted, the way in which it has adapted and changed, and the perceptions the population has about its future needs. Otherwise, everything may change superficially, but basically things will remain the same.

The Harasiis, as all nomadic pastoral tribes, have adapted, and continue to adapt, to the changes in their physical, social, and material environment. The individual's material dependence on livestock as the main source of livelihood has fluctuated in the past and will do so in the future. This fact has created a problem for scholars and development experts as they grapple with how to define nomadic pastoralists, particularly when they have lost their livestock. Today the cultural self-definition of the individual or society is proving a most promising approach to an understanding of these people and their way of life (see Eickelman 1981:74). As Dahl writes, "People are pastoralists to the extent that they feel that a secure subsistence for them can best be achieved through dependence on livestock, and that such dependence is the best way for them to live a worthy life, achieving what they consider to be fundamental human values" (1990:1). For many dispossessed pastoralists, their belief in their ability to reenter pastoral life is the focus of their cultural self-definition. This is very obvious among the poor rural "Bedouin" laborers, found throughout Lebanon, Syria, Jordan, and, perhaps, part of Iraq, who are obviously dispossessed of their livestock through a combination of poor management, loss of land rights, and perhaps climatic conditions. For others, their pastoral identity is a kind of ethnic badge that does not have any relation to actual dependence on livestock (see Layne 1994:12–17).

Thus, in Jordan and parts of Syria, wealthy families in trade, industry, or other modern commercial enterprise often identify themselves as Bedouin. What has become clear in the past two decades of study is that pure pastoralism does not exist (Chatty 1972, 1990). Pastoralism presupposes the existence of adjacent subsistence systems that are often an integral part of the total culture of pastoralists. The recent study by Dahl discusses the more typical subsistence forms pastoralism takes today. Rather than a monodimensional dependence on one type of resource, pastoralists exhibit a flexibility that combines different resources (also see Salzman 1969). To survive as pastoralists (in the cultural sense) within a long time perspective, the specialized livestock rearers have had to integrate take-a-chance farming or small-scale irrigation, famine year hunting, trade, etc., into their own general system of activities and opportunities or maintain close contacts with other groups pursuing complementary activities. "Pastoralism" economically taken thus covers a wide range of such combinations, particularly of cultivation and livestock rearing (Dahl 1990:1).

The relationship of the Harasiis tribe with central authority has gone through several phases as the interests of the state have changed. While other tribal segments of the population were at various times caught up in numerous political struggles for control of the country, the Harasiis tribe was not involved. Its very remoteness, its uncontested right to the hostile landmass of the Jiddat-il-Harasiis, and its relatively small population size made it an insignificant actor on the political stage. Its leadership was recognized by the government, and the ruling Sheikh made annual trips to the palace of the Sultan to receive money and gifts in kind, along with the heads of other tribes in the country. Thus the Sultan was the paramount tribal leadership figure who dispensed largesse and demanded loyalty.

Between 1954 and 1980, however, when oil exploration first reached the Jiddat, relations with the central authority changed dramatically. During this period the Harasiis elders saw an opportunity to gain some benefits from the sudden interest in their tribal land. Demands were made for control over the hiring of laborers from the tribe for any oil company work in the Jiddat-il-Harasiis. They also saw an opportunity to gain greater access to the most scarce resource of all, water, and made the appropriate demands to the oil company. The government and the oil company were, to the minds of the Harasiis tribesmen, one and the same. In actual fact, government activity in the desert was oil company activity, and only when relations between the tribesmen and the oil company became explosive was the Sultan asked to intervene or set policy.[10]

Politically, this was an important period for both the government and the oil company, since uncontested rights over the desert land needed to be established over what previously had been exclusively tribal territory.

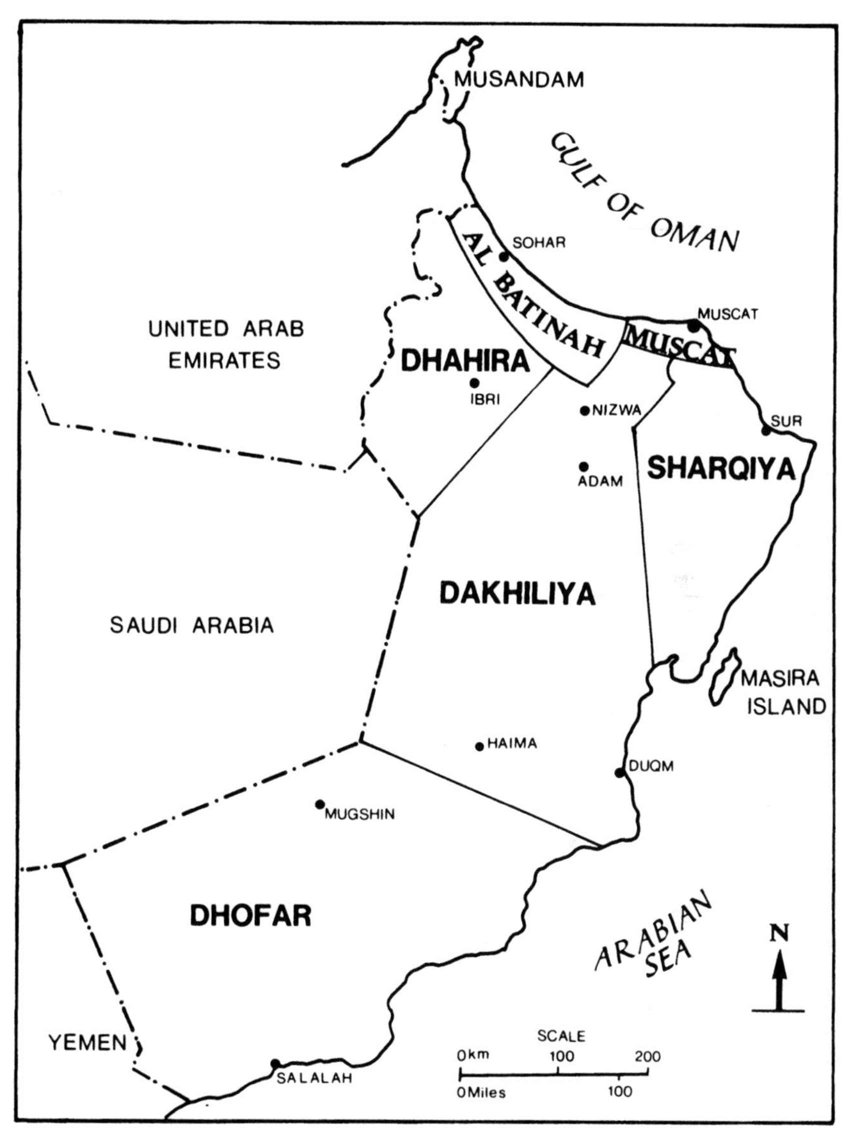

MAP 6 Administrative Regions Before 1991

It was vital to the interests of the government that areas near the borders with the United Arab Emirates and Saudi Arabia be populated by nomadic pastoralists with an allegiance to the Sultan. Thus, in the early years of oil exploration, the Duru tribe's leadership, on whose tribal territory oil was first found, received generous hand-outs, gifts, and concessions for drilling water wells. An extensive housing scheme was also built between Ibri and the border with the United Arab Emirates. These measures were a confirmation of the government's interest in keeping the Duru tribe attached to Oman.

This government concern extended to all the tribes that held territory near the border areas and included the Harasiis, the Beit Kathir, and the Har-Rashid. Important government infrastructure was set up along the border shared with Saudi Arabia. To the south the government established offices and schools in Fasad for the Har-Rashid; further north it opened a tribal administrative center at Mughshin that included low-cost housing, a school, and a hospital;[11] in the middle section, the Haima tribal administrative center was opened. These measures served many purposes. They were unquestionably an economic and service boon for the populations in the areas. For the government, they served the important political function of establishing—with some flexibility—the borders of the country.

As oil exploration pointed increasingly to more and more fields in the central desert area, its significance to the government increased and in 1991 the provinces of the country were redrawn to create a central province in addition to the northern and southern ones. This province, called Al-Wusta, stretches across the entire middle of the country from Mahout to the Empty Quarter and from Jazir across to the Saudi Arabian border (see maps 6 and 7). Haima, which began its life as a simple water well dug by the oil company in 1958 and grew into an economic and social focus for the Harasiis tribe after its establishment as a government tribal center in 1981, is now set to become the capital of the central province. For the Harasiis tribe, the benefits will be myriad. Infrastructural development and expansion of the road systems are likely, employment and education opportunities, as well as simplified access to government officials, will increase. The appeal of Haima as not only a tribal capital but now also as a government capital, albeit a provincial one, will create a renewed focus on the tribe in government circles and elsewhere.

How the individual tribespeople will adapt to these developments in

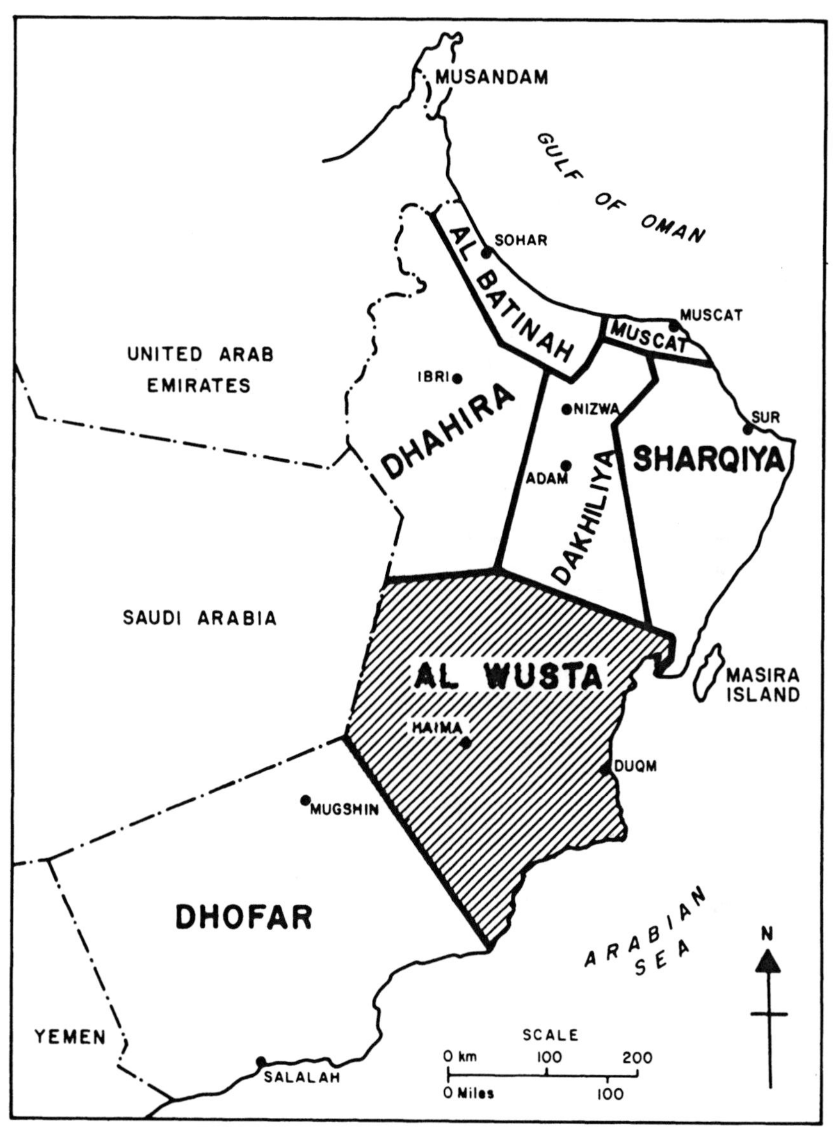

MAP 7 Administrative Regions After 1991

the middle of the Jiddat-il-Harasiis is more problematic. Here are a people caught in the modern postcolonial world of development and planning. It is a world where the current focus is on saving the planet and its plants and animals. Their tribal rights to part of their territory have already been ceded to the government by its leaders in order to provide a suitable spot to reintroduce the white Arabian oryx after its extermination in the early 1970s. Much of the rest of their territory—with the exception of a seventy-five-kilometer radius of Haima—was declared a "national nature reserve" in 1986 by royal decree. This was the outcome of a concerted effort by the expatriate adviser to the Sultan on conservation (and on the oryx reintroduction effort). The purpose of this nature reserve was to protect the potential home range of the oryx. No Harasiis were consulted and few government officials understood the implications of the decree, which was only the first step in having the entire region registered as a World Heritage Site with UNESCO.

For a region to be accepted as a World Heritage Site, it must be shown that infrastructural planning and development within that area would be very rigorously discouraged, if not prohibited. Thus, in spite of the remoteness, the marginality, and the isolation that characterizes the Harasiis and their tribal lands, they are now beginning to face problems similar to the nomadic pastoral tribes of the rest of the peninsula. Their lands have been, in a sense, confiscated as in the rest of the Middle East and are controlled de facto and de jure by the nation-state. Recent infrastructural growth has meant that they have access to and are affected by developments hundreds of kilometers away. Motor transport and motorized water pumping facilities have revolutionized their lives, as have telecommunications. Many have had the opportunity to leave and take up new lives. Some have, but many have chosen to remain. This situation is not very different from other parts of the peninsula.

Although each country in the Arabian Peninsula has to face different sets of economic, political, and social factors, a feature that is found in common throughout is the plight of the subsistence nomadic pastoralists. Without exception, their territorial usufruct is no longer recognized by the central government; their struggle to subsist has required that they acquire modern forms of transport that can only be supported through some form of wage labor. This, in turn, often means the household head spending long periods of time away from the pastoral household, leaving the management of the herds to other, often younger and less experienced, members of the family. At the same time, entrepreneurs, often from politically powerful families, have seized the opportunity to profitably use the open rangelands by moving extremely large herds on to it until the graze and browse is totally depleted. These herds often have little significance for the hired laborers other than as a pay packet at the end of their contract. The animals do not provide subsistence for any nomadic pastoral families. They simply feed off the land, giving little if anything back to the human group handling them. The benefit is to the absentee owner, whose profit is strictly from commercial sale of the animal for meat. The immediate effect of this type of activity is rangeland destruction, which is then inevitably blamed on the subsistence nomadic pastoralist and not on the commercial entrepreneurs.

This situation, which characterizes the current crises in the Dhofari region of Oman as well as in large parts of the Middle East, threatens the livelihood and well-being of subsistence nomadic pastoralists everywhere. Where the problem of rangeland destruction or deterioration has been taken up by governments and international agencies, the tendency remains to blame the subsistence pastoralists for the sins of the commercial entrepreneurs. The reality of the situation is the same as I described two decades ago, a cultural gap between the officials and planners in a region and the nomadic pastoralist utilizing the otherwise barren arid land.[12] The national officials feel that they understand the situation and do not require foreign experts to tell them about their own region. Their negative appraisal of the situation is easily reaffirmed by mounting evidence of grass and rangeland destruction. The subsistence nomadic pastoralists are blamed for a situation that is no longer in their control, as land use and, in particular, water rights—two of the three most important factors in the success of a common property system—are actually controlled by central authority (Ensminger and Rutten:1991).[13]

The situation in the Jiddat-il-Harasiis is a reflection of this reality. The government, facing very extensive grassland deterioration in the southern region of the country, has sought international assistance to try to reverse the rapid decline of that unique ecosystem. The blame for this destruction, in the eyes of government officials and local planners, rests with the population on the grasslands and in the mountain meadows. The fact that control over the resources that once underpinned the local political economy now rests with the government itself is not being addressed. More ominous is the increasing tendency among government planners and visiting advisers to view problems of the Jiddat-il-Harasiis through the same lens with which the overgrazing and misuse of resources in Dhofar is seen.

A few government advisers and experts have also begun to speak of the overgrazing and destruction of the "rangelands" of the Jiddat-il-Harasiis by vehicle tire tracks. The fact that recent studies exist on this population (Chatty 1984, 1989, 1990; Jaafer 1989; Sammane 1990), which establish a fairly accurate record of animal and human population size and attempt to explain the rational economics of the society, does not seem to affect the national "development expert circles" and theories currently in fashion. As elsewhere in the region, assumptions of pastoral-induced damages to the rangeland and claims of overgrazing are being used without careful presentation of proof or their relevance to the specific situation.

In the past decade, much criticism has been raised against the way concepts such as overgrazing and carrying capacity are mechanically applied in many situations in East Africa and elsewhere (Dahl 1990:2). The fierce discussion concerning the drying up of Africa—the most serious consequence of which is the degradation of the basic resources—has ominous overtones for the situation in the Middle East. In Africa the victims, particularly the nomadic pastoralists, were blamed. Among specialists, however, there has been a shift in thought, and the great force of climatic change is now held by some physical geographers, such as Rapp and Mattson (1988), to reflect changes on a continental scale related to Atlantic rates of wind and water circulation.[14] However, this academic absolving of guilt of the nomadic pastoralists has yet to reach the people who decide their future. For, in the Middle East, in East Africa, and elsewhere, conventional wisdom rather than careful consideration of specific cases forms the framework upon which development decisions, particularly at the national level, are made. This conventional wisdom generally reflects outdated scientific understanding as well as ethnocentric preconceptions.

Development Planning for the People, Not by Them

In 1991 an important book on rural development was published by the World Bank in a revised second edition. It reflected the lessons learned in development planning in the 1970s and 1980s. Its title, *Putting People First: Sociological Variables in Rural Development*, dramatically highlighted the seriousness of the lag with which new knowledge trickles down to those who actually design and plan development schemes. Putting people first is often regarded as little more than a goodwill appeal to the humanitarian feelings of project planners at the national level. It is, in fact, much more. As Cernea argues, putting people first is a "scientifically grounded request to policymakers, planners and technical experts to explicitly recognize the centrality of what is the primary factor in development processes" (1991b:7). When this requirement is addressed to those who currently design projects, it is tantamount to asking for a *reversal* of the conventional approach to project making, where technical factors or economic models so overwhelmingly dominate and the characteristics of the social organization and the very actors are dealt with as an afterthought (1991b:7).

In an earlier book on the development process, Chambers (1983) also tries to come to terms with the seeming inability of planners to consider the target population. As he explains, in trying to see what to do, nonrural outsiders are trapped by core-periphery perception and thinking. Looking outward and downward toward the remote and powerless, their vision is blurred. They see most clearly what is close by; they see action starting from where they are. The very words reflect the problem: "remote" means distant from urban and administrative centers, from where most of the outsiders are; and "what to do" implies initiatives taken by them in the centers of power. However much the rhetoric changes to "participation," "participatory research," "community involvement," and the like, at the end of the day there is still an outsider seeking to change things. A stronger person wants to change things for a person who is weaker (1983:141).

Both Chambers and Cernea are writing from experiences among rural populations. Most of their case material was derived from agricultural development planning—projects designed to improve existing technology or to increase crop production. In the case of nomadic pastoral societies—those remote, marginal, difficult-to-reach populations that have been particularly recalcitrant and resistant to outside domination—the situation is more bleak. As the East African experience has shown, nomadic pastoral societies are an evolutionary response to environmental pressure. These societies exhibit a pattern for survival that has proved successful insofar as pastoral populations continue to exist. These East African nomadic pastoral societies were almost obliterated at the turn of the century by epidemic disease and were badly hit by drought in the 1920s, 1960s, and 1970s. For centuries, and perhaps millennia, spatial movement and periodic devastation of human and livestock population were essential features of these societies and have proved to be successful survival strategies.

Over the last two decades, however, a new pattern for survival has appeared, based on the technical rationale brought in from the outside but not yet adjusted to social factors nor subjected to the test of time. It is in East Africa, among a population devastated by drought, by the death of livestock, and by loss of control over land and water, that the problems of development planning are most prominent today. The results of the past two decades in pastoral development have been disappointing. The frustrations and disappointments felt by those people intimately involved with East African livestock development does not mean that lessons have not been learned and that the basic sociological contentions put down on paper should not now be implemented. For slowly a recognition has come to international as well as national development planners that pastoral systems are not as modest as their simple tools would imply. And, moreover, that they are not as inefficient as their herd structures first suggested to Westerners raised on a livestock taxonomy of beef ranches and dairy farms. Finally, it is being recognized that these people employ a highly complex strategy for survival in a severely fluctuating environment. The problem is how the national government can achieve the "political and economic integration of pastoral populations without destroying their special skills and cultural variety and without causing human misery" (Dyson-Hudson 1991:237).

Government policy in Oman reflects this concern. By decree of the Sultan, government is enjoined to find a way of extending to the pastoral populations the same basic social services that have reached the rest of the country's citizens, but without forcing these people to give up their way of life. In Oman, as is the case wherever pastoral populations form a remote minority, policy planners do the planning *for* the people. The pastoral populations are treated as simply mobile versions of the agrarian-based sector of the population, and the assumptions made about them reflect the national planners' entrenched ideas that these peoples are simply poor, illiterate versions of themselves. Given half a chance and a little agricultural education, planners believe they would become properly settled oases dwellers.

The grounds for this ethnocentric assumption are shaky when the evidence is examined. Up to the present time—and with the exception of the limited success of the project OMA/80/WO1—development planning *for* the nomadic pastoralists in Oman has meant little that has not already been extended to its rural agrarian-based population. Numerous housing units have been built in the desert for these populations. These "social housing" projects are exact replicas of constructions elsewhere in the country. They are, without much exception, tightly packed units of twenty to thirty two-story town houses that require substantial adjustments for a villager to comfortably occupy, let alone a nomadic pastoralist. No concession is made for livestock, small or large, in the patch of land between the house and the walls of the garden. Only when the selected recipients refuse to move into these units are questions raised as to what might be lacking. And, as often as not, a bad plan is made worse. In two recent cases, the planners decided to bring in piped water and electricity in a bid to entice the nomadic pastoralists to settle into the houses. No one came.

That a home need not be a cement house but can be something as simple as the creation of shade is simply not accepted as legitimate by national development planners. The needs and problems of the nomadic pastoral population of Oman and elsewhere are perceived, even in the 1990s—and despite numerous studies to the contrary—as what the planners themselves regard to be the problems. Thus, if a family has no physical home, a house is what should be provided. Never mind that they neither want nor need one. The fundamental problem—the cultural gap spoken of earlier—is that the reality of existence in the desert is simply not grasped by national planners. The media in Oman and elsewhere exacerbates the situation by continuously referring to the "villages and villagers" in the desert. That there are no villages and villagers in the open gravel plain deserts of the country is inconceivable, just as a man with no house is an incomprehensible entity. The reality of the nomadic pastoral existence thus runs counter to all the accepted cultural norms and standards exhibited by the majority society in the country; the nomadic pastoralist who is perpetually in motion, with no fixed place of abode, is simply not officially recognized. Occasionally one or another government official, after serious effort and study, begins to come to terms with the very different mentality and way of life that nomadic pastoralists exhibit. Such individuals are rare and as often as not do not remain in the same position in the government bureaucracy long enough to be able to implement or follow through any program specifically designed for the desert communities.[15]

Ill-conceived development planning only adds to the poor impression most planners have of these societies as negative, conservative, and backward populations. Yet nomadic pastoralists themselves, in Oman and elsewhere, continue to change, to adapt, and at times to spontaneously adopt techniques, technologies, and ideas they perceive to be in their own interest. This book has described the many innovations that have dramatically altered, simplified, and consolidated daily life among the Harasiis. Yet all of these changes were the result of spontaneous efforts within the society. Some individuals initiated the changes. When the change proved valuable to the group, others adopted the idea, often improving and refining along the way. All the changes, small or large, insignificant or momentous, needed a "native" spark. Earlier in this chapter a partial cultural definition of pastoralism was discussed. Within the concept was that of "worthiness," encompassing traits such as a good degree of self-reliance, independence, self-control, foresight, generosity, and bravery. All these features are brought into play when change is introduced in a community, whether it be in a harsh, inhospitable desert or a simple agrarian community. Among the pastoral community, however, innovators derive particular benefit from their efforts, that is, an increased worthiness in the eyes of the community.

The Intermediate Culture in Development

Development planning for nomadic pastoral populations requires the intimate involvement of an intermediary culture. There is the local population, the nomadic pastoralists themselves, the national community of development planners and policy makers with a culture of their own, and, finally, the international body of development or technical assistance experts. At the most basic level, evidence is mounting to show that in rural development putting people first "is a necessary condition for good performance whenever local people are involved" (Chambers 1991:515). At the intermediate and highest tier—the national and international communities of planners—the popular adage for technical assistance experts seems to hold true. To see a plan or program implemented, it is considered important for the technical assistance expert to make "them" believe it is their own idea; "them" referring to both the government and the target population.

In the case of the remote and increasingly marginalized pastoral populations of the Middle East, neither "putting people first" nor "make them believe your idea is theirs" ever necessarily applies. Recently, in Oman, for example, a branch of the government requested a two-month study of the needs and problems of the country's nomadic pastoralists. This study was a prerequisite—following UNDP regulations—to developing a program for these communities. Having prepared a similar study five years earlier, I was asked to undertake the assignment. Water, in the final analysis, turned out to be a deeply felt and most urgent problem, and a number of local suggestions were put forward in the report to help alleviate the situation. The completed technical report was sent to UN headquarters for clearance and comment before being submitted to the appropriate authorities in the government.

Four months later the report was returned to Oman for submission to the government with a modification from the technical backup unit at UNDP headquarters. "If water is such a problem then the Omani government should move the people to other areas," wrote the Arab-born, but naturalized, American technical expert. Here not only was the local involvement in solving the problem being ignored but the unusually enlightened, if not unique, position of the government of *not* trying to force these peoples to settle was also being overlooked. That report was distributed among a very small government circle, and in the following year a second study was commissioned, with the same terms of reference, that resulted in nearly identical findings. No policy, plan, project, or action has come about as a result of either study.

International and national development experts and planners continue to write papers and commission studies. And the local pastoral population moves on, adapting, adjusting, experimenting, and at times adopting innovations that *they* perceive to be in their best interests—though not always regarded as such on a national or international level. Is it any wonder, then, that after four decades of a "nomad" problem among the government circles of the Middle East, the "problem" has yet to be solved?

Development planners at the national and international level need to closely study the nomadic pastoralists' responses to their particularly unstable and capricious environments. For in their responses and native strategies lies the way to a solution to the problems. Up until the present time, the problems have been the focus of world attention. Once the international community shifts its attention from the problems to the *people*, viable and sustainable solutions can emerge.

This study of the Harasiis population and the peripheral interaction of a small development program is just one case in point. By accident, mismanagement, and force of circumstances, the people have—by and large—been left to find their own solutions. Their dependence upon government or outside agencies has remained superficial, and the society continues to adjust and adapt to changes in its environment; ever searching for a meaningful and viable existence for themselves and their family herds.

As detailed in earlier chapters, Harasiis household subsistence patterns have changed to accommodate the demands that have been made upon it. With the adoption of the four-wheel-drive vehicle, households were forced to enter the cash economy for no other reason than to find a means of operating their machines. Petrol costs alone swallowed most of the locally available monthly wages. Within a decade of adopting the vehicle, long periods of absence for higher wage labor by the young adult men became common, and a form of debt management arose whereby local tribal creditors provided support to families on the understanding that debts would be cleared annually either through the sale of larger livestock, through the prize money of a racing camel, or through the employee gratuities that were commonly awarded at the end of a year's service.

With the growing absence of young male household heads over long periods of time, it has become increasingly common to find hired household laborers from the Indian subcontinent looking after the needs of the larger livestock and undertaking the arduous task of hauling water long distances for the household and the herds. Women have become more mobile, using the vehicles to move and search for smaller livestock as well as to visit other women locally. Income-generating activities have begun to attract women's attention and a spontaneously implemented activity begun in the mid-1980s—the production of car key chains, stick shift covers, and other decorative items using traditional skills—has found some success in a few tourist outlets in the capital area.

Group self-reliance and interdependence among households sharing the same grazing areas is increasing. One can almost speak of neighborhood associations where the larger animal herds' needs for fodder and water are met in common, where increasing carpooling to the tribal center of Haima helps cut down on expenses, where short brief visits by both men and women among each other's households is greatly increased, and where information that once took days to travel across the Jiddat now takes but hours. Still the herds, the camels, goat, and sheep, form the centrality of daily existence, and the Harasiis continue to search for the optimal adjustment to gain the best of both worlds—the modern cash-oriented economy and the one they know best.

Depending upon the definition or measure that is used, nomadic pastoralists are either thinning out or dying out altogether. Throughout the region, similar changes to those discussed here are taking place. In Jordan, Syria, Saudi Arabia, and Iraq, large-scale, ranching type systems operate at the expense of the small-scale pastoralists. The abuse of natural resources, the overgrazing and destruction of the grasslands, is finally in the 1990s being attributed to these large-scale entrepreneur livestock owners, who are generally not subsistence pastoralists. The Harasiis are, however, far removed from rich grazing lands, and, with no human competition for the extremely harsh lands they consider their own, they operate against simpler pressures. However, they, as pastoralists everywhere, hope for a better standard of living within their environment.

Until 1958 this small, remote nomadic pastoral community was totally isolated from the rest of the country by the sheer distances that had to be traversed before settled communities were reached. Nevertheless, they have adjusted to the very rapid changes in their physical, social, and technical universe. These adjustments continue with an internal logic that is often not understood or grasped at the national or international level. However, their very remoteness and inaccessibility has allowed the community to search, experiment, and, on occasion, adopt new ideas and tools in their fight for a meaningful pastoral existence in the midst of a rapidly changing world. Haima was a water hole in the 1970s, a tribal administrative center in the 1980s, and a promising provincial government capital in the 1990s. It has, in many ways, been the making of the Harasiis tribe.

Notes

1. Introduction: The Stirrings of a Development Plan

1. From now on I will use the less cumbersome term *Middle East* to mean Arabian Peninsula and Fertile Crescent.

2. At one time, tribute (*khuwa*) was exacted from sedentary farmers generally in the form of crops in return for protection from raids (*ghazu*) by their tribe or others in the surrounding areas. This tribute-raid relationship was a simple business proposition whereby the pastoralists received a needed produce (grain) and the farmer gained a scarce service (security). In principle, it was not very different from a more widespread relationship whereby animal products were exchanged for dates or grain.

3. By 1880 this modern weaponry, especially the Martini and Remington, was in the hands of the Bedouin as well (Lewis 1987:210).

4. The northern region of the country can be divided into three distinct geographic/ecological zones—a narrow coastal strip, mountain ranges, and interior foothills. Similar features characterize the southern region known as Dhofar. Between them lies a great expanse of desert shrub land covering nearly two hundred thousand square kilometers. The population of the country is unevenly dispersed throughout these zones—about 25 percent lives in the capital area of Muscat and the Batinah, another 10 percent in Salalah, the main urban center of Dhofar, and the remaining 65 percent is found in the rural ecological zones referred to above.

5. For a fascinating analysis of a similar phenomenon see Stephen Pastner and Carrol McC. Pastner's study, "Clients, Camps, and Crews."

6. These experts' understanding of social and political organization in society was so rudimentary that they could write, "The lifestyles and values of sedentarization and freedom from tribal and kinship ties are gradually replacing those of nomadism and maintenance of strong kinship and tribal ties" (UNESCO 1973:32, cited in Bocco 1990:110).

7. Among the nomadic pastoral tribes of the Middle East, and in particular among the Bedouin, mobility has long been a distinguishing factor in tribal clas-

sification. The dignity of a tribe was in direct proportion to its range of movement and mobility. Tribes raising camels deep in the interior of the desert were the "noble" tribes. The "common" tribes were the sheep- and goatherders who had to stay near agricultural lands and necessarily found themselves at the mercy of those more wide-ranging than themselves. The noble tribes felt they had—and were widely conceded to have—greater prestige than any other people in the area. The boundaries between these forms of pastoralism have never been rigid, but rather fluid and susceptible to modification as the environment changed. The categories of noble and common, however, have been less amenable to change. Individuals can do what they like. But what others think of them is more difficult to alter. Thus those that had an ascribed notion of nobility tended to keep it even when they changed the type of animal they herded. And those that aspired to achieve noble status by changing their herd animal rarely accomplished it in their own lifetime.

8. Perhaps because of earlier successes, the bedouin sheep cooperatives were amalgamated into the Peasant Unions in 1974. By the end of the decade the political rivalry between these two sectors resulted in a serious decline in range management on the Syrian steppe (Masri 1991).

2. Developing a Plan: United Nations Project OMA/80/WO1

1. Letter of the UNDP resident representative to the sultan's adviser on the Conservation of the Environment, dated November 17, 1985. The latter's interest in the report was simply due to the fact that his office was operating an animal reintroduction project for the arabian oryx in the heart of the Jiddat-il-Harasiis.

2. This is a paraphrasing of Grazel's statement that "when we speak of development, we should not forget that we are concerned, ultimately, with life, and not with economic parameters or production per se" (1986:162, cited in Gow 1993:393).

3. Malinowski wrote extensively about practical anthropology (now labeled applied anthropology). He along with many of his students suggested that anthropologists should be involved in policy considerations along with the preparation of background information for administrators. A committee on applied anthropology was established at the Royal Anthropological Institute in an attempt to have anthropology's voice heard on the world stage. According to Mair (1992:290), this position was fairly unsuccessful as only Mayer and Nadel—and Malinowski before them—were regularly asked to give advice on policy questions.

4. Hereafter project OMA/80/WO1 will be referred to as simply *the project.*

5. January 1968 speech of Sultan Saiid bin Taimur on the financial position of the country. In the private archives of J. Townsend, as quoted in his book *Oman: The Making of the Modern State.*

6. Throughout the 1980s the government was regularly forced to initiate a number of measures to shore up the pastoral economy of the mountains of Dhofar. In 1981 the government found it necessary to begin a program of subsi-

dizing animal feed for a population that was no longer able to make full use of its seasonal pastures. With the equilibrium of human, animal, and pasture thrown more askew by the 50 percent government animal feed subsidy, it was not long before a government program had to be launched to reduce the swollen herd sizes of the Dhofari pastoralists. This off-take program, as well as others, continued for a number of years. Finally, in 1988, the government requested UN assistance to save the seriously threatened pastures, and a land management project was initiated the following year with that goal in mind.

7. This disconcerting request was granted without hesitation by the Ministry of Social Affairs and Labor.

8. Interoffice memorandum dated June 26, 1981, from the program coordinator to the Program Management Officer for the Middle East (DTCD).

3. Implementing a Plan: Transforming a Water Well Into a Tribal Center

1. The identification of project problem areas occasionally reflects political pressure at the national level (see, for example, Seddon, in Pottier 1993:71–109).

2. I had not yet come to appreciate the important influence that the anthropological fieldworker sometimes has in shaping the cultural and political transformations of the community under study (see Turner 1991:285–313).

3. This was a quick survey undertaken by an Egyptian social worker to determine whether or not the Harasiis tribe wanted to have low-cost cement block housing. I have not been able to locate the study, but have been informed by government officials that his findings were that everyone in the Jiddat-il-Harasiis wanted a house.

4. The director of Curative Services at the Ministry of Health as well as the head of the Nizwa Hospital had arrived at Haima early in October to discuss the UN project's health component. Before the meeting could take place, the director was badly injured in a road accident just outside of Haima. The medical officer-in-charge of Haima at the time asked our help in arranging an air medical evacuation of the injured, as the police seemed unable to get through on their radio set. This we were able to accomplish through personal contacts. The project team's assistance on that evening was to swing the majority to our side, and, shortly thereafter, the Haima clinic agreed to run a joint immunization effort with us.

5. The occasions when the Harasiis community gather in large numbers are few. These are limited to weddings, funeral services, and, more recently, camel races. Also during the month of fasting—Ramadan—a number of families will camp together in order to share the work of preparing the special meals associated with that religious festival.

6. This was an obvious result of a request put to him during his annual "meet the people" tour on the border area of the Jiddat-il-Harasiis a short time earlier.

7. I hesitate to use the word *demand* in relation to the requests that began to rain down on the project team. They were more in the line of aspirations, hopes,

and wishes. As one elderly Harsiis man explained to me after seeing my discomfort, the requests for welfare, tents, water and animal feed, and so on were made in the hope they would materialize. If they didn't request anything, then nothing would happen. But by making known their desires, they were that much closer to seeing them fulfilled.

8. The Harasiis tribesperson—as well as many Omanis—finds it difficult to deal with an impersonal bureaucracy. As in many traditional societies, the individual link, the personal relation, is the key to success. When petitions are presented to the appropriate authority, most tribesmen feel it is necessary to see the minister or his deputy as well, in order to give the petition a better chance of success. A sudden windfall from the government, such as an increase in welfare payments, is not perceived as a routine administrative procedure, but rather due to the personal intervention of a friend, patron, or the sultan himself.

9. This transformation of their social consciousness has parallels in the changes that Turner records for the Kayapó (1991:285–313).

10. This letter is quoted in the beginning of chapter 2.

4. Employment on the Side: The Changing Nature of Pastoralism in the Jiddat-il-Harasiis

1. See Stanley Price (1989:68–81) for greater detail on the geomorphology, climate, and vegetation of the Jiddat-il-Harasiis.

2. Roughly 80 percent of the population present on the Jiddat between 1981 and 1983 was interviewed in a general socioeconomic survey (167 families). A 10 percent random sample was selected for further in-depth surveys, interviews, and participant observation (seventeen households).

3. Unlike some nomadic pastoral tribes in Oman, Harasiis families generally purchased dates if they required any in addition to their own holdings. They rarely worked in other date gardens for payment in kind.

4. Among camel herding people, the often great distances between the camel herd and the residential camp seem to ensure that the milking of camels and the tending of their young are more frequently specified as male tasks. In some places, such as the Horn of Africa, the association between males and camel tending is reinforced by strong ritual sanctions. Such rules tend to be combined with a definition of goat milking and kid care as belonging to the female domain (see Dahl and Hjort 1976: 251).

5. Harasiis nutrition is far superior to that of the average Omani village household because milk is such an important part of the Harasiis diet.

5. The Modern Harasiis Household: The Traditional and the Innovative

1. I have elsewhere described and analyzed the importance of the truck for a pastoral household (Chatty 1976, 1986). There are a number of studies that deal

with the effect of technology on social organization. Those of particular interest here are: Sharp, "Steel Axes for Stone-Age Australians," Hall, "The 'Iron Dog' in Northern Alaska," and Pelto, *The Snowmobile Revolution: Technology and Social Change in the Artic.*

2. Layne discusses in some depth the transformations in the concept of space among tribal peoples in Jordan (1994:61–73).

3. Only jewelry for women and rifles for men seemed to hold a private exclusive value. Vehicles, though they were privately owned and registered with the police force, were regularly borrowed and loaned out. Seeing a tribesman driving a vehicle did not automatically mean it belonged to him—in fact more often than not it didn't.

4. This process is what Pelto calls "de-localization," the irreversible growth of dependence on nonlocal sources of energy. Delocalization expands the geographical scope within which people actively appropriate artifacts, with extensive implications for social and cultural change (Pelto 1973:165–181).

5. The impact of modern technology on "traditional societies" is a field of study in itself. Pfaffenberger (1988, 1992) powerfully reveals the preconceptions in Western discourse that depict technology as the cause of social transformations. This discourse disguises the social choices and social relations that figure in the adoption of any "modern" technology. The essay by Schaniel (1988) on the Maori appropriation of iron artifacts and Sharp's analysis of steel axes for stone-age Australians illustrate the danger of reading too much technological determinism into a single case. For the Bedouin, for the Lapps, and for the Harasiis, the transportation revolution has produced extensive modifications in economic and social patterns of behavior. But individual differences and social relations reveal that people are the active appropriators and not the passive victims of transferred technology.

6. He was measured for leg callipers in 1982, but a local medical decision was made to put him on wooden crutches instead, as the desert environment was deemed unsuitable for such sophisticated equipment. Within a few months the child was moving about by himself, and beginning to lend some assistance to the family.

6. Entrepreneurship and Marginality: Harasiis Brokers and the Outside World

1. In northern Alaska, for example, Hall records how the snowmobile became popular as a winter recreational vehicle—a weekend leisure toy—in Canada and the United States during the late 1950s. In 1960 the first snowmobile was sold to a white resident in Kotzebue, the main distribution center of northwest Alaska. In 1965 a white man came through the small, mainly native Alaskan village of Noatak on a snowmobile. But little local interest was expressed in this technology. In February 1966 an *acculturated* (emphasis mine) Noatak Eskimo purchased a snowmobile. By 1966–1967 eight more snowmobiles were purchased by Noatak

Eskimo, and in 1967–1968 nine more appeared in the village (1971:242). The rest is history and is recorded in the work of Pelto (1968, 1972, 1973).

2. Until 1988 the produce from the PDO experimental station at Wadi Arah was mainly available to local Dhofari tribes. Although there was no specific ban, few Harasiis tribesmen made the journey, except under special circumstances, such as when a bulk purchase for the Yalooni oryx project was being undertaken. Since 1988 Harasiis tribesmen in the southern part of the Jiddat regularly buy feed from the station particularly for their racing camels.

3. The State Consultative Council of Oman was created in 1981. It is not a parliament or a legislature, but rather a strictly consultative body that allows some scope for select Omani citizens to participate in the task of formulating opinion and advice on the country's economic and social development. For a full discussion of the SCC, see Eickelman 1984. In 1991 this council was disbanded and a similar "elective" council was formed in its place.

7. Harbingers of Change: Women and the Quest for Education

1. This association derives from Western philosophical arguments that women, due to their very physiology and anatomy, were closer to nature, while men were closer to culture. At its roots were the basic dualism of Western philosophy and theology—flesh and spirit, body and mind, nature and culture, emotion and reason, female and male (Fernea 1987). This male/female opposition eventually came to be regarded as a struggle between the forces of tradition and those of modernization (Jordanova 1980).

2. I take *status* to mean the degree to which individuals have authority or power in the domestic and/or public domain (Sanday 1974:191).

3. I have suggested earlier that this development was a borrowing from the enclosure introduced at the oryx reintroduction project at Wadi Yalooni. As Shamma tells it, she first heard about it while visiting her sister, who was married to a ranger at the oryx project. Returning home a few months later, she told her husband about it, and not long thereafter he had acquired a similar door for their campsite.

4. In the early months of my fieldwork, this trademark brightness of color that Shamma wore helped me to identify her. For with the burqa'—the full face mask of indigo-dyed cloth—which only exposed the eyes, the black head, neck, and shoulder covering, the generally somber-colored dresses, and black outer garment, it was difficult to distinguish one adult woman from another. I was often confused, until I learned to recognize women using their eye shape as a primary marker.

5. The Harasiis maintain that only Muslim men may ritually slaughter an animal correctly, that is in the tradition of halal. I can find no reference in the Koran to justify this position, and assume therefore that it is—like many other Harasiis traditions, such as the prohibition on women milking camels—related to ideas of pollution and biological functions.

6. Among the Harasiis, men not only slaughter a goat or a camel for a ritual meal, they also prepare the ensuing meal of rice and meat. They serve it and oversee the distribution of the meat, thus effectively reversing the normal division of labor. This ultimate ritual of generosity—when a beast is slaughtered and prepared in honor of a guest—is strictly a male preserve among the Bedouin of Arabia (Marx 1987; Abu Rabia 1994).

7. On my earlier trips into the Harasiis tribal area before commencing fieldwork, I regularly wore shirt and trousers. This seemed to disquiet the community in some way, and I was repeatedly asked by women why I was dressed as a man. I decided that if my clothing was going to disturb the community, I would change it and fashion myself something more suitable.

8. After Hamad's father was killed, his herd of camels was divided between his wife and sons, following the Harasiis interpretation of Islamic inheritance rules. Hamad managed his mother's camels within his own herd.

9. The contraceptive effect of frequent nipple stimulation is widely written about in specialist journals and World Health Organization technical reports. One good general study is by S. Thapa, R. V. Short, and M. Potts, "Breast Feeding, Birth Spacing and Their Effects on Child Survival," in *Nature* (1988), 335:679–82.

10. Teshoona approached me at this time to ask me to look out for a second-hand, cheap, small four-wheel-drive vehicle. She felt that she and Hamad might be able to tempt their oldest son to remain in school if they offered to buy him his own car. It would make him feel independent and more adult, she said. I was struck by how quickly they seemed to be adopting an approach so similar to middle-class Western parents, though for entirely different reasons.

11. Bukhaita was an unlikely candidate to take such affirmative action. I had first met her as a shy, young mother of three girls in 1982. Then she was overshadowed by her brothers, of whom two worked with the national oil company and were effectively making a name for themselves as progressive and resourceful employees marked for promotion and training. Her older sister had been married, but had been unable to bear children and had successfully turned her energies to becoming a traditional healer. The Ministry of Health had considered recruiting this sister into the health service, but she rejected the offer because government work hours would, she felt, severely curtail her freedom to move about.

12. In 1993 the first dormitory for high school girls was opened in the Musandam, the remote, mountainous terrain of Oman's northern province. This community is isolated and difficult to reach and hence is affected less by the ideas and cultural constraints regarding women prevalent in the Sultanate.

8. Looking to the Future: Pastoralists in Oman and the Middle East

1. Neville Dyson-Hudson reports that the African livestock development programs of the past two decades have been aimed at increasing livestock production, raising the standard of living of the human population, and improving the

environment itself. The entire process could be seen as an effort "towards transforming subsistence pastoralism into the beginnings of commercial livestock production" (1991:220).

2. The project cycle generally has a set of fixed stages as discussed in chapter 2. In the case of the Jiddat-il-Harasiis project, the earlier stages of problem identification and assessment of alternatives were not formalized steps. The actual Harasiis project cycle commenced only after a policy had been formulated by the Sultan. Later problem identification had to be assessed in terms of the policy already in place.

3. Lorimer's *Gazetteer* estimated that the Harasiis numbered only 250 arms-bearing men in 1905. Later writers took these figures as fact and simply elaborated upon them (as found, for example, in the PDO uncatalogued papers, 1948–1975).

4. In Syria nomadic pastoralists have built cement houses, which they occupy for part of the year, and raise crops (Leybourne, Jaubert, and Tutwiler 1993:7–10). In Jordan, according to Layne, where cement housing projects have been introduced with numerous social services, pastoralists are making the transition and becoming agriculturalists as well (1994:45).

5. This response is similar to that of the women among the Syrian Bedouin tribes who began making tassels and other decorations for cars in the 1970s (Chatty 1986:105).

6. These cultural beliefs can be attributed to Arab tribal society as a whole, but are generally accepted to be more pronounced among nomadic pastoral Bedouin groups than among urbanized Arabs (Chatty 1986:43–53).

7. In spite of this relative stability in animal numbers over the last decade, and with no figures to prove their case, visiting development experts and ecologists to the white oryx project at Yalooni are already making pronouncements about "overgrazing" and "destruction of the rangeland" in the Jiddat-il-Harasiis.

8. Between February 1991 and January 1992, there was no rain in any part of the Jiddat, and even the successfully reintroduced Arabian oryx herd suffered unexpected losses because of this drought.

9. Harasiis regularly clear up their debts before making the pilgrimage to Mecca, a time in which purity also means settling one's affairs on earth. Devout Muslims in their own way, numerous Harasiis men and women have made the pilgrimage more than once in their lifetime.

10. This is described and analyzed in detail in Chatty 1983.

11. Mughshin is the point at which Wilfred Thesiger set off in his quest to cross the Empty Quarter in 1946–1947.

12. In 1991 an FAO-sponsored workshop of development experts, government officials, and academics interested in and involved with nomadic pastoral tribes in the region was held in Amman. The findings of the workshop revealed that the age-old dichotomy between those who are in support of this culture and way of life and those who are opposed to it still exists. Academics have, over the past two decades, accepted the fact that nomadic pastoralism presupposes a multire-

source form of exploitation. Few government officials and policy planners, however, accept this position. Even as we enter the 1990s, some government advisers—particularly the representatives of countries with large nomadic pastoral sectors—hold the position that as there are no longer any *nomadic* pastoralists, there is no longer a "nomad" problem. The implication of this stance is what many academics have referred to in the past few decades—the existence of a wide cultural gap between government administrators and pastoral populations in the same country (Chatty 1972, 1986; Barth 1961; Salzman and Galaty 1990; Galaty, Aronson, Salzman, and Chouinard 1981).

13. Ensminger and Rutten provide striking evidence of the effects of ancillary controls in development planning with the recent case in Botswana. Here development planners noted that the lack of water limited the number of cattle. Planned programs to dramatically increase water resulted in an increase in cattle as desired, but also in the destructive overuse of the land. This was "not the tragedy of the commons; but the tragedy of making common what had been private" (1991:698).

14. The debate about the issue of desertification has many sides. For example, Nicholson (1989) argues that climate has become drier during the last century and Olsson (1985) states that there has been no observable trend toward land degradation in central Sudan for the last two decades.

15. Throughout most of the 1980s the responsibility for low-cost housing rested with the Ministry of Social Affairs. Each time permanent housing was proposed for the Harasiis tribe I was able to convince ministry officials how much more effectively the financial output could be put to the disbursement of annual tents/tarpaulin to the population, as they themselves had requested. When a separate ministry for housing was created in the late 1980s, I made an effort to put forward the viewpoint of the pastoral population, but it was not possible to fight the deeply held state ideology that all nationals were entitled to a house.

Glossary

asabiyah	sense of group unity or solidarity
badia	semiarid steppeland and desert of Northern Arabia
bedu	inhabitant of the badia; nomadic pastoralist
beit / buyut	house or home; sublineage
burqa'	indigo-dyed cloth face mask
dar	tribal territory, homeland
dishdasha	a long, ankle-length shift worn by men and male children
donum	an Ottoman land measure. One donum equals 1,000 square meters.
falaj / aflaj	system for distributing water supply, irrigation canal
filly	woven goat hair panel
Firqat	government organized tribal militia in Dhofar
ghazu	raiding
hadhar	settled people, civilization
halaal	that which is allowed; ritually correct slaughter of livestock
hema	protected pastureland
Hijra	settlements set up in 1920s in Saudi Arabia
Ikhwan	Bedouin forces attached to Abdul Aziz in 1920's
khuwa	tribute paid for protection to a more powerful tribe; brotherhood
mafkook	an animal left free to graze
mihrab	prayer niche, a recess indicating the direction of prayer
Omani Rial	one rial is approximately $2.58
ooma	dried sardine fish
rashiid/rushada'	tribal elder
Rub' al-Khali	the Empty Quarter
sa'af	dwarf palm frond
sirwaal	loose, baggy trousers

References

Abdulrahman, S. 1979. "The Transition from a Tribal Society to a Nation State." Ph.D. diss., University of Missouri, Columbia.

Abu Jaber, K., et al. 1978. *The Bedouin of Jordan: A People in Transition.* Amman: Royal Scientific Society.

Abu Jaber, K., and F. Gharaibeh. 1981. "Bedouin Settlement: Organizational, Legal, and Administrative Structures in Jordan." In J. Galaty, D. Aronson, and P. Salzman, eds., *The Future of Pastoral Peoples.* Ottowa: International Development Research Center.

Abu-Lughod, L. 1985. "A Community of Secrets: The Separate World of Bedouin Women." *Signs* 10:637–657.

— 1986. *Veiled Sentiments: Honor and Poetry in a Bedouin Society.* Berkeley: University of California Press.

Abu-Rabia, A. 1994. *The Negev Bedouin and Livestock Rearing.* Oxford: Berg.

Altorki, S., and D. Cole. 1989. *Arabian Oasis City: The Transformation of Unayzah.* Austin: University of Texas Press.

Appleby, G. 1988. "Using Central-Place Methods to Evaluate Agricultural Development Projects." *Practicing Anthropology* 10:24–26.

Aronson, D. 1980. "Must Nomads Settle? Some Notes Toward Policy on the Future of Pastoralism." In P. Salzman, ed., *When Nomads Settle.* New York: Praeger.

Attwood, D. 1979. "Why Some of the Poor Get Richer: Economic Change and Mobility in Rural Western India." *Current Anthropology* 20:495–514.

Awad, M. 1959. "Settlement of Nomads and Semi-Nomadic Tribal Groups in the Middle East." *International Labor Review* 79(1):25–56.

— 1962. "Nomadism in the Arab Lands of the Middle East." *The Problems of the Arid Zone.* Paris: UNESCO Proceedings no. 18.

Barnett, H. 1956. *Anthropology and Administration.* Evanston, Ill.: Row, Peterson.

Barth, F. 1961. *Nomads of South Persia: The Basseri Tribe of the Khamseh Confederacy.* Boston: Little, Brown.

— 1962. "Nomads in the Mountain and Plateau Areas of South West Asia." *The Problems of the Arid Zone.* Paris: UNESCO Proceedings no. 18.

Behnke, R., and I. Scoones. 1993. "Rethinking Range Ecology: Implications for Rangeland Management in Africa." In R. Behnke, I. Scoones, and C. Kervan, eds., *Range Ecology at Disequilibrium.* London: Overseas Development Institute.

Bennett, J. 1988. "Anthropology and Development: The Ambiguous Engagement." In J. Bennett and J. Bowen, eds., *Production and Autonomy: Anthropological Studies and Critiques of Development.* Lanham, Md.: University Press of America.

Bocco, R. 1989. "Espaces Étatiques et Espaces Tribaux dans le Sud Jordanien: Legislation Foncière et Redefinition des Liens Sociaux." *Maghreb-Machrek* (January-March), no. 123, pp. 144–163.

— 1990. "La Sédentarisation des Pasteurs Nomads: Les Experts Internationaux Face à la Question Bedouine dans le Moyen-Orient Arabe (1950–1970). *Cahiers des Sciences Humaines* 26(1–2):97–117.

Bonfiglioli, A. 1992. *Pastoralists at a Crossroads: Survival and Development Issues in African Pastoralism.* Project for Nomadic Pastoralists in Africa. Nairobi: UNICEF/UNSO.

Bonnenfant, P. 1977. "L'Evolution de la Vie Bedouine en Arabia Centrale." *Revue de l'Occident et de la Mediterranee Musalmane* 23(1):111–176.

Boserup, E. 1971. *Women's Role in Economic Development.* London: George Allen and Unwin.

Bossen, L. 1975. "Women in Modernizing Societies." *American Ethnologist* 2(4):587–601.

Brokensha, D., and P. Little, eds. 1988. *Anthropology and Development and Change in East Africa.* Boulder, Colo.: Westview.

Caplan, P., ed. 1987. *The Cultural Construction of Sexuality.* London: Tavistock.

Caskel, W. 1954. "The Bedouinization of Arabia." In G. von Grunebaum, ed., *Studies in Islamic Culture.* Washington: American Anthropological Association Memoir no. 76.

Caton, S. 1990. *Peaks of Yemen I Summon: Poetry as Cultural Practice in a North Yemeni Tribe.* Berkeley: University of California Press.

Cernea, M. 1991a. *Using Knowledge from Social Science in Development Projects.* Washington, D.C.: World Bank.

Cernea, M., ed. 1991b. *Putting People First: Sociological Variables in Rural Development.* 2d ed. New York: Oxford University Press.

Chambers, E. 1989. *Applied Anthropology: A Practical Guide.* 2d ed. Prospect Heights, Ill.: Waveland.

Chambers, R. 1983. *Rural Development: Putting the Last First.* London: Longman.

— 1991. "Shortcut and Participatory Methods for Gaining Social Information for Projects." In M. Cernea, ed., *Putting People First: Sociological Variables in Rural Development.* New York: Oxford University Press.

Chatty, D. 1972. "Structuring Forces of Pastoral Nomadism in S.W. Asia". *Development and Change* 4:51–72.

— 1976. "From Camel to Truck: A Study of Pastoral Adaptation." *Folk* 18:113–128.

— 1978. "Changing Sex Roles in Bedouin Society in Syria and Lebanon." In L. Beck and N. Keddie, eds., *Women in the Muslim World.* Cambridge: Harvard University Press.

— 1980. "The Pastoral Family and the Truck." In P. Salzman, ed., *When Nomads Settle.* New York: Praeger.

— 1983. "The Bedouin of Central Oman." *Journal of Oman Studies* 6:149–162.

— 1984. *Women's Component in Pastoral Community Assistance and Development: A Study of the Needs and Problems of the Harasiis Population.* DTCD Project Findings and Recommendations. New York: United Nations.

— 1986. *From Camel to Truck: The Bedouin in the Modern World.* New York: Vantage.

— 1989. *Bedouin Population Development: Findings and Proposed Work Program.* DTCD. New York: United Nations.

— 1990. "Tradition and Change Among the Pastoral Harasiis in Oman." In M. Salem-Murdock, M. Horowitz, and M. Sella, eds., *Anthropology and Development in North Africa and the Middle East.* Boulder, Colo.: Westview.

Chatty, D., M. Zaroug, and A. Osman. 1991. *Pastoralists in Oman.* FAO/ESH Working Papers on Pastoral and Agro-Pastoral Societies. Rome: FAO.

Clay, J., and B. Holcomb. 1986. Politics and the Ethiopian Famine, 1984–1985. *Cultural Survival Report 20.* Cambridge, Mass.: Cultural Survival.

Cole, D. 1971. "The Social and Economic Structure of the Al-Murrah: A Saudi Arabian Bedouin Tribe." Ph.D. diss., University of California, Berkeley.

Conlin, S. 1985. "Anthropological Advice in a Government Context." In R. Grillo and A. Rew, eds., *Social Anthropology and Development Policy.* London: Tavistock.

Coon, C. 1951. *Caravans: The Story of the Middle East.* New York: Holt, Rinehart and Winston.

Cornwall, A., and N. (Tapper) Lindisfarne, eds. 1994. *Dislocating Masculinity: Comparative Ethnographies.* London: Routledge.

Cunnison, I. 1977. "Nomads in the 1960s." Inaugural lecture, University of Hull.

Curtis, D. 1985. "Anthropology in Project Management: On Being Useful to Those Who Must Design and Operate Rural Water Supplies." In R. Grillo and A. Rew, eds., *Social Anthropology and Development Policy.* London: Tavistock.

Dahl, G. 1990. "Pastoral Strategies After Drought." Paper prepared for the Sub-Regional Workshop on Dynamics of Pastoral Land and Resource Tenure: Changes in Countries Affected by the Recent Droughts in the Horn of Africa. Rome: FAO.

Dahl, G., and A. Hjort. 1976. *Having Herds: Pastoral Herd Growth and Household Economy.* Stockholm: University of Stockholm.

Dalton, W. 1973. "Economic Change and Political Continuity in a Saharan Oasis Community." In *Man* 8(2):266–284.

Draz, O. 1977. *Role of Range Management and Fodder Production.* Beirut: UNDP Regional Office for Western Asia.

Dresch, P. 1989. *Tribes, Government, and History in Yemen.* Oxford: Clarendon Press.

Dyson-Hudson, N. 1991. "Pastoral Production Systems and Livestock Development Projects: An East African Perspective." In M. Cernea, ed., *Putting People*

First: Sociological Variables in Rural Development. 2d ed. New York: Oxford University Press.

Eickelman, D. 1989. *The Middle East: An Anthropological Approach.* 2d ed. Englewood Cliffs, N.J.: Prentice-Hall.

— 1984. "Kings and People: Oman's State Consultative Council." *Middle East Journal* 38(1):51–71.

Ensminger, J. 1987. "Economic and Political Differentiation Among Galole Orma Women." *Ethnos* 52 (1–2):28–49.

Ensminger, J., and A. Rutten. 1991. "The Political Economy of Changing Property Rights: Dismantling a Pastoral Commons." *American Ethnologist* 18:683–699.

Escobar, A. 1991. "Anthropology and the Development Encounter: The Making and Marketing of Development Anthropology." *American Ethnologist* 18:658–682.

FAO (Food and Agriculture Organization). 1972. *Expert Consultation on the Settlement of Nomads in Africa and the Near East.* Cairo.

— 1985. *Pastoralism: An Overview of Practice, Process, and Policy.* Rome: FAO/ESH Working Papers on Pastoral and Agro-Pastoral Societies.

— 1988. *Major Issues in Pastoral Development with Special Emphasis on Selected African Countries.* Rome: FAO/ESH Working Papers on Pastoral and Agro-Pastoral Societies.

— 1989. *Rehabilitation Alternatives for Pastoral Populations in the Sudan.* Rome: FAO/ESH Working Papers on Pastoral and Agro-Pastoral Societies.

Fara, O. 1973. "The Effects of Detribalizing the Bedouin on the Internal Cohesion of an Emerging State: The Kingdom of Saudi Arabia." Ph.D. diss., University of Pittsburgh.

Fernea, E. 1987. "Women's Studies," MESA presidential address. Middle East Studies Association Annual Meeting.

Fernea, R. 1970. *Shaykh and Effendi: Changing Patterns of Authority among the El-Shabana of Southern Iraq.* Cambridge: Harvard University Press.

Galaty, J. 1980. "The Maasai Group Ranch: Politics and Development in African Pastoral Society." In P. Salzman, ed., *When Nomads Settle.* New York: Praeger.

Galaty, J., D. Aronson, P. Salzman, and A. Chouinard, eds. 1981. *The Future of Pastoral Peoples: Proceedings of a Conference Held in Nairobi, Kenya.* Ottowa: International Development Research Center.

Gavrielides, N. 1993. "Sedentarisation des Bedouins et Construction de l'Etat au Kuwait." In R. Bocco, R. Jaubert, and F. Metral, eds., *Steppes d'Arabies: Etats, Pasteurs, Agriculteurs et Commerçants: Le Devenir des Zones Seches.* Paris: Presses Universitaires de France.

Gilles, J., and J. Gefe. 1990. "Nomads, Ranchers, and the State: The Sociocultural Aspects of Pastoralism." In J. Galaty and D. Johnson, eds., *The World of Pastoralism.* London: Guilford.

Glubb, J. 1942. *Handbook of the Nomads, Semi-Nomads, Semi-Sedentary Tribes of Syria.* London: G.S.I., 9th Army.

Goldstein, M., and C. Beall. 1991. "Change and Continuity in Nomadic Pastoralism on the Western Tibetan Plateau." *Nomadic Peoples* 28:105–122.

Gow, D. 1993. "Doubly Damned: Dealing with Power and Praxis in Development Anthropology." *Human Organization* 52(4):380–393.

Green, C., ed. 1986. *Practicing Development Anthropology*. Boulder, Colo.: Westview.

Grillo, R., and A. Rew, eds. 1985. *Social Anthropology and Development Policy*. London: Tavistock.

Gritzinger, D. 1990. "Developing Egypt's Western Desert Oases: Anthropology and Regional Planning." In M. Salem-Murdock, M. Horowitz, and M. Sella, eds., *Anthropology and Development in North Africa and the Middle East*. Boulder, Colo.: Westview.

Grotsch, K. 1972. "Technical Change and the Destruction of Income in Rural Areas." *American Journal of Agricultural Economics* 54:326–341.

Gulliver, P. 1985. "An Applied Anthropologist in East Africa during the Colonial Era." In R. Grillo and A. Rew, eds., *Social Anthropology and Development Policy*. London: Tavistock.

Hall, E. 1971. "The "Iron Dog" in Northern Alaska." *Anthropologica* 13(1–2): 237–254.

Hebdige, D. 1981. "Object as Image: The Italian Scooter Cycle." *Block* 4:39–56.

Hobart, M., ed. 1993. *An Anthropological Critique of Development: The Growth of Ignorance*. London: Routledge.

Hobbs, J. 1989. *Bedouin Life in the Egyptian Wilderness*. Austin: University of Texas Press.

Hoben, A. 1982. "Anthropologists and Development." *Annual Review of Anthropology* 11:349–375.

Hopkins, N. 1990. "Water-User Associations in Rural Central Tunisia." In M. Salem-Murdock, M. Horowitz, and M. Sella, eds., *Anthropology and Development in North Africa and the Middle East*. Boulder, Colo.: Westview.

Horowitz, M. 1988. "Anthropology and the New Development Agenda." *Development Anthropology Newsletter* 6:1–4.

Hourani, A. 1991. *A History of the Arab Peoples*. London: Faber and Faber.

Hurskainen, A. 1990. "Levels of Identity and National Integrity: The Viewpoints of the Pastoral Maasai and Parakuyo." *Nomadic Peoples* 25–27:79–92.

Ibn Khaldun. 1958. *The Muqqadimah*. Trans. F. Rosenthal. New York: Pantheon.

Innes, N. 1987. *Minister in Oman*. London: Oleander.

International Labor Organization. 1962. *On Indigenous and Tribal Populations*. Geneva.

Jaafer, M. 1989. *Bedouin Population Development: A Report on Desert Plants and Fodder*. Muscat: Ministry of Social Affairs, Local Community Development.

Janzen, J. 1983. "The Modern Development of Nomadic Living Space in Southeast Arabia—The Case of Oman." *Geoforum* 14(3):289–309.

— 1986. *Nomads in the Sultanate of Oman: Tradition and Development in Dhofar*. Boulder, Colo.: Westview.

— 1990. *Land Tenure and Land Use in the Pastoral Living Areas of Dhofar Sultanate of Oman.* Rome: FAO.

Johnson, D. 1969. "The Nature of Nomadism." Department of Geography. Chicago: University of Chicago.

Johnstone, T. 1977. *Harsuusi Lexicon and English-Harsuusi Word-list.* London: Oxford University Press.

Jordanova, L. 1980. "Natural Facts: A Historical Perspective on Science and Sexuality." In C. MacCormack and M. Strathern, eds., *Nature, Culture, and Gender.* Cambridge: Cambridge University Press.

Justice, J. 1986. *Policies, Plans and People: Culture and Health Development in Nepal.* Berkeley: University of California Press.

Kuper, H. 1975. "What Have We in Common?" A paper delivered at the International Conference of Women. La Crosse, Wisconsin.

Lancaster, W. 1981. *The Rwala Bedouin Today.* Cambridge: Cambridge University Press.

Layne, L. 1989. "The Dialogics of Tribal Self-Representation in Jordan." *American Ethnologist* 16(1):24–39.

— 1994. *Home and Homeland: The Dialogics of Tribal and National Identity in Jordan.* Princeton: Princeton University Press.

Lewis, N. 1987. *Nomads and Settlers in Syria and Jordan, 1800–1980.* Cambridge: Cambridge University Press.

Leybourne, M., R. Jaubert, and R. Tutwiler. 1993. "Changes in Migration and Feeding Patterns Among Semi-Nomadic Pastoralists in Northern Syria." *Pastoral Development Network Paper 34a.* London: Overseas Development Institute.

Lorimer, J. 1986 [1908]. *Gazetteer of the Persian Gulf, Oman, and Central Arabia.* Gerrards Cross, Buchinghamshire: Reprinted Archives Editions.

McClelland, D. 1977. "The Psychological Causes and Consequences of Modernization: An Ethiopian Case Study." In M. Nash, ed., *Essays on Economic Development and Culture Change in Honor of Bert F. Hoselitz.* Chicago: University of Chicago Press.

Mair, L. 1992. *An Introduction to Social Anthropology.* 2d ed. Oxford: Clarendon.

Marx, E. 1987. "Relations Between Spouses Among the Negev Bedouin." *Ethnos* 52(1–2):156–179. Stockholm: Ethnographical Museum of Sweden.

Mason, J. 1990. "An Anthropologist's Contribution to Libya's National Human Settlement Plan." In M. Salem-Murdock, M. Horowitz, and M. Sella, eds., *Anthropology and Development in North Africa and the Middle East.* Boulder, Colo.: Westview.

Masri, A. 1991. *The Tradition of Hema as a Land Tenure Institution in Arid Land Management: The Syrian Arab Republic.* Rome: FAO.

Mead, M. 1935. *Sex and Temperament in Three Primitive Societies.* New York: William Morris.

Meir, A. 1987. "Comparative Vital Statistics Along the Pastoral Nomadism Sedentarism Continuum." *Human Ecology* 15(1):81–103.

Mernissi, F. 1975. *Beyond the Veil: Male and Female Dynamics in a Modern Muslim Society*. New York: Schenkam.

Miles, S. 1966 [1919]. *The Countries and Tribes of the Persian Gulf.* London: Frank Cass.

Ministère des Affairs Etrangères. 1923–1937. "Rapport sur la Situation de la Syria et du Liban Soumis au Conseil de la Société des Nations." Paris.

Morales-Gomez, D. 1992. "Agents of Change: Children in Development." *IDRC Reports* (January), 19:4–6.

Morris, T. 1991. *The Despairing Developer: Dairy of an Aid Worker in the Middle East.* London: I. B. Taurus.

Morton, A. 1990. "Brokering Social Science in Development: Experiences in Morocco." In M. Salem-Murdock, M. Horowitz, and M. Sella, eds., *Anthropology and Development in North Africa and the Middle East.* Boulder, Colo.: Westview.

Nelson, C. 1974. "Public and Private Politics: Women in the Middle Eastern World." In *American Ethnologist* (August), vol. 1, no. 3.

Nicholson, S. 1989. "Long-Term Changes in African Rainfall." *Weather* 44:446–456.

Nutting, A. 1964. *The Arabs.* London: Hollis and Carter.

Olmstead, J. 1975. "Farmer's Wife, Weaver's Wife: Women and Work in Two Ethiopian Communities." *African Studies Review* 18(3):85–98.

Olsson, L. 1985. *An Integrated Study of Desertification.* Lund, Sweden: University of Lund, Department of Geography.

Oppenheim, M. 1939. *Die Beduinen.* 4 vols. Leipzig: Otto Harrassowitz.

Ortner, S. 1974. "Is Female to Male as Nature Is to Culture?" In M. Rosaldo and L. Lamphere, eds., *Women, Culture, and Society.* Stanford: Stanford University Press.

Partridge, W., ed. 1984. *Training Manual in Development Anthropology.* Washington, D.C.: American Anthropological Association.

Partridge, W., and D. Warren. 1984. "Introduction: Development Anthropology and the Life Cycle of Development Projects." In W. Partridge, ed., *Training Manual in Development Anthropology.* Washington, D.C.: American Anthropology Association.

Pastner, McC., C. 1978. "The Status of Women and Property on a Baluchistan Oasis in Pakistan." In L. Beck and N. Keddie, eds., *Women in the Muslim World.* Cambridge: Harvard University Press.

Pastner, S., and C. McC. 1982. "Clients, Camps, and Crews: Adaptational Variation in Baluch Social Organization." In S. Pastner and S. Flam, eds., *Anthropology in Pakistan: Recent Socio-Cultural and Archaeological Perspectives.* South Asia Occasional Papers and Theses. South Asia Program. Cornell University.

Pelto, P. 1968. "The Snowmobile Revolution in Lapland." *Journal of the Finno-Ugric Society* 69:3–42.

— 1972. "Snowmobiles: Technological Revolution in the Arctic." In H. Bernard and P. Pelto, eds., *Technology and Social Change.* New York: Macmillan.

— 1973. *The Snowmobile Revolution: Technology and Social Change in the Arctic.* Menlo Park, Cal.: Cummings.

Peterson, J. 1978. *Oman in the Twentieth Century: Political Foundations of an Emerging State.* London: Croom Helm.

Petroleum Development (Oman) Limited (PDO). 1948–1975. Uncatalogued papers on tribes, geology, and labor recruitment policy. Mina-al-Fahl, Muscat and Shell International, The Hague.

Pfaffenberger, B. 1988. "Fetishised Objects and Humanised Nature: Towards an Anthropology of Technology." *Man* 23:236–52.

— 1992. "Social Anthropology of Technology." *Annual Review of Anthropology* 21:491–516.

Pottier, J. 1993. "Introduction: Development in Practice." In J. Pottier, ed., *Practising Development.* London: Routledge.

Pottier, J., ed. 1993. *Practicing Development.* London: Routledge.

Poulin, R., G. Appleby, and Q. Cao. 1987. *Impact Evaluation of Project North Shaba.* Kinshasa: United States Agency for International Development.

Price, D. 1989. *Before the Bulldozer: The Nambiquara Indians and the World Bank.* Cabin John, Md.: Seven Locks.

Rapp, A., and J. Mattson. 1988. "The Recent Sahelo-Ethiopian Droughts in a Climatic Context." Paper presented at the International Conference on Environmental Stress and Security. Stockholm: Royal Swedish Academy of Sciences.

Rickson, R., J. Western, and R. Burdge. 1990. "Social Impact Assessment: Knowledge and Development." *Environmental Impact Assessment Review* 10:1–10.

Rogers, B. 1980. *The Domestication of Women: Discrimination in Developing Societies.* London: Routledge.

Rosaldo, M., and L. Lamphere, eds. 1974. *Women, Culture, and Society.* Stanford: Stanford University Press.

Rubin, G. 1975. "The Traffic in Women: Notes on the 'Political Economy' of Sex." In R. Reiter, ed., *Toward an Anthropology of Women.* New York: Monthly Review Press.

Sacks, K. 1974. "Engles Revisited: Women, the Organization of Production and Private Property." In M. Rosaldo and L. Lamphere, eds., *Women, Culture, and Society.* Stanford: Stanford University Press.

Sahlins, M. 1967. "The Segmentary Lineage: An Organization of Predatory Expansion." In J. Middleton and R. Cohen, eds., *Comparative Political Systems.* Garden City: American Museum Sourcebooks in Anthropology.

Saleh, M. 1990. "Pastoralism and the State in African Arid Lands: An Overview." *Nomadic Peoples* 25–27:7–18.

Salzman, P. 1969. "Multi-Resource Nomadism in Iranian Baluchistan." Paper presented at the annual meeting of the American Anthropolgical Association. New Orleans.

Salzman, P., and J. Galaty, eds. 1990. *Nomads in a Changing World.* Naples: Istituto Universitario Orientale.

Sammane, M. 1990. *Bedouin Population Development: Findings and Recommendations.* DTCD. New York: United Nations.

Sanday, P. 1974. "Female Status in the Public Domain." In M. Rosaldo and L. Lamphere, eds., *Woman, Culture, and Society.* Stanford: Stanford University Press.

Sanford, S. 1983. *Management of Pastoral Development in the Third World.* London: Overseas Development Institute.

Schaniel, W. 1988. "New Technology and Culture Change in Traditional Societies." *Journal of Economic Issues* 22:493–98.

Schneider, H. 1959. "Pakot Resistance to Change." In W. Bascom and M. Herskovits, eds., *Continuity and Change in African Cultures.* Chicago: University of Chicago Press.

Seddon, D. 1993. "Anthropology and Appraisal: The Preparation of Two IFAD Pastoral Development Projects in Niger and Mali." In J. Pottier, ed., *Practising Development.* London: Routledge.

Sharp, L. 1952. "Steel Axes for Stone Age Australians." *Human Organization* (Summer), 17–22.

Shoup, J. 1990. "Middle Eastern Sheep Pastoralism and the Hima System." In J. Galaty and D. Johnson, eds., *The World of Pastoralism.* London: Guilford.

Skeet, I. 1974. *Muscat and Oman: The End of an Era.* London: Faber and Faber.

Stanley Price, M. 1989. *Animal Re-introductions: The Arabian Oryx in Oman.* Cambridge: Cambridge University Press.

Strathern, M. 1988. *The Gender of the Gift.* Berkeley: University of California Press.

Swagman, C. 1990. "Doing Development Anthropology: Personal Experience in the Yemen Arab Republic." In M. Salem-Murdock, M. Horowitz, and M. Sella, eds., *Anthropology and Development in North Africa and the Middle East.* Boulder, Colo.: Westview.

Sweet, L. 1970. "Camel Raiding of Northern Arabian Bedouin: A Mechanism of Ecological Adaptation." In L. Sweet, ed., *Peoples and Cultures of the Middle East.* Garden City: Natural History Press.

Tapper, N. (Lindisfarne). 1978. "The Women's Subsociety Among the Shahsevan Nomads of Iran." In L. Beck and N. Keddie, eds., *Women in the Muslim World.* Cambridge: Harvard University Press.

— 1991. *Bartered Brides.* Cambridge: Cambridge University Press.

Thapa, S., R. V. Short, and M. Potts. 1988. "Breast Feeding, Birth Spacing, and Their Effects on Child Survival." *Nature* 335:679–682.

Thesiger, W. 1950. "The Badu of Southern Arabia." *Journal of the Royal Central Asian Society* 37(1):53–61.

Thomas, B. 1929. "The South Eastern Borderlands of the Rub'al Khali." *Geographical Journal* 73(3):193–215.

— 1937. "Four Strange Tongues from South Arabia: The Hadara Group." *Proceedings of the British Academy,* vol. 23.

Thomas, E. M. 1958. *The Harmless People.* New York: Random House.

Townsend, J. 1977. *Oman: The Making of the Modern State.* London: Croom Helm.

Turnbull, C. 1962. *The Forest People.* New York: Simon and Schuster.

Turner, T. 1991. "Representing, Resisting, Rethinking: Historical Transformations of Kayapó Culture and Anthropological Consciousness." In G. Stocking, ed., *Colonial Situations: Essays on the Contextualization of Ethnographic Knowledge.* Madison: University of Wisconson Press.

UNESCO. 1961. *A History of Land Use in Arid Regions.* Arid Zone Research no. 17. Paris: UNESCO.

— 1962. *Problems of the Arid Zone.* Arid Zone Research no. 18. Paris: UNESCO.

— 1963. *Problems of the Arid Zone.* Arid Zone Research no. 19. Paris: UNESCO.

UNESOB. 1970. "Nomadic Populations in Selected Countries in the Middle East and Related Issues of Sedentarization and Settlement." *Studies on Selected Countries in the Middle East.* Beirut: UNESOB.

Volney, M. 1959 [1787]. *Voyage en Egypte et en Syrie.* Le Haye: Mouton.

Warriner, D. 1959. *Land and Poverty in the Middle East.* London: Oxford University Press.

Webster, R. 1991. "The Al Wahiba: Bedouin Values in an Oil Economy." *Nomadic Peoples* 28:3–17.

Weulersse, J. 1946. *Paysans de Syrie et du Proche-Orient.* Paris: Gallimard.

Wilkinson, J. 1972. "The Origins of the Omani State." In D. Hopwood, ed., *The Arabian Peninsula: Society and Politics.* London: George Allen and Unwin.

— 1977. *Water and Tribal Settlement in South-East Arabia: A Study of the Aflaj of Oman.* Oxford: Clarendon.

— 1987. *The Imamate Tradition of Oman.* Cambridge: Cambridge University Press.

World Bank. 1988. *Rural Development, World Bank Experience, 1965–1986.* Working paper. Washington: World Bank.

Wulff, R., and J. Fiske, 1987. *Anthropological Praxis: Translating Knowledge Into Action.* Boulder Colo.: Westview.

Yacoub, S. 1970. *Sedentarization of the Nomadic Populations in the Countries of the* UNESOB Region. Beirut: UNESOB.

— 1972. *A Socio-Economic Survey of the Settler-Candidates in the Qatrana Irrigated Farming Pilot Project in East Jordan.* Beirut: UNESOB.

Index